THE ART OF COURTLY LOVE

Records of Civilization

THE ART OF
COURTLY LOVE

By Andreas Capellanus

WITH INTRODUCTION,
TRANSLATION, AND NOTES BY
JOHN JAY PARRY

COLUMBIA UNIVERSITY PRESS
New York

Columbia University Press
New York   Oxford
Copyright © 1990 Columbia University Press
All rights reserved

Library of Congress Cataloging-in-Publication Data

Andre, le chapelain.
    [De amore et amoris remedio. English]
    The art of courtly love / by Andreas Capellanus ; with
introduction, translation, and notes by John Jay Parry.
    p.   cm.—(Records of civilization)
Translation of: De amore et amoris remedio.
Includes bibliographical references.
ISBN 0-231-07305-4 (alk. paper)
    1. Courtly love.   I. Parry, John Jay, 1889–1954.   II. Title.
III. Series: Records of civilization (Unnumbered)
PA8250.A236D413   1990
306.7—dc20   89-71284
                CIP

Casebound editions of Columbia University Press books are Smyth-sewn
and printed on permanent and durable acid-free paper

Printed in the United States of America

p 10 9 8 7 6 5 4

PREFACE

THIS TRANSLATION was originally undertaken, some fifteen years ago, for the use of students in a course in medieval literature in translation. It is now published in the hope that it may prove useful to others who desire some acquaintance with one of the significant books of the Middle Ages, but who are unable to read the medieval Latin in which it is written. My primary aim has been to preserve the ideas of Andreas, and to keep close to what he says, even though it has been necessary, at times, to use somewhat awkward English in doing so. My secondary aim has been to reproduce something of his style. This is in general colloquial, but it is colored with Biblical expressions, and at times it becomes almost pompous when he tries to reproduce the speech of the upper classes. In one respect, however, it seemed best not to follow him. Andreas is very fond of loose, straggling sentences strung together with "and," "but," "for," "so," or some similar connective. Medieval rhetoric was much more tolerant of such sentences than modern readers are, but Andreas seems to go beyond the practice of his contemporaries. In my translation such sentences have been broken up into shorter, more manageable units.

The basis of the translation is Trojel's edition of the text; Pagès's reprint is convenient to use, but it has no independent authority. For the Biblical quotations I have followed the Douay-Rheims translation, since this represents most closely the version that was in use in the time of Andreas. Sometimes the Vulgate references differ materially from those of the King James version. In such cases I have added in parentheses references to the latter text. The translations from classical and medieval authors are mostly my own, although I have checked them by other translations when these were accessible. Such parallel passages are cited to throw light upon the text of Andreas, but without any attempt to assert that he made use of them.

An intensive investigation of his sources was no part of my plan.

For several of these references and for other assistance and encouragement I am indebted to Professor Arpad Steiner of Hunter College. Professor Roger S. Loomis of Columbia has made a number of valuable suggestions, and I believe the book is the better because of them. Greatest of all is my debt to the editor of the series, Professor Austin P. Evans. He has read the whole work carefully, in manuscript and again in proof, and his vigilance has saved me from a number of errors, and his knowledge and judgment have helped me over many difficult places.

J. J. P.

Urbana, Ill.
August 18, 1941

CONTENTS

Contents

BOOK TWO: HOW LOVE MAY BE RETAINED

INTRODUCTION

INTRODUCTION

OF THE *Treatise on Love* [1] of Andreas the Chaplain (Andreas Capellanus) a recent French scholar has written, "It is, like Brunetto Latini's *Trésor* or the *Speculum Majus* of Vincent of Beauvais, one of those capital works which reflect the thought of a great epoch, which explain the secret of a civilization." [2] It is from this point of view that a translation of the work is here presented. Andreas is not a great literary figure like his friend and fellow citizen Chrétien de Troyes, but perhaps for that very reason he brings us closer to the actual life of the time than does Chrétien. From his work we get a vivid picture of life in a medieval court like that of Troyes or Poitiers; to the student of medieval manners such a picture is especially valuable, because in these courts was taught, and probably also practiced, that strange social system to which Gaston Paris has given the name of "courtly love." [3] This developed in the twelfth century among the troubadours of southern France, but soon spread into the neighboring countries and in one way or another colored the literature of most of western Europe for centuries. Its influence did not cease with the Renaissance, and even today,

[1] Sometimes called *The Art of Courtly Love* (De arte honeste amandi).

[2] Robert Bossuat, *Drouart la Vache, traducteur d'André le Chapelain* (Paris: Champion, 1926), p. 31.

[3] "L'Amour courtois," in *Romania*, XII (1883), 519. Other discussions of the system are to be found in: Lewis Freeman Mott, *The System of Courtly Love* (Boston: Athenaeum Press, 1896); Joseph Anglade, *Les Troubadours* (2d ed., Paris: Colin, 1919), chap. iv.; Tom Peete Cross and William Albert Nitze, *Lancelot and Guenevere: a Study on the Origins of Courtly Love* (Chicago: University of Chicago Press, 1930), chap. iv; Alfred Jeanroy, *La Poésie lyrique des troubadours* (Toulouse: Privat, 1934), I, 90–100, II, 94–113; C. S. Lewis, *The Allegory of Love* (Oxford: Clarendon Press, 1936), chap. i; Ramón Menéndez-Pidal, "El Amor cortés," *Bull. Hisp.*, XL (1938), 401–406; Sidney Painter, *French Chivalry* (Baltimore: Johns Hopkins Press, 1940), chap. iv; Thomas A. Kirby, *Chaucer's Troilus, a Study in Courtly Love* (University, La.: Louisiana State Univ. Press, 1940), chaps. i–iv. Some of these works do not distinguish sufficiently between the system as it existed in the time of Andreas and the system as it later developed.

although it would scarcely be correct to speak of courtly love in our present-day society, some phases of it still linger on in our modern attitude toward romance.[4]

For all practical purposes we may say that the origin of courtly love is to be found in the writings of the poet Ovid who lived in Rome in the time of the Emperor Augustus. Among his poems are *The Art of Love* (Ars amatoria), *The Cure for Love* (Remedia amoris), and the *Amours* (Amores), all dealing, as their names imply, with the subject of love. *The Art of Love* was a sort of parody on the technical treatises of Ovid's day—a bit of fooling which should never have been taken seriously, but often was. The *Amours* supplement this with accounts of some of Ovid's own experiences in the art, and *The Cure for Love* shows those who are anxious to terminate a love affair how they may do so. Ovid does not present his ideas as a formal system (although he does speak of his "system"),[5] but from his writings men in later times derived the materials to make a system.

Love as Ovid conceived it is frankly sensual [6] ("merry sensuality" Lewis calls it [7]), and there is little or no trace in his work of the romantic affection of later times. It is extramarital and does not contemplate matrimony as its object.[8] Ovid is careful to say that the love he has in mind is not that of maidens or married women, but only such as modesty and the laws permit,[9] and much ingenuity has been expended [10] in showing that his doctrine is really not very immoral according to our present standards. But in the Middle Ages it was assumed as a matter of course that the *vir* who must be deluded, and whom Ovid delighted to delude, was the woman's husband,[11] and his statements that husbands and wives cannot love each other [12] and that

---

[4] Lewis, *op. cit.*, pp. 3–4.

[5] "What used to be an impulse is now a system (*ratio*)": *The Cure for Love*, l. 10.

[6] *The Art of Love* III. 27; *The Cure for Love*, ll. 385–86.

[7] *Op. cit.*, p. 4.   [8] *The Art of Love* III. 585–86.

[9] *Ibid.* I. 31–34; II. 599–600.

[10] For example by F. A. Wright in *Ovid: the Lover's Handbook*, 2d ed., pp. 72–83.

[11] *Amours* I. iv; *The Art of Love* I. 577 ff.; *The Cure for Love*, l. 34.

[12] *The Art of Love* II. 153–55; III. 585–86.

even Penelope may be seduced if one is persistent [13] and his approving accounts of how Venus and Helen deceived their husbands [14] helped to confirm the impression. Whatever may have been Ovid's real meaning—and his sincerity on this point is not beyond question—the men of the Middle Ages thought that they had his approval for the dictum that the best partner in a love affair is another man's wife. Ovid does not restrict either men or women to one affair at a time, but he does point out that the matter is greatly complicated if one woman learns of her lover's affair with another. [15] Trouble arises, too, if the lady's husband learns that she is in love with another man, so there is good reason for keeping such an affair secret; moreover, the very fact that it is secret makes it much pleasanter. [16]

Other ideas of Ovid which influenced the conception of courtly love are: Love is a kind of warfare, and every lover is a soldier. Cupid is the generalissimo, [17] and under him are the women whose power over the men is absolute. A man should deceive a woman, if he can, but he must never appear to oppose her slightest wish. [18] To please her he must watch all night before her doors, [19] undergo all sorts of hardships, [20] perform all sorts of absurd actions. [21] For love of her he must become pale and thin and sleepless. [22] No matter what he may do, or from what motives, he must persuade her that it is all done for her sake. [23] If in spite of all these demonstrations of affection she still remains obdurate, he must arouse her jealousy; he must pretend to be in love with some other woman, and when the first one thinks she has lost him, she will probably capitulate and he can clasp her sobbing to his breast. [24]

Of the circulation of Ovid's poems in the early Middle Ages we know comparatively little. But in the twelfth and thirteenth centuries

---

[13] *Ibid.* I. 477.
[14] *Ibid.* II. 359 ff.; 562 ff.; *Amours* II. v. 28.
[15] *The Art of Love* II. 387 ff.
[16] *Ibid.* I. 275.
[17] *Amours* I. ix. 1.
[18] *The Art of Love* I. 629 ff.
[19] *Ibid.* II. 523 ff.; *Amours* II. xix. 21 ff.
[20] *The Art of Love* II. 233–50; *Amours* I. ix.
[21] *The Art of Love* II. 198 ff.
[22] *Ibid.* I. 727–36; *Amours* I. vi. 5–6, ix. 8.
[23] *The Art of Love* II. 288 ff.
[24] *Ibid.* II. 443 ff.; compare III. 593–94.

so popular was his work [25] that Ludwig Traube used to call this period the *aetas Ovidiana,* as the two preceding periods were the *aetas Vergiliana* and the *aetas Horatiana.*[26] In this revival the *Art of Love* had its full part. It circulated both in Latin and in the vernaculars, and it was rewritten to adapt it to the changed conditions of medieval society. Much of the literature of France and England was colored by its ideas,[27] although a certain amount of the sensuality was glossed over. Even if courtly love had never developed, Ovid's influence would have been profound. Among the troubadours of southern France, however, this influence took on a special character. The Ovidian material was combined with other elements, and the whole combination was infused with a new spirit. It is to this new combination as it developed in the south and as it spread to other lands that we refer when we speak of "courtly love." No one of the troubadours produced even an approach to a treatise on the art; [28] we have to get our idea of it from their lyric poems. Yet in spite of individual differences and of the changes that took place with time, we can get a fairly coherent picture of the system.

The basis of it is the familiar material: love is an art and has its rules; lovers take service in the army of Cupid, and in this service they become pale and thin and sleepless; one cannot love one's own wife but must love the wife of some other man, so of necessity the affair must be kept secret; love cannot exist apart from jealousy. But

[25] Arturo Graf, *Roma nella memoria . . . del medio evo* (Torino: Loescher, 1882), II, 296–315; Max Manitius, "Beiträge zur Geschichte des Ovidius und anderer römischer Schriftsteller im Mittelalter," *Philologus,* Supplementband VII (1899), 723–58; J. E. Sandys, *A History of Classical Scholarship* (3d ed., Cambridge: Cambridge University Press, 1921), I, 638–41; Rudolph Schevill, "Ovid and the Renascence in Spain," pp. 6–27; Lester K. Born, "Ovid and Allegory," *Speculum,* IX (1934), 362–79.

[26] Edward Kennard Rand, *Ovid and His Influence* (New York: Longmans, 1928), pp. 12–23; Born, *op. cit.,* p. 363.

[27] Cross and Nitze, *op. cit.,* chap. iv; Urban Tigner Holmes, Jr., *A History of Old French Literature from the Origins to 1300* (Chapel Hill: Linker, 1937), pp. 302 ff.; Karl Voretzsch, *Introduction to the Study of Old French Literature* (translated by Francis M. Dumont, Halle: Niemeyer, 1931), pp. 244 ff., 450 ff.

[28] *Las Leys d'amors* is a text book on grammar and the art of poetry, not a treatise on love.

the spirit that connects these ideas is wholly different from that of Ovid. The lover and his lady are no longer playing a game of mutual deceit. She is now his feudal suzerain, and he owes allegiance to her, or to Cupid through her. Her status is far above his, and although in theory he holds to the precept of Ovid that love levels all ranks, in practice he seldom dares to presume upon this equality, and his addresses to the lady are full of the deepest humility.[29] This difference in tone is a not unnatural result of the great social differences between Rome in Ovid's day and France in the twelfth century. The source of the other modifications of Ovid's doctrine is not so easy to discover. The matter is still in dispute, but of the various possibilities that have been suggested [30] the most reasonable seems to be that the troubadours were influenced by the culture of Moslem Spain, where many of these elements can be found before they appear among the Christians.[31]

After the fall of the Califate of Cordova in 1031 the territory of the Moors was divided among twenty petty kings whom the Spanish historians in derision have called "kings of parts" (*reyes de taïfas*).[32] Until the coming of the Almoravides from Africa in 1086 there was no religious fanaticism, and Moslems and Christians lived side by side on practically an equal footing. The period was one of pleasure and luxury, of wine and love, but it was also a period of culture. Because among the Arabs the encouragement of literature was one of the traditional manifestations of royal power, each of these petty kings had his court poets. The smaller towns and villages also produced their own poets, who came from all walks of life. All these poets were trained in the classical Arabic tradition—some even went to Arabia to perfect themselves in the art—but the life they depicted in their poems was Spanish. For the traditional camp in the desert they substituted the

---

[29] Jeanroy, *op. cit.*, I, 90–93.

[30] *Ibid.*, I, 64–80, and Holmes, *op. cit.*, pp. 171–73, and the authorities there cited.

[31] Opposition to the theory of Arabic influence seems to be due largely to the reluctance of the modern school of French scholars to admit that French literature is indebted to any source outside its own country and ancient Rome.

[32] The following sketch is based largely upon "La Poésie andalouse du XIe siècle," by Georges Marçais in *Journal des Savants*, 1939, pp. 14–30.

gardens of Andalusia, and they described with care and interest the beauties of their own country. Their poetry has the classical Arabic emphasis upon form, but it is at the same time both national and popular.

Communication between these Moslem states, with their Mozarabic subjects, and the adjoining Christian states was both easy and frequent. Often the poets themselves were the mediums of communication. Because they had been trained in the art of saying things well, they were often employed on missions both to Mohammedan and to Christian sovereigns. Secretaries and ambassadors were often chosen from among their ranks. But such employment was precarious, and many of them changed masters either through necessity or in the hope of bettering their condition. A set of wandering poets came into existence, who passed from one court to another or sometimes found shelter with some bourgeois lover of verse. The situation is very much like that which developed a century later in France.

Not only does Moslem Spain show us a type of civilization which may well have given the impetus to that in Provence and Limousin, but even the metrical forms and the themes of the Spanish poets are like those that were later used by the troubadours.[33] The metrical similarities do not concern us here, except that they fill in the picture; but the similarities in content do, for here we find almost all the elements which, when combined with the ideas of Ovid, give us courtly love. We find among the Arabs two different attitudes toward the subject of love: they have a sensual tradition, perhaps native although colored by the work of Ovid, and another more spiritual tradition, which appears to be based upon the work of Plato as it had come down through the commentaries of Arabic scholars. As a presentation of this second point of view we may consider the book called *The Dove's Neck-Ring,* which was written about the year 1022 by the Andalusian

[33] Menéndez-Pidal in *Revista cubana,* VI (1937), 5–33, and in *Bulletin hispanique,* XL (1938), 337–423; A. R. Nykl, *A Book Containing the Risala Known as The Dove's Neck-Ring about Love and Lovers composed by Abu Muhammad 'Ali ibn Hazm al-Andalusi* (Paris: Geuthner, 1931), pp. lxxviii-ciii.

Ibn Hazm at the request of a friend who had asked him for a discussion of the subject.[34]

Ibn Hazm admits that the ways of the Bedouins and of the ancients, in the matter of love, "are different from ours" (4), and even in his own day there was a great deal of dispute and much lengthy discussion about its nature (7). He is familiar with the Ovidian conventions that the lover must sigh and weep and become pale and thin and that he cannot eat or sleep (xxvi, 14–15), and he adds to these the sudden trembling in the presence of the loved one (12), but he thinks that the lengths to which the Arabs have carried these conventions are absurd (143). He agrees with Ovid that the very secrecy of a love affair helps to make it pleasant, and he is in practical agreement with him as to the effect of jealousy, although he speaks of it under the heading "avoidance brought about by coquetry" (65). In a later book, *Kitab-al-akhlaq*, he says definitely, "When jealousy fades out you can be sure that love has faded out," but here he thinks of jealousy as the result of love rather than its cause (xxv).

Ibn Hazm's concept of love, however, is in its main aspects very different from Ovid's and more resembles that of Plato. He defines love as a reunion of parts of souls which were separated in the creation (7). Its usual cause is an outwardly beautiful form, "because the soul is beautiful and passionately desires anything beautiful, and inclines toward perfect images" (9). This kind of love cannot be felt for more than one person although the other type, which is really passion and is improperly called love, may (24–25). True love does not ignore the physical aspect (58), but the union of souls is a thousand times finer in its effects than that of bodies (92). True love is not forbidden by religious law, and it makes the lover better in many ways, for he tries with all his power to do what he was incapable of doing before, in order to show his good qualities and to make himself desirable. "And how many a stingy one became generous, and a gloomy

[34] Nykl, *op. cit.* Roman numerals refer to pages of Nykl's introduction, and Arabic numerals to the paging of Petrof's text, which Nykl retains in his translation. On pp. ciii ff. he gives a brief summary of earlier works in the same Platonic tradition.

one became bright-faced, and a coward became brave, and a grouchy-dispositioned one became gay, and an ignoramus became clever, and a slovenly one in his personal appearance 'dolled up,' and an ill-shaped one became handsome" (12–13). Ibn Hazm does not say specifically, as Andreas does, that love ennobles the character, but this seems clearly implied by his definition of love and by such remarks as, "Among the praiseworthy natural gifts and noble character and excellent characteristics in love and elsewhere is faithfulness" (71–72). Certainly in his system true love and nobility of character go hand in hand.

This type of love may be felt for a woman who is powerful and of high rank (22, 50), or it may be felt for a slave girl (75, 78, 85),—the position of slave girls in Moslem society was one which seems very strange to us today.[35] In its purely spiritual aspect such a love may exist between two men without blame, but the question is complicated for us by the fact that among the Arabs public opinion required that if the beloved was a woman she must, "for decency's sake," be spoken of as a man and referred to by masculine pronouns, adjectives, and verbs.[36] Ibn Hazm disapproves of the practice which some poets indulged in of addressing their love poems to the daughters of their lords (35), and upon one point he is most emphatic—one must not make love to a married woman; "Moslems have come together on this point unanimously, only heretics not fulfilling it" (128).

Whether the beloved was of high or of low rank, the lover was always abject before her. "The surprising thing which happens in love is the submissiveness of the lover to his beloved" (39–40). "I have [trod] the carpets of khalifs and [seen] circles of kings, and I never saw a timid respect which would equal that of a lover toward his beloved" (66). If the woman's soul, wrapped in its earthly veil, does not recognize its other half (8, 24) and she is not favorable to him,

---

[35] There is some doubt as to whether the word *garija* always means "slave girl," although in most cases it certainly does. *Archivum Romanicum*, XIX (1935), 235.

[36] See the authorities cited by Nykl, *op. cit.*, p. cxviii. There may be some connection between this convention and the practice of the troubadour of addressing his lady as "my lord" (*midons* or *senhor*). Jeanroy, *op. cit.*, I, 91; Nykl, *op. cit.*, pp. cii f.

or if circumstances prevent the union of the lovers, the man seeks for contentment in what he has and hopes for more favors later (89). When he does receive anything, he is filled with joy; but he does not pretend, as the troubadours sometimes did, that he finds joy in the mere fact that his devotion is not rewarded. There are differences between Ibn Hazm's conception of love and that of the troubadours, but there is no justification for the statement of Jeanroy that "there is no trace, for example, in Ibn Hazm of the ennobling power of love, nor of the amorous vassalage, nor of the superiority of the lady over her lover, that is to say, of the courtly theories." [37] There is much more than a trace of each of these.

In his view of love Ibn Hazm is by no means unique among the Arabs. We find similar ideas in the works of the philosophers who preceded him, and we find them over and over again in the works of the poets of the eleventh century. [38] There was a definite school among them which advocated what Pérès calls "platonic love," but which resembles more closely what Andreas (p. 122) designates as "pure love." These poets taught that a man shows his good character and his good breeding by practicing a chaste love (*al-hawa al-ʿudri*) rather than a sensual love. [39] But true love, whether "pure" or "mixed," had an ennobling influence upon the lover, making a man of the humblest birth the equal of the noble lady whom he addressed (p. 427), for among the Arabs courtly manners were not the exclusive prerogative of the upper class (p. 425). But the lover, whether of higher or lower rank than his beloved, speaks of himself as her slave—a form of slavery which does honor to him (pp. 411 ff.); he addresses the lady as "my lord" (*sayyidi*) or "my master" (*mawlaya*) (p. 416) and loves her even when she tortures him. He finds contentment when she rejects him

---

[37] *Op. cit.*, II, 367. He is answered by Nykl in *Archivum Romanicum*, XIX (1935), 227 ff.

[38] Henri Pérès, *La Poésie andalouse en arabe classique au XIᵉ siècle* (Paris: Maisonneuve, 1937), see especially pp. 397–431, "La Femme et l'amour." Pérès says (p. 411) that the material is so abundant that he finds it difficult to select.

[39] For more specific details see Pérès, *loc. cit.* This institution should be compared with that of the *subintroducta* among the early Christians.

and joy when she shows him any kindness (415). One poet, Ibn 'Ammar, even says that love's delights are made of its burning torments (427), a form of expression which is almost identical with that of some of the later Christian poets.

In spite of what Ibn Hazm says about the fact that Moslems avoided love affairs with married women, we find that some of the poets did address their amatory verses to the wives of other men, and Pérès believes that this was not due to pure fancy, but that the verses reflect the actual social condition of the time (419). There are abundant evidences of the freedom which women, even married women, enjoyed in Andalusia at this period (398 ff.). We even know that Wallada, daughter of the Caliph Al-Mustakfi, established, after her father's death, a sort of salon which was a gathering place for literary men and other people of prominence. She was criticized, it is true, but the fact that such a state of things was tolerated at all shows a great deal about the freedom of the Mohammedan women (399).[40]

Even if we accept the theory that courtly love is a fusion of Latin and Moorish elements—and not all scholars are willing to admit this— still we have not solved the problem of how and why it developed. In France the first troubadour of whom we have any record was Duke William of Aquitaine, who had some acquaintance with Moslem Spain. His early poetry is by no means courtly, but traces of courtliness begin to appear in his later poems; Appel says, indeed, that they contain all the elements of courtly love.[41] There are some indications that the actual fusion of the various elements took place at the court of his friend and vassal, Viscount Ebles II of Ventadorn.[42] Ebles himself was a poet, although none of his verses has come down to us, and he

---

[40] In this Arabic poetry there are still other resemblances to the poetry of the troubadours: the use of the assumed name to conceal the lady's identity (417); the use of the epithet "jealous one" to designate the husband (418–19); and the references to the evil work of slanderers (420). There are also references to the religion of love and its laws (421), and what are practically decisions in problems of love.

[41] Review of Nykl's book in *Zeitschrift für romanische Philologie*, LII (1932), 771.

[42] Cross and Nitze, *op. cit.*, p. 92; Holmes, *op. cit.*, pp. 172–73; Jeanroy, *op. cit.*, I, 156; II, 16–17.

was surrounded by poets, the most famous of whom were Bernart de Ventadorn and Peire Rogier. Both Bernart and Marcabrû seem to be referring to a new courtly style of poetry when they speak of the poetic school of Ebles, but the style was soon adopted by poets in other parts of the country.

The ideas were introduced into the north when Duke William's granddaughter, Eleanor of Aquitaine, married Prince Louis of France and later, after her divorce from him, Prince Henry of England, in each case becoming queen within a short time. Bernart de Ventadorn followed her and doubtless helped her to introduce her ideas on love into the north. In Paris this was done, apparently, against considerable opposition on the part of King Louis and some of his advisors, but in London, with a second husband who was more in sympathy with her ideals, her influence was considerable. Thomas of Britain wrote his *Tristram and Ysolt* under her inspiration, perhaps definitely for her. Wace dedicated to her his *Brut,* and it is generally believed that she is the noble lady to whom Benoît de Sainte-More dedicated his romance of Troy. It seems probable that Marie de France was connected with the English court, and perhaps also Chrétien de Troyes.[43] Three of Queen Eleanor's sons, Henry, Geoffrey, and Richard, were patrons of literature and at Poitiers kept up the family tradition; Richard also wrote poetry of his own.

But an even more influential role was played by the two daughters of Eleanor and King Louis. They were both married in the same year (1164), Marie to Count Henry the Liberal of Champagne, and Alix to his brother, Count Thibaut of Blois, and both carried on their mother's social and literary interests.[44]

Countess Marie was particularly active in this respect, and Troyes, her husband's capital, was, even before her marriage, something of a literary center. Its most famous literary figure was that Chrétien about

---

[43] This is the conjecture of Gustave Cohen, *Chrétien de Troyes et son œuvre* (Paris: Boivin, 1931), pp. 82, 89. See also Holmes, *op. cit.,* p. 164, n.

[44] Adèle of Champagne, sister of Henry and Thibaut, had already (in 1160) become the third wife of King Louis VII, the father of Marie and Alix.

whom we know so little that we are forced to call him, as he once called himself (*Erec*, l. 9), Chrétien de Troyes. His *Erec and Enide* was almost certainly written before Marie came to Troyes, and perhaps also his story of "King Mark and Iseult the Blond" and those translations from Ovid which he mentions in the introduction to *Cligès*, but which have not come down to us.[45] It is possible that the Ovidian translations were written after Countess Marie came to Troyes; *Cligès* almost certainly was, for scholars have detected in it references to the *Heraclius* of Gautier of Arras, and that, as we know from a reference to Countess Marie, was written after her marriage.[46] There is nothing in the love casuistry of *Cligès* that Chrétien could not have developed for himself out of Ovid, but it seems most natural to attribute the difference in tone between this poem and the *Erec and Enide* to the growing influence of the countess.

As to his next poem, *The Knight of the Cart* (sometimes called *Lancelot*), there is no doubt whatever. He tells us plainly that the countess furnished him with both the subject matter (*matière*) and the manner of treatment (*sens*) and that he is simply trying to carry out her desire and intention. His statement is phrased as a compliment, but it is not difficult to see beneath the surface a note of apology for writing on a theme with which he is not wholly in sympathy. The poem is an elaborate illustration of the doctrine of courtly love as it was introduced into northern France by Eleanor and Marie. Here for the first time in Chrétien's extant works we find the glorification of the love of one man for another man's wife, a situation which Fenice, in *Cligès*, had declared to be intolerable. Chrétien clearly found the theme distasteful and left the poem unfinished; the conclusion is by Godefroy de Laigny. It is to this same period that we must refer Chrétien's lyrics of courtly love, written in the style of the troubadour

---

[45] There is no general agreement as to the dates of Chrétien's poems, although their order is fairly certain.

[46] But Holmes (*op. cit.*, p. 167) dates it about 1162 on the basis of some references to German affairs, and Cohen (*op. cit.*, p. 87) before 1164, because Marie is not mentioned but the library at Beauvais (which was dependent upon Count Henry) is.

poets.[47] In his next poem, the *Yvain*, he rejects the idea of an adulterous love, which he did not like, but retains the other conventions of courtly love, which apparently he did. In his last work,[48] *The Story of the Grail*, he departs even further from the ideas and the ideals of courtly love. The story, he tells us, he got from a book which Count Philip of Flanders had given him,[49] and from this fact it is generally assumed that Chrétien had now left Troyes and was living at Philip's court. But this does not necessarily follow; we know that Philip made a number of visits to Troyes at about this time,[50] and it may have been on one of these occasions that Chrétien obtained from him the book he speaks of. Chrétien died before he finished the poem; the continuations are by other hands.

Chrétien's literary career shows us the nature, and in some measure the extent, of the influence which Countess Marie exerted upon her circle at Troyes. At least once during this period she seems to have left her capital to seek renewed inspiration from her mother at Poitiers. In 1167 King Henry had appointed his son Richard, then a boy of eleven, Duke of Aquitaine, and Richard's mother accompanied him when he went to reign over this territory. He can hardly have been more than a figurehead at first, while his mother was Duchess of Aquitaine in her own right; so it was she who was the actual ruler, and as such she sought to revive the former glories of her ancestors. The ducal palace at Poitiers was rebuilt to provide some of the luxuries with which she

[47] Modern criticism has left him only two of those formerly attributed to him; one of these is modeled in part upon a poem by Bernart de Ventadorn.

[48] The place in the scheme of *William of England*, if that is by Chrétien, is difficult to determine; perhaps it belongs between the *Yvain* and the *Story of the Grail*. F. E. Guyer (*Romanic Review*, XII [1921], 247) places it early because of its attitude toward love.

[49] According to Gaston Paris (*La Littérature française au moyen âge*, § 57) Count Philip had been in England in 1172. Chrétien's *Story of the Grail* is variously dated from 1174 to 1184, the preference apparently being for the earlier date, and Philip may have brought him the book from England.

[50] L.-A. Vigneras, "Chrétien de Troyes Rediscovered," *Modern Philology*, XXXII (1935), 341 f. In 1182 Philip proposed marriage to the countess, whose husband had died the year before, but ended by marrying his nephew Baldwin to her daughter Marie.

had become acquainted when she visited Byzantium as Queen of France. To her court came the lords and ladies of her dominions, and here she was able, for the first time, to establish in a wholly congenial atmosphere a court of love on a grand scale. In so doing, if we may judge from the book of Andreas, she was assisted by her daughter Marie, also an ardent devotee of the art of love, by her niece Isabelle of Flanders,[51] whose devotion to its precepts was soon to involve her in trouble with her husband, and perhaps by Marie's sister-in-law Adèle of Champagne, who was now Queen of France, and who, as we know from a poem of Conan de Béthune, was fond of presiding over assemblies where amorous verse was recited.[52] But the experiment was soon to come to an end, for in the summer of 1174 King Henry came to Poitiers, took Queen Eleanor back to England, where she was imprisoned for a time, and sent the other ladies to their homes.[53]

In the year 1181 Count Henry of Champagne died, leaving Countess Marie to act as regent during the minority of their sons. She was now able, free from all interference, to revive in a small way her mother's social experiment. Troyes was not as congenial soil for courtly love as Poitiers, with its memories of Count William the Troubadour, had been, yet her influence was great, and in some measure it persisted down to the time of her grandson, Thibaut the Great, who became King of Navarre and is best known for his love lyrics on the courtly model and for his romantic affection for Queen Blanche of Castille. The period of Marie's regency was a period of literary activity at Troyes. Conan de Béthune sang at her court, and the poet Gace

---

[51] She is sometimes referred to as Elizabeth; apparently the two names were looked upon as the same and were interchangeable during the Middle Ages (*Notes and Queries,* CLXXVIII [1940], 81, 268). For the story that was commonly told about her see p. 20, below.

[52] *Chansons,* III, 5–14, cited by Holmes, *op. cit.,* p. 11, and G. Paris, in *Romania,* XII, 523, 525.

[53] For a reconstruction of this whole episode see the article by Amy Kelly in *Speculum,* XII (1937), 3 ff. Part of her work is based upon inference, but I have no doubt that it is substantially correct. Andreas assigns the leading role to Countess Marie, but this probably does not represent the real situation; it is only flattery, no more subtle than that with which Chrétien introduces his story of *The Knight of the Cart.*

Brulé was one of her vassals. Aubouin de Sézanne wrote for her. The anonymous long paraphrase of the psalm *Eructavit* belongs to this period, and so does Éverat's verse translation of Genesis, although it was not completed until after her death. Chrétien may still have been at Troyes, working on his *Story of the Grail*, and it is almost certainly at this period that the treatise on *The Art of Courtly Love* was written by her chaplain Andreas.

Of this Andreas the Chaplain we know almost nothing aside from his book. His name is signed as a witness to seven charters dated between 1182 and 1186, and one of these charters was granted by the Countess Marie, which serves to confirm, if confirmation were needed, the fact that he knew her.[54] In the latter part of his book he refers to himself as "chaplain of the royal court,"[55] and although no evidence to substantiate this claim has ever been found, it may well have been true, in view of the close relations between Troyes and Paris which existed at the time.[56]

It is clear that Andreas, like Chrétien, wrote his book by direction of the countess, but unlike Chrétien he seems to have felt little repugnance for the doctrines embodied in it. He takes care to remind gentlemen that they should be attentive to the services of the Church and generous in giving, but he is more concerned with establishing the fact that the clergy, by virtue of their cloth, rank above even the higher nobility. He does admit, grudgingly, that this kind of nobility, granted them by God and not to be taken away from them by men, cannot give them especial privilege in a love affair, so that in love a clerk can claim no more consideration than his original social status entitled

---

[54] Vigneras, *loc. cit.*

[55] The statement of Jeremiah de Montagnone (a statement followed by some of the early printed editions) that Andreas was chaplain of Pope Innocent IV is doubtless due to a confusion between him and that other Andreas who wrote a book called *De dissuasione uxorationis* and who was Innocent's chaplain. See Pio Rajna, "La questione della data del libro di Andrea Capellano" in *Studj di filologia romanza,* XIII (1890), 225 ff.

[56] King Philip Augustus was a half brother of Countess Marie, and the Queen mother was a sister of her husband, Count Henry.

him to; nevertheless a clerk makes the best lover because he has "an experienced knowledge of all things." Andreas boasts of his own skill in "the art of soliciting nuns" and smacks his lips over an adventure he once had with one of them; very regretfully he was forced to decline her proffered advances because of the very severe penalties which, in this world and the next, are inflicted upon a man who carries on a love affair with a nun. The picture we get of Andreas from his book is that of a man who is connected with the Church, but for whom spiritual affairs are not the first consideration.

Even the last section of the book, "The Rejection of Love," does little to change this picture. Such a retraction was called for by the scheme of Ovid, which in a general way Andreas was following,[57] and there are plenty of precedents in ecclesiastical tradition to justify his misogyny.[58] The early Fathers of the Church taught that virginity was preferable to marriage and attempted to popularize the celibate life by dwelling on the vices of women. St. Jerome, for example, angered by Jovinian's statement that, other things being equal, a virgin was no better in the sight of God than a wife or a widow, attempted to prove him wrong by setting forth all the wickedness of women and so provided the Middle Ages with a convenient compendium of anti-feminist literature. Probably there was no age that did not furnish such attacks upon women, but in the period just before Andreas wrote they seem to have been especially numerous. John of Salisbury,[59] Bernard of Morlaix, Hildebert of Le Mans, and Marbod of Rennes all contributed to the campaign, and it is possible that Andreas made some use of the work of the last two. It has been pointed out that his satire,

[57] One may compare also what Asin (quoted by Nykl, *op. cit.*, p. liii) calls the "brutal antifeminism" of Ibn Hazm's later life.

[58] Eve's sin was generally looked upon as the cause of the downfall of mankind, for without it Adam would not have sinned; Solomon was unable to find a single good woman; Paul held that it was good for a man not to touch a woman, and so forth.

[59] Chapter xi of Book VIII of John's *Policraticus* is taken largely from Jerome. For the other works see August Wulff, *Die frauenfeindlichen Dichtungen in den romanischen Literaturen des Mittelalters bis zum Ende des XIII. Jahrhunderts*, Halle: Niemeyer, 1914. The discussion of Andreas is on pp. 65–72.

caustic as it is, is somewhat milder than that of the others. Doubtless he was attempting to appease his ecclesiastical superiors, who may well have been offended by the tone of the first two books, but the third is not on a much higher spiritual level than the rest.[60]

Andreas's knowledge of the Bible is about what one might expect of a none too sincere cleric. With the work of the Church Fathers he seems to have had some slight acquaintance, but it is difficult to determine the exact nature of his indebtedness to them. Many of their ideas had become commonplaces of religious instruction, and he himself may not have known where he picked them up. For the same reason it would be rash to venture a statement concerning his familiarity with the theological writers of his own day. I have cited a number of passages which resemble some of his, but they may be parallels only and not sources. His quotations from the classical Latin writers are, at first sight, somewhat impressive, but most, if not all of these, are taken at second hand. Even the passages he quotes from Ovid (an author whom one would expect him to know) are those which are repeated over and over in the literature of the time—in florilegia, in arts of poetry, and even in goliardic verse. Walter of Châtillon, for example, has a poem of eighty lines in which he includes twenty "auctoritates" or quotations from Latin authors. Of these twenty passages, four (one from Lucan, one from Claudian, one from the *Metamorphoses,* and one from *The Cure for Love*) and an echo of a fifth appear in the work of Andreas. It is generally believed that Walter knew the classics at first hand, but it seems almost equally certain that Andreas derived his knowledge from Walter or from some other contemporary writer.[61]

The other features of the book, including the exposition of courtly love, are, I am sure, due to Countess Marie and her associates. The

[60] Andreas may have been influenced by still other currents: the sixth satire of Juvenal, which Wulff thinks he knew, the satires of Marcabrû, who had been a vassal of Queen Eleanor's father (Jeanroy, *op. cit.,* I, 151; II, 23 ff.), the oriental tales which served as exempla for the priests, and so forth.

[61] F. J. Raby, *A History of Secular Latin Poetry in the Middle Ages* (Oxford: Clarendon Press, 1934), II, 196–98; see also II, 190, 205, 213.

style, it seems to me, rises at times above anything of which Andreas is capable, as though he were writing from dictation. The only date given in the book is May 1, 1174, which is the date of the letter supposed to have been written by the Countess of Champagne in answer to an inquiry on a problem of love. The date falls toward the end of Queen Eleanor's domination at Poitiers, and the book is undoubtedly intended to present us with a picture of life in her circle there. One of the decisions it records was rendered by "a court of ladies convened in Gascony," and the only lady outside the family whose decisions are quoted is Ermengarde, Countess of Narbonne, a southern lady. Since Andreas distinguishes between "the Queen" and "Queen Eleanor," the former must have been Adèle (Aélis) of Champagne, who was married to King Louis of France in 1165 and was left a widow in 1180.[62] The Countess of Flanders (also mentioned as one of the circle) was at this time Isabelle of Vermandois. Her mother was Petronille of Provence, sister of Queen Eleanor, and her father was a distant cousin of King Louis. In 1156 she married Philip, eldest son of Count Thierry of Flanders, and in 1168 Philip became count; in the preceding year his wife had become Countess of Vermandois in her own right. In 1175, according to the story as it has come down to us, she was accused by her husband of encouraging the attentions of Walter of Fontaines, a knight who shone out among his fellow knights as the morning star among the other stars. He was put to death, and she was disgraced.[63] Gaston Paris remarks that after this episode she would not have ventured to pronounce a decision in a love affair, but there is nothing in the recorded accounts to indicate that she had offended in any way against the code of courtly love, whatever her husband may have thought of her conduct. In fact the troubadours who mention the

[62] Gaston Paris believes that after her husband's death she would not have been referred to as "the Queen." He forgets that Andreas is supposed to be reporting decisions she rendered before her husband's death when she still was the Queen.

[63] Miss Kelly (*loc. cit.*) discreetly says that he was "drawn and quartered," but his death as described by both Ralph de Diceto, her source, and by Benedict of Peterborough was a much more ignominious and a much less romantic one.

matter blame her for hardness of heart rather than for easy yielding.[64] Andreas may here be trying to vindicate her memory (she died in 1182) from the slurs that had been cast upon it.

Although Andreas's book was almost certainly intended to portray conditions at Queen Eleanor's court at Poitiers between 1170 and 1174, the actual writing of it must have taken place some years later, when Marie was at Troyes ruling as regent for her son after her husband's death. We may determine the date rather exactly from a comment which one of the characters makes upon a Hungarian marriage. The reference is obviously to the marriage between King Béla III of Hungary and Marguerite, daughter of King Louis (and of his second wife Constance of Castille) and widow of Prince Henry, eldest son of Queen Eleanor and of King Henry II. Andreas refers to this marriage as one that was contemplated but had not actually taken place, so that this part of the book must have been written, or at least revised, between 1184, when King Béla sent to Paris an account of his income, and August, 1186, when the marriage took place.[65] This date is not inconsistent with anything else that we know of the work.

There is no external evidence that helps us to verify this date. The manuscripts are all late, although Rajna believed that he found evidence that two of them are copies of an exemplar that was written in 1209 or 1210.[66] Albertanus of Brescia quotes from it in his *De dilectione Dei et proximi* (1238) and in his *De Arte loquendi et tacendi* (1245), and it seems to have influenced the *Art of Love* of Jacques d'Amiens, who wrote at about the same time. By March 7, 1277, it was so widely known that Bishop Stephan Tempier of Paris felt obliged to condemn some of its errors, referring to it as "Librum De amore sive

---

[64] It is very doubtful whether the suffering lover was really Walter of Fontaines, and somewhat doubtful whether there was any truth at all in the story, although it spread rather widely. See *Revue des langues romanes*, XXXII (1888), 286–88, and *Romania*, XVII (1888), 591–95.

[65] Arpad Steiner, in *Speculum*, XIII (1938), 308.

[66] Pio Rajna, "Il libro di Andrea Capellano in Italia nei secoli XIII e XIV," *Studj di filologia romanza*, XIII (1890), 206–207.

de Deo amoris qui sic incipit: *Cogit me multum,* etc. et sic terminatur: *Cave igitur, Gualteri, amoris exercere mandata.*" [67]

That the work of Andreas enjoyed considerable popularity is also shown by the number of manuscripts that have been preserved [68] and by the translations into the vernaculars. There is also an early printed edition, published apparently at Strasburg in 1473 or 1474, and two later editions printed in Dortmund in 1610 and 1614.[69] Of the translations, the earliest is one into French, selections from which are included in *La Doctrine d'amor* by a certain Enanchet or Annanchet (the name may be a pseudonym), about whom nothing further is known. On linguistic grounds we assume that the translation was made in the neighborhood of Verona in the first half of the thirteenth century; the sole surviving manuscript was finished on the fourteenth of June, 1287. This translation wholly changes the tone of Andreas's work, giving to certain passages a religious significance which they did not bear in the original and even explaining that the lady whose love one seeks is the Virgin Mary.[70] The other French translation is in verse and is the work of a man who in an acrostic at the end of the poem gives his name as Drouart la Vache. He tells us that on the Sunday after the Exaltation of the Holy Cross (September 17) in the year 1290 one of his companions gave him a copy of a book in Latin. After he had read a little of it, he found the book so pleasing and he laughed so much over it that a friend urged him to translate it into French. His lady added her entreaties, and he assented; he finished his task on the Wednesday before the feast of Saint Martin (November 8) in the same year. His translation is on the whole a competent and facile piece of work; it covers the whole of Andreas's volume, although with many omissions.[71]

---

[67] *Speculum,* VII (1932), 75 ff.

[68] Twelve complete or nearly so (twice as many as we have of Chrétien's *Knight of the Cart*), besides a number which contain extracts. For particulars see Trojel's introduction, p. xx.

[69] For details of the printed editions see the Bibliography.

[70] Rajna, *op. cit.*, p. 209.

[71] No thorough study of the influence of Andreas in France has ever been made;

The references to the work of Andreas by Albertanus of Brescia, Jeremiah de Montagnone, and others, and the citation of extracts by Enanchet testify to the spread of the work in Italy.[72] There are, in addition, two translations into Italian. One is contained in a single manuscript written in the middle of the fifteenth century, but Rajna believes that the work itself is of the fourteenth. The other, attributed without any good reason to Andrea Lancia, is of about the same period and is found in four manuscripts, and portions of it are in several others. Part of this was printed in 1561 under the name of Giovanni Boccaccio.[73]

In Spain the work of Andreas served as a textbook for those courts of love that were established in Barcelona by King Juan of Aragon (1350–1396) and his wife Violant de Bar. These courts were supposed to be a revival of those that had formerly been conducted by Queen Eleanor and Countess Marie, but the spirit of the Catalan courts was quite different from that which had animated the earlier ones, for here it was the rule that no gentleman could pay court to a lady without first obtaining the permission of her husband, and most of the affairs seem to have consisted only of lengthy discussions of elaborate problems of love casuistry. These courts reached their height during the years 1387–1389, when King Juan fell under the influence of Na Carrosa de Vilaragut, and it appears that the Catalan translation of Andreas's book was made at this time. The work was probably done by Domenec Mascó, the Vice-Chancellor. Apparently he translated all of the first two books of Andreas's Latin, but the one surviving manuscript has lost a number of leaves, so that there are now several gaps in the text.[74]

In medieval Germany there were two translations, both dating from the fifteenth century. The first was made in the year 1404 by Eber-

---

Trojel's introduction gives some references. This influence lasted as late as the time of Rabelais, who in a dialogue between Panurge and a lady of Paris burlesques one of the speeches of Andreas.

[72] It was often referred to as the work of Walter.

[73] Rajna, *op. cit.*, 203–24; Trojel, *op. cit.*, Introduction, pp. xvii–xix.

[74] Pagès, Introduction to the Catalan text, pp. ix–xxxi.

hardus Cerlne (Kellner) of Minden, but was not printed until the nineteenth century. The second, by Dr. Johann Hartlieb of Munich, was made "by request and procurement of a prince of Austria." This prince was Archduke Albrecht VI, and as Hartlieb lived in Vienna during the years 1431–1440 presumably the work was done during this period.[75] This translation has been preserved in six manuscripts; it was printed in Augsburg in 1482 and again in 1484, and there is also an edition printed in Strasburg in the latter year. There is likewise a modern translation into German made by Hanns Martin Elster. Except for a few scattered passages, Andreas's work has never been translated into English.

[75] Hans Georg Wieczorek, *Johann Hartliebs Verdeutschung von des Andreas Capellanus Liber de reprobatione amoris,* Breslau diss., 1929, p. 3; *Euphorion,* XXV (1924), 226–27.

Genealogical Table

Genealogical Table

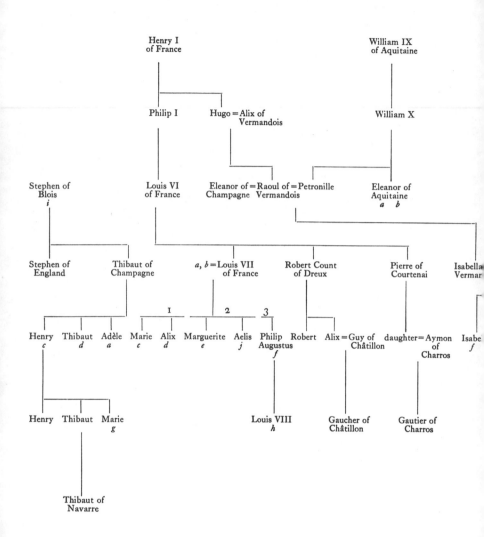

a. King Louis of France married: (1) Eleanor of Aquitaine; (2) Constance of Castille; (3) Adèle of Champagne.
b. Eleanor of Aquitaine married: (1) Louis VII of France; (2) Henry II of England.
c. Henry Count of Champagne married Marie, daughter of Louis VII.
d. Thibaut Count of Blois married Alix, daughter of Louis VII.
e. Marguerite of France married: (1) Prince Henry of England; (2) King Béla III of Hungary.

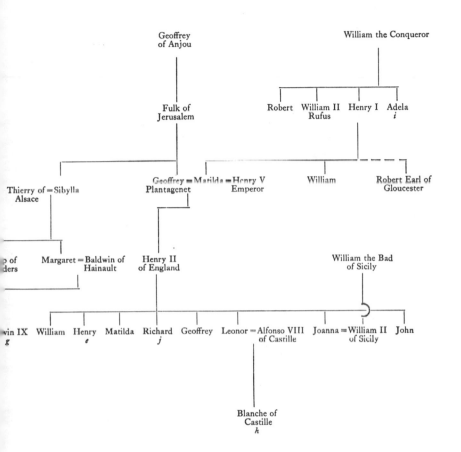

King Philip Augustus married Isabella of Hainault.
Count Baldwin of Flanders married Marie, daughter of Henry of Champagne.
King Louis VIII of France married Blanche of Castille.
Adela of England married Stephen Count of Blois.
Aelis of France was betrothed to Prince Richard of England.

THE ART OF COURTLY LOVE

AUTHOR'S PREFACE

I AM greatly impelled by the continual urging of my love for you, my revered friend Walter,[1] to make known by word of mouth and to teach you by my writings the way in which a state of love between two lovers may be kept unharmed and likewise how those who do not love may get rid of the darts of Venus that are fixed in their hearts. You tell me that you are a new recruit of Love, and, having recently been wounded by an arrow of his, you do not know how to manage your horse's reins properly and you cannot find any cure for yourself. How serious this is and how it troubles my soul no words of mine can make clear to you. For I know, having learned from experience, that it does not do the man who owes obedience to Venus's service any good to give careful thought to anything except how he may always be doing something that will entangle him more firmly in his chains; he thinks he has nothing good except what may wholly please his love. Therefore, although it does not seem expedient to devote oneself to things of this kind or fitting for any prudent man to engage in this kind of hunting, nevertheless, because of the affection I have for you I can by no means refuse your request; because I know clearer than day that after you have learned the art of love your progress in it will be more cautious, in so far as I can I shall comply with your desire.

[1] This Walter has never been satisfactorily identified. Andreas tells us that he is a young man of the highest nobility, but he may be only a lay figure created to give life to the book. Trojel, who believes that he was a real person, points out (*Middelalderens Elskovshoffer*, pp. 105 ff.) that the title "venerandus" was applied only to bishops and to members of the French royal family, and Walter can hardly have been a bishop. The colophon of one manuscript states that he was "nepos" (nephew?) of the king of France. The only Walter (Gautier) found in the royal family at this time was a grandson of Pierre de Courtenai and therefore grandnephew of King Louis VII (Trojel, *op. cit.*, genealogical tables), but he was apparently too young to have been addressed by Andreas. Trojel believed that the person addressed was Gaucher III of Châtillon, grandson of Count Robert I of Dreux (see p. 74), and therefore another grandnephew of King Louis. But Gaston Paris (*Journal des Savants*, 1888, p. 673) objected on the ground that Gautier and Gaucher were different names, and in his edition of Andreas, Trojel seems to have withdrawn his suggestion.

BOOK ONE

Introduction to the Treatise on Love

WE MUST first consider what love is, whence it gets its name, what the effect of love is, between what persons love may exist, how it may be acquired, retained, increased, decreased, and ended, what are the signs that one's love is returned, and what one of the lovers ought to do if the other is unfaithful.

CHAPTER I. WHAT LOVE IS

Love is a certain inborn suffering derived from the sight of and excessive meditation upon the beauty of the opposite sex, which causes each one to wish above all things the embraces of the other and by common desire to carry out all of love's precepts in the other's embrace.

That love is suffering is easy to see, for before the love becomes equally balanced on both sides there is no torment greater, since the lover is always in fear that his love may not gain its desire and that he is wasting his efforts. He fears, too, that rumors of it may get abroad, and he fears everything that might harm it in any way, for before things are perfected a slight disturbance often spoils them. If he is a poor man, he also fears that the woman may scorn his poverty; if he is ugly, he fears that she may despise his lack of beauty or may give her love to a more handsome man; if he is rich, he fears that his parsimony in the past may stand in his way. To tell the truth, no one can number the fears of one single lover.[2] This kind of love, then, is a suffering which is felt by only one of the persons and may be called "single love." But even after both are in love the fears that arise are

[2] Ovid *Art of Love* II. 517 ff.

just as great, for each of the lovers fears that what he has acquired with so much effort may be lost through the effort of someone else, which is certainly much worse for a man than if, having no hope, he sees that his efforts are accomplishing nothing, for it is worse to lose the things you are seeking than to be deprived of a gain you merely hope for. The lover fears, too, that he may offend his loved one in some way; indeed he fears so many things that it would be difficult to tell them.

That this suffering is inborn I shall show you clearly, because if you will look at the truth and distinguish carefully you will see that it does not arise out of any action; only from the reflection of the mind upon what it sees does this suffering come. For when a man sees some woman fit for love and shaped according to his taste, he begins at once to lust after her in his heart; [3] then the more he thinks about her the more he burns with love, until he comes to a fuller meditation. Presently he begins to think about the fashioning of the woman and to differentiate her limbs, to think about what she does, and to pry into the secrets of her body, and he desires to put each part of it to the fullest use. [4] Then after he has come to this complete meditation, love cannot hold the reins, but he proceeds at once to action; straightway he strives to get a helper and to find an intermediary. He begins to plan how he may find favor with her, and he begins to seek a place and a time opportune for talking; he looks upon a brief hour as a very long year, because he cannot do anything fast enough to suit his eager mind. It is well known that many things happen to him in this manner. This inborn suffering comes, therefore, from seeing and meditating. Not every kind of meditation can be the cause of love, an excessive one is required; for a restrained thought does not, as a rule, return to the mind, and so love cannot arise from it.

[3] Compare Paul the Deacon *Exhortation to Henry, Count of Forum Julii:* "Do not let the beauty of a body seduce you; do not let death enter into your soul through the windows of your eyes."

[4] Compare Ovid *Metamorphoses* VI. 490–93.

CHAPTER II. BETWEEN WHAT PERSONS LOVE MAY EXIST

Now, in love you should note first of all that love cannot exist except between persons of opposite sexes. Between two men or two women love can find no place, for we see that two persons of the same sex are not at all fitted for giving each other the exchanges of love or for practicing the acts natural to it. Whatever nature forbids, love is ashamed to accept.

Every attempt of a lover tends toward the enjoyment of the embraces of her whom he loves; he thinks about it continually, for he hopes that with her he may fulfill all the mandates of love—that is, those things which we find in treatises on the subject. Therefore in the sight of a lover nothing can be compared to the act of love, and a true lover would rather be deprived of all his money and of everything that the human mind can imagine as indispensable to life rather than be without love, either hoped for or attained. For what under heaven can a man possess or own for which he would undergo so many perils as we continually see lovers submit to of their own free will? We see them despise death and fear no threats, scatter their wealth abroad and come to great poverty. Yet a wise lover does not throw away wealth as a prodigal spender usually does, but he plans his expenditures from the beginning in accordance with the size of his patrimony; for when a man comes to poverty and want he begins to go along with his face downcast and to be tortured by many thoughts, and all joyousness leaves him. And when that goes, melancholy comes straightway to take its place, and wrath claims a place in him; so he begins to act in a changed manner toward his beloved and to appear frightful to her, and the things that cause love to increase begin to fail. Therefore love begins to grow less, for love is always either decreasing or increasing. I know from my own experience that when poverty comes in, the things that nourished love begin to leave, because "poverty has nothing with which to feed its love." [5]

[5] Ovid *The Cure for Love*, l. 749.

But I do not tell you this, my friend, with the idea of indicating by what I say that you should follow avarice, which, as all agree, cannot remain in the same dwelling with love, but to show you that you should by all means avoid prodigality and should embrace generosity with both arms. Note, too, that nothing which a lover gets from his beloved is pleasing unless she gives it of her own free will.

CHAPTER III. WHERE LOVE GETS ITS NAME

Love gets its name (*amor*) from the word for hook (*amus*), which means "to capture" or "to be captured," [6] for he who is in love is captured in the chains of desire and wishes to capture someone else with his hook. Just as a skillful fisherman tries to attract fishes by his bait and to capture them on his crooked hook, so the man who is a captive of love tries to attract another person by his allurements and exerts all his efforts to unite two different hearts with an intangible bond, or if they are already united he tries to keep them so forever.

CHAPTER IV. WHAT THE EFFECT OF LOVE IS

Now it is the effect of love that a true lover cannot be degraded with any avarice. Love causes a rough and uncouth man to be distinguished for his handsomeness; it can endow a man even of the humblest birth with nobility of character; it blesses the proud with humility; and the man in love becomes accustomed to performing many services gracefully for everyone. O what a wonderful thing is love, which makes a man shine with so many virtues and teaches everyone, no matter who he is, so many good traits of character! There is another thing about love that we should not praise in few words: it adorns a man, so to speak, with the virtue of chastity, because he who shines with the light of one love can hardly think of embracing another woman, even a

[6] Isidore of Seville says (*Etymologies* X. i. 5), "A friend (*amicus*) is so called from the word for hook (*hamus*), that is, a shackle of affection; therefore they are also called hooks because they hold."

beautiful one. For when he thinks deeply of his beloved the sight of any other woman seems to his mind rough and rude.

I wish you therefore to keep always in mind, Walter my friend, that if love were so fair as always to bring his sailors into the quiet port after they had been soaked by many tempests, I would bind myself to serve him forever. But because he is in the habit of carrying an unjust weight in his hand, I do not have full confidence in him any more than I do in a judge whom men suspect. And so for the present I refuse to submit to his judgment, because "he often leaves his sailors in the mighty waves." But why love, at times, does not use fair weights I shall show you more fully elsewhere in this treatise.[7]

CHAPTER V. WHAT PERSONS ARE FIT FOR LOVE

We must now see what persons are fit to bear the arms of love. You should know that everyone of sound mind who is capable of doing the work of Venus may be wounded by one of Love's arrows unless prevented by age, or blindness, or excess of passion. Age is a bar, because after the sixtieth year in a man and the fiftieth in a woman, although one may have intercourse his passion cannot develop into love; because at that age the natural heat begins to lose its force, and the natural moisture is greatly increased, which leads a man into various difficulties and troubles him with various ailments, and there are no consolations in the world for him except food and drink. Similarly, a girl under the age of twelve and a boy before the fourteenth year do not serve in love's army.[8] However, I say and insist that before his eighteenth year a man cannot be a true lover, because up to that age he is overcome with embarrassment over any little thing, which not only interferes with the perfecting of love, but even destroys it if it is well perfected. But we find another even more powerful reason, which is that before this age a man has no constancy, but is changeable in every way, for such a tender

---

[7] See pp. 47, 50.

[8] "Young men before they are fourteen years old, and girls before they are twelve, may not, according to the laws, enter into marriage." Hugo of St. Victor *Summa sententiarum* VII. XV.

age cannot think about the mysteries of love's realm. Why love should kindle in a woman at an earlier age than in a man I shall perhaps show you elsewhere.

Blindness is a bar to love, because a blind man cannot see anything upon which his mind can reflect immoderately, and so love cannot arise in him, as I have already fully shown. But I admit that this is true only of the acquiring of love, for I do not deny that a love which a man acquires before his blindness may last after he becomes blind.

An excess of passion is a bar to love, because there are men who are slaves to such passionate desire that they cannot be held in the bonds of love—men who, after they have thought long about some woman or even enjoyed her, when they see another woman straightway desire her embraces, and they forget about the services they have received from their first love and they feel no gratitude for them. Men of this kind lust after every woman they see; their love is like that of a shameless dog. They should rather, I believe, be compared to asses, for they are moved only by that low nature which shows that men are on the level of the other animals rather than by that true nature which sets us apart from all the other animals by the difference of reason. Of such lovers I shall speak elsewhere.

CHAPTER VI. IN WHAT MANNER LOVE MAY BE ACQUIRED, AND IN HOW MANY WAYS

It remains next to be seen in what ways love may be acquired. The teaching of some people is said to be that there are five means by which it may be acquired: a beautiful figure, excellence of character, extreme readiness of speech, great wealth, and the readiness with which one grants that which is sought. But we hold that love may be acquired only by the first three, and we think that the last two ought to be banished completely from Love's court,[9] as I shall show you when I come to the proper place in my system.

[9] "There are also other less creditable [reasons for marriage] such as the good looks of the man or the woman which often drive those whose minds are inflamed by love to enter into marriage so that they may carry out their desires. The love of property or of

A beautiful figure wins love with very little effort, especially when the lover who is sought is simple, for a simple lover thinks that there is nothing to look for in one's beloved besides a beautiful figure and face and a body well cared for. I do not particularly blame the love of such people, but neither do I have much approval for it, because love between uncautious and unskilled lovers cannot long be concealed, and so from the first it fails to increase. For when love is revealed, it does not help the lover's worth, but brands his reputation with evil rumors and often causes him grief. Love between such lovers seldom lasts; but if sometimes it should endure it cannot indulge in its former solaces, because when the girl's chaperone hears the rumors, she becomes suspicious and watches her more carefully and gives her no opportunities to talk, and it makes the man's relatives more careful and watchful, and so serious unfriendliness arises. In such cases, when love cannot have its solaces, it increases beyond all measure and drives the lovers to lamenting their terrible torments, because "we strive for what is forbidden and always want what is denied us." [10]

A wise woman will therefore seek as a lover a man of praiseworthy character—not one who anoints himself all over like a woman or makes a rite of the care of the body, for it does not go with a masculine figure to adorn oneself in womanly fashion or to be devoted to the care of the body. It was people like this the admirable Ovid meant when he said,

> Let young men who are decked out like women stay far away from me,
> A manly form wants to be cared for within moderate limits. [11]

Likewise, if you see a woman too heavily rouged you will not be taken in by her beauty unless you have already discovered that she is good company besides, since a woman who puts all her reliance on her rouge usually doesn't have any particular gifts of character. As I said about men, so with women—I believe you should not seek for beauty so much as for excellence of character. Be careful therefore, Walter, not

---

riches is a frequent cause, and so are certain other things which any one who will look carefully can notice for himself." Hugo of St. Victor, *op. cit.*, VII. i.

[10] Ovid *Amours* III. iv. 17. [11] Ovid *Heroides* IV. 75–76.

to be taken in by the empty beauty of women, because a woman is apt to be so clever and such a ready talker that after you have begun to enjoy the gifts you get from her you will not find it easy to escape loving her. A person of good character draws the love of another person of the same kind, for a well-instructed lover, man or woman, does not reject an ugly lover if the character within is good. A man who proves to be honorable and prudent cannot easily go astray in love's path or cause distress to his beloved. If a wise woman selects as her lover a wise man, she can very easily keep her love hidden forever; she can teach a wise lover to be even wiser, and if he isn't so wise she can restrain him and make him careful. A woman, like a man, should not seek for beauty or care of the person or high birth, for "beauty never pleases if it lacks goodness," and it is excellence of character alone which blesses a man with true nobility and makes him flourish in ruddy beauty. For since all of us human beings are derived originally from the same stock and all naturally claim the same ancestor, it was not beauty or care of the body or even abundance of possessions, but excellence of character alone which first made a distinction of nobility among men and led to the difference of class.[12] Many there are, however, who trace their descent from these same first nobles, but have degenerated and gone in the other direction. The converse of this proposition is likewise true.

Character alone, then, is worthy of the crown of love. Many times fluency of speech will incline to love the hearts of those who do not love, for an elaborate line of talk on the part of the lover usually sets love's arrows a-flying and creates a presumption in favor of the excellent character of the speaker. How this may be I shall try to show you as briefly as I can.

To this end I shall first explain to you that one woman belongs to the middle class, a second to the simple nobility, and a third to the higher nobility.[13] So it is with men: one is of the middle class, another of the

---

[12] "All men descend from the same original stock; no one is better born than another, except in so far as his disposition is nobler and better suited for the performance of good actions." Seneca *Benefits* III. xxviii.

[13] The ranks designated by *plebeia, nobilis,* and *nobilior* apparently correspond to

nobility, a third of the higher nobility, and a fourth of the very highest nobility. What I mean by a woman of the middle class is clear enough to you; a noblewoman is one descended from a vavasor or a lord, or is the wife of one of these, while a woman of the higher nobility is descended from great lords. The same rules apply to men, except that a man married to a woman of higher or lower rank than himself does not change his rank. A married woman changes her status to match that of her husband, but a man can never change his nobility by marriage. In addition, among men we find one rank more than among women, since there is a man more noble than any of these, that is, the clerk.

First Dialogue

A man of the middle class speaks with a woman of the same class

Now let a man of the middle class approach a woman of the same class and address her in this manner. First he should greet her in his usual way; this, however, should always be done, and all lovers must realize that after the salutation they should not immediately begin talking about love, for it is only with their concubines that men begin in that way. On the contrary, after the man has greeted the woman he ought to let a little time elapse, so that she may, if she wishes, speak first. If she does begin the conversation, you have good reason to rejoice, unless you are a fluent talker, because her remark will give you plenty to talk about. There are men who in the presence of ladies so lose their power of speech that they forget the things they have carefully thought out and arranged in their minds; they cannot say anything coherent, and it seems proper to reprove their foolishness, for it is not fitting that any man, unless he is bold and well-instructed, should enter into a conversation with ladies. But if the woman waits too long before beginning the conversation, you may begin it yourself, skillfully.

-----

the *bourgeoisie* (not the peasants), the *simple noblesse,* and the *noblesse titrée;* in England they might be the tradespeople, gentry, and nobility.

First you should say things that have nothing to do with your subject—make her laugh at something, or else praise her home, or her family, or herself. For women, particularly middle-class women from the country, commonly delight in being commended and readily believe every word that looks like praise. Then after these remarks that have nothing to do with your subject, you may go on in this fashion:

"When the Divine Being made you there was nothing that He left undone. I know that there is no defect in your beauty, none in your good sense, none in you at all except, it seems to me, that you have enriched no one by your love. I marvel greatly that Love permits so beautiful and so sensible a woman to serve for long outside his camp. O if you should take service with Love, blessed above all others will that man be whom you shall crown with your love! Now if I, by my merits, might be worthy of such an honor, no lover in the world could really be compared with me."

The woman says: "You seem to be telling fibs, since although I do not have a beautiful figure you extol me as beautiful beyond all other women and although I lack the ornament of wisdom you praise my good sense. The very highest wisdom ought not to be required of a woman descended from the middle class."

The man says: "It is a habit of wise people never to admit with their own mouths their good looks or their good character, and by so doing they clearly show their character, because prudent people guard their words so carefully that no one may have reason to apply to them that common proverb which runs, 'All praise is filthy in one's own mouth.' You, like a wise woman, not wishing to fall foul of this saying, leave all praise of you to others; but there are so many who do praise you that it would never be right to say that any of them meant to tell fibs. Even those who do not love you for the sake of your family are, I know, diligent in singing your praises. And besides, if you think you are not beautiful, you should believe that I must really be in love, since to me your beauty excels that of all other women; and love makes even an

ugly woman seem very beautiful to her lover. You said, too, that you
come of a humble family. But this shows that you are much more de-
serving of praise and blessed with a greater nobility, since yours does
not come from your descent or from your ancestors, but good character
and good manners alone have given to you a more worthy kind of
nobility. In the beginning the same nature created all men, and to this
day they would have remained equal had not greatness of soul and
worth of character commenced to set men apart from each other by the
inequality of nobility."

The woman says: "If I am as noble as you are trying to make out, you,
being a man of the middle class, should seek the love of some woman
of the same class, while I look for a noble lover to match my noble
status; for nobility and commonalty 'do not go well together or dwell
in the same abode.' " [14]

The man says: "Your answer would seem good enough if it were only
in women that a lowly birth might be ennobled by excellence of character. But since an excellent character makes noble not only women but
men also, you are perhaps wrong in refusing me your love, since my
manners, too, may illumine me with the virtue of nobility. Your first
concern should be whether I lack refined manners, and if you find my
status higher than you would naturally expect, you ought not deprive
me of the hope of your love. For one whose nobility is that of character
it is more proper to choose a lover whose nobility is of the same kind
than one who is high-born but unmannerly. Indeed, if you should find
a man who is distinguished by both kinds of nobility, it would be better
to take as a lover the man whose only nobility is that of character. For
the one gets his nobility from his ancient stock and from his noble father
and derives it as a sort of inheritance from those from whom he gets his
being; but the other gets his nobility only from himself, and what he
takes is not derived from his family tree, but springs only from the best
qualities of his mind. You should therefore approve the second man's

---

[14] Compare Ovid *Metamorphoses* ii. 846.

nobility more than that of the other. For I notice that we consider more worthy of praise and reward that king who received a small realm from his ancestors and afterwards by his virtuous rule brought countless nations under his sway than the king who retains undisturbed the many kingdoms which he inherited. If, therefore, you recognize that I enjoy nobility of manners, incline your excellence toward me and give me at least the hope of your love, which I have so long desired, so that I may live; for there is no hope of saving me if you cause me to despair of your love."

The woman says: "You may deserve praise for your great excellence, but I am rather young, and I shudder at the thought of receiving solaces from old men."

The man says: "Old age is certainly not a thing to disapprove of, since we are all drawing near to it at the same speed, and the same nature that not one of us can resist is bringing us to it. I was not able to oppose the Divine Power and make it change its plan and postpone my nativity and bring me later into the world. Therefore I am not in the least to blame for the fact that I am so far advanced in life, and it ought not to be considered to my disadvantage; I will even say that if you were at all wise, my advanced age would be of great weight in obtaining your love, because in such a long period I have done many praiseworthy deeds, extended many courtesies, offered numberless services to everybody I could, and done many other good things which no one would have been able to do in a short space of time, and so I deserve great rewards and should be honored with the greatest recompense. On the other hand, if I had lived but a short time I would not deserve such a reward, because in a brief space of time very few good deeds can be done. And that he who serves more and has done many services deserves greater rewards than a man who has done fewer laudable deeds is clear enough from the fact that in the court of the Heavenly King, as well as all those of earthly princes, we see that all men are rated according to the rule that he who does more service gets the greater rewards. I do not say this with the idea of asserting that I possess the glory of old age, but only to disabuse you of the error that a man who has passed the age of adolescence should be driven out of Love's service, when, at that age there is hardly anybody who is not vacillating and inconstant in everything. It is not proper to assume that a man is old because his hair is white, for we constantly see many men who grow white when they are not old, while others who are decrepit with age have not grown white at all. Therefore you should judge a man's age more by his heart than by his hair."

But if, on the other hand, some man happens to be still young, the woman might use against him an objection like this. "You haven't yet arrived at the age where you may properly ask for the love of a woman of good sense, and so it seems I must consider you very forward in asking for that of which you are found wholly unworthy. For a man who seeks for the love of a woman of good character should be of excellent character himself and should have many good deeds to his credit. What signs there are that you have such a character or what good deeds commend you, to cause your unworthiness to seek so boldly for such great things, I cannot see, nor have I heard from anyone else. If I should wish to take service in Love's army, there are many men whom I meet regularly who are really famous and of fine character from among whom I might choose a suitable lover. Therefore, before you ask for such a gift you must exert yourself to do deeds which are considered worthy of the rewards you are asking for."

The man says: "If I didn't think that you said this in jest or to make me blush for modesty, I would say that your good sense had deserted you. I admit that good deeds when done deserve great rewards, but all men agree that no one does a good or courteous deed in the world unless it is derived from the fount of love. Love will therefore be the origin and cause of all good, and when the cause ceases, its effect must necessarily cease. Therefore no man could do good deeds unless the persuasion of love impelled him, and you ought to grant me the love I seek, so that men will think you did it to make me do well and that through you my manners may be improved and may ever remain so. For I know that it will be considered more to your credit if out of your grace alone you give me your love, or the hope of it, than if you grant it to me in payment for what I have done; that would be like paying a debt, but the other remains pure generosity. Again, doesn't a teacher who by his instruction makes a prudent man out of one who has never had any instruction deserve more honor and praise than one who teaches more wisdom to a man who is already wise? That is why I, a new recruit in Love's service and awkward in love, ask you to be my teacher and to train me more fully by your instruction. For it will be considered greatly to your credit if by your good sense you make a trained soldier out of me who am now awkward and untaught. It is fitting that an awkward, untaught man should serve a lover by whose industry he may hide his heedless youth."

The woman says: "You don't have the proper understanding of love, since your statements seem to go directly counter to its rules. We are taught by Love's precept that the man who has done more good deeds ought to enjoy the greater honor and obtain the greater rewards. But if we were to accept your statements as true, good deeds would be harmful to those who do them, while other men would seem to profit by having refrained from well-doing and by having done nothing good. You say that you wish to submit to my instruction in this matter, but I absolutely refuse the task, because it seems to me that I ought to choose a lover who is already trained rather than one whom I must go to the trouble of training. You should plan to go to Paris for your education, rather than to be tutored by a woman, because an awkward, untaught man who seeks the love of a sensible, well-taught woman seems to be laboring too much in ignorance."

The man says: "I marvel at your words and that you try so sophistically to find fault with what I said. You don't seem to have understood correctly what I did propose. What I said about it being more to your credit to grant your love as a gift rather than to give it in payment for good deeds that somebody had done, you must understand as meaning that if there are two men, one of whom has done many good deeds, while the other has done none, although he is of full age and has had an opportunity to do them but has taken no advantage of it, you ought to reject the man who has done no good deeds and to accept as your lover the man who has done them. But if you assume that the man who has done no good deeds is still in his youth and has had no opportunity to do any, in that case the young man who has done none should be chosen, not because he is more worthy of being loved than the man who has done much good, but because this course is more profitable to society. For as the Heavenly King rejoices over the conversion of one sinner more than over ninety-nine just,[15] because of the good that follows therefrom, so a woman does better if she takes a man who is none too good, makes him praiseworthy through her good character, and by her instruction adds him to the court of Love, than if she makes some good man better. In other words, just as there is more profit to God in the conversion of one sinner than in the improvement of the ninety-nine just, so society gains more when one man who is not good is rendered excellent than when the worthy character of some good man is increased.

"As for what I said about choosing the love of a man who has done no good deeds rather than one who has done many, you must understand this as not applying to the fourth stage of love, but only to the three preceding ones. In case this isn't clear to you, I will explain my meaning. From ancient times four distinct stages have been established in love: the first consists in the giving of hope, the second in the granting of a kiss, the third in the enjoyment of an embrace, and the fourth culminates in the yielding of the whole person. Therefore, when I said 'If there are two men, one of whom has done many good deeds and the other none, you should preferably choose for your lover the man who has done none,' you should understand me as not referring to the fourth

[15] Luke 15: 7.

stage—the yielding of the whole person—but to the first—the giving of hope. For if a woman wants to select a lover in the fourth stage, all at once without waiting to think it over, then it is profitable for her to select the man who has done many good deeds instead of the one who hasn't done any; this is because she is sure of the goodness of the first and not at all sure of that of the second, and people are often cautious and give up uncertainties in favor of certainties. But it is not seemly for wise women to give themselves so hastily to anyone, passing over the preliminary stages and jumping at once to the fourth. Women usually proceed in this order: first a woman should make use of the granting of hope, and then if she sees that her lover, after receiving this, improves in conduct, she need not fear to go on to the second stage. And so step by step she may come to the fourth stage, if she finds that he is in every respect worthy of it. If you should ask why, in the case I have mentioned, a young man who has done no good deeds should be chosen as a lover in the first stage but in the other case the one who has done many good deeds should be chosen in the fourth stage, the reason clearly is that until the third stage is passed a woman may withdraw without blame; but if love has been established in the fourth stage, after that she ought not to go back except for the very best of reasons, not only because she has ratified her love, which is done by the fourth step, but also because of the great thing that the yielding of her person is to a woman. For what greater thing can a woman give than to yield herself to the mastery of someone else?

"As for your remark about preferring to save trouble by selecting a lover who has been trained rather than one you must go to the trouble of training, that deserves a good reprimand, for anyone ought to find that fruit taken from his own plantation tastes sweeter than what he gets from his neighbor's tree, and we value more what we have got with great labor than that which comes easily, for 'without great labor great things cannot be won.' " [16]

[16] Jakob Werner, *Lateinische Sprichwörter und Sinnsprüche des Mittelalters*, p. 1, No. 17.

The woman says: "If great things cannot be won without great labor, since what you are seeking is one of the greatest you will have to be exhausted by a great deal of labor before you get what you want."

The man says: "I give you all the thanks of which I am capable that you have so prudently promised that after much labor I may have your love, and I hope that neither I nor anyone else may enjoy the love of a woman as worthy as you are until I have acquired it with much labor. It is not likely that so prudent a woman as you would give her love hastily to anyone, nor would she permit the efforts of any worthy man in her behalf to go unrewarded; for it would seem unreasonable if good deeds did not bring suitable rewards to those who do them."

Second Dialogue

A man of the middle class speaks with a woman of the nobility

If a man of the middle class should seek the love of a noblewoman, he may follow this plan. If he finds that the woman, although noble, is not sophisticated, all the things will serve which were given in the dialogue between the man and the woman of the middle class, except that here commendation of the nobility of her family may claim a place. But if the woman should be wise and shrewd, he ought to be careful not to overdo the praise of her beauty. For if he should praise a noble and prudent woman beyond all measure, she will think that he isn't very good at the art of conversation or that he is making up all this flattery and thinks her a fool. So after he has begun the conversation in the usual way, let him come down to words of love in this manner. "If I could shut up my heart within the bounds of my will, I would, perhaps, pass over in silence many things which I am urgently driven to say. But my heart drives on my will with sharp spurs, diverting it from its natural path and causing it to wander and to seek things too great for me to express. So if love compels me to say anything aimless or foolish, I ask Your Nobility to endure it patiently and to reprove me gently.

I know well that Love is not in the habit of differentiating men with titles of distinction, but that he obligates all equally to serve in his (that is, Love's) army, making no exceptions for beauty or birth and making no distinctions of sex or of inequality of family, considering only this, whether anybody is fit to bear Love's armor. Love is a thing that copies Nature herself, and so lovers ought to make no more distinction between classes of men than Love himself does. Just as love inflames men of all classes, so lovers should draw no distinctions of rank, but consider only whether the man who asks for love has been wounded by Love. Supported by this unanswerable argument, I may select for my beloved any woman I choose so long as I have no depravity of character to debase me.

"So if you will give me a patient hearing, I shall try to ask only what you can have no good reason for denying me, and if my remarks offend you in any way and you use harsh words in defending yourself, that will be an unbearable misfortune to me and the cause of all sorts of grief.

"You must know, then, that many days ago I was smitten with the arrow of your love, and that I have tried with all my might to conceal the wound, not because I consider myself an incompetent soldier of Love, but because I am afraid of Your Highness's wisdom. The sight of your face so terrifies my spirit and disturbs my mind that I completely forget even those things I have carefully thought out in my mind. With reason, therefore, I tried to hide my grief, but the more I sought to cover up my wound, the more the pain of it increased. Yet the wound did remain hidden so long as the pain of it was not too much for me; but after I was overcome by the strength of it, by its mighty power it forced me to ask for great things and to seek for a cure for my ever-present pain. You are the cause of my suffering and the cure for my mortal pain, for you hold both my life and my death shut up in your hand.[17] If you grant what I ask, you will give me back the life I have lost and much solace in living, but if you deny me, my life will be a

[17] Compare Peter Alphonsus *Clerical Instruction*, Ex. ii.

torment to me, and that is worse than if I met with sudden death; for a quick death would be preferable to suffering continually such terrible torture. I cannot tell you all the things my soul thinks should be told, but God knows the words that the dumb man wishes to speak."

The woman says: "I am very much surprised—it is enough to surprise anyone—that in such a great upsetting of things the elements do not come to an end and the world itself fall into ruin. If I were not determined to ignore the shame you cast on my nobility, I would rebuke you very bitterly; but since it is too unladylike for a noblewoman to speak harsh and discourteous words to anyone, no matter who he is, my soul endures with patience your crazy remarks and gives you a soft answer. Who are you that you ask for such great gifts? I know well enough what you look like, and the family you come from is obvious. But where can one find greater effrontery than in a man who for the space of a whole week devotes all his efforts to the various gains of business and then on the seventh day, his day of rest, tries to enjoy the gifts of love and to dishonor Love's commands and confound the distinctions of classes established among men from of old? It is not without cause or reason that this distinction of rank has been found among men from the very beginning; it is so that every man will stay within the bounds of his own class and be content with all things therein and never presume to arrogate to himself the things that were naturally set aside as belonging to a higher class, but will leave them severely alone. Who are you, then, to try to defile such ancient statutes and under the pretense of love to attempt to subvert the precepts of our ancestors and so presumptuously go beyond the limits of your own class? If I should so far forget my senses as to be induced to assent to what you say, your heart would not be able to endure such great things. Did a buzzard [18] ever overcome a partridge or a pheasant by its courage? It is for falcons and hawks to capture this prey, which should not be annoyed by cow-

[18] What bird Andreas means by *lacertiva avis* is unknown; the translation is merely conjectural.

ardly kites. Your folly needs to be sharply checked, because you seek a love from the upper class, although you are not worthy of her.

"Nor can what you have just said support your opinion. You said that Love makes no distinction of classes, but forces all to love who are found fit to bear his arms, and that lovers likewise should not distinguish beyond asking whether the man who seeks for love has been wounded by Love. Now without attempting to contradict you, I admit that Love forces everyone, without distinctions, to love, but that which follows (that a lover ought not to distinguish beyond asking whether he who seeks for love is in love) I do not accept, because it rests wholly on a falsehood. If it were true, it would rule out the saying that Love carries an unequal weight in his hand. When the conclusion of this assumption is disproved, you will be refuted; therefore you see my contention firmly established. And if you should try to say, what many have boldly said, that we should all call Love an unjust judge, since he carries unequal weights,[19] I shall refute you with this answer. Although Love does carry unequal weights, yet he may truly be called a just judge, for he does not use them except when compelled by the best of reasons. Although he sees that all men are by the natural desire of their passions drawn to anybody of the opposite sex, he considers it shameful for him to pitch his tents at once over against the other person, so that she whose love is sought must immediately be driven to love. If he did this, any rough, shaggy person who spent his time in farming or in begging his bread publicly in the streets might impel a queen to love him. But lest such an impropriety or absurdity happen, Love regularly leaves it to the choice of each woman either to love or not, as she may wish, the person who asks for her love. And if this rule you mention, that everyone who loves is always loved, were kept unbroken without any exceptions, it would in the natural course of events run foul of another rule. Any man would rather seek his love in a higher class than in his own or a lower one, and on the other hand the woman whose love is sought,

[19] Lev. 19: 36; Deut. 25: 15.

because of the same rule and her natural inclination, would gladly have a lover from her own or a higher class, lest people think that she is unjustly excepted from the regular rule of love. From this it should be clear that your efforts are worse than useless, and when you finish you will see that you have spent your labor in vain."

The man says: "You show your great worth by giving me a kindly and gentle answer, since you choose to act in accordance with your character and to suit your words to your rank. Nothing is more suited to the character of a well-born woman than to use gentle words when she speaks, and nothing seems more contrary to a noble character and more degrading to nobility of blood than to use harsh, discourteous ones. But I marvel greatly at your remark that the family I come from is as apparent as my face; I see that in this Your Prudence is going wrong, since you seem to agree with those mistaken people who reject worth of character if it is unaccompanied by good birth or beauty, but who accept physical beauty and noble blood without any character. How grave and troublesome an assertion this is to make, how absurd to speak of, is shown beyond all contradiction by the law which says that nobility came in the beginning only from good character and manly worth and courtesy. If, then, it is only good character which can give men the privileges of nobility and allow them to take the name 'well-born', you must lay aside completely this error I have mentioned and let good character alone induce you to love.

"As for your objection that it is a disgrace for me to engage in business, if you will listen attentively to what I say you will certainly see that this cannot justly be held against me. That I devote myself to the honorable gains of business is, I contend, devotion to my position in life; because I am trying to do those things that are accordant with my nature and thereby to avoid the murmur of the crowd, which is in the habit of saying, 'Everybody ought to do the things suitable to his birth and his social position.' [20] I do not say that I pile up these gains dis-

---

[20] "That which is most consistent with each man's nature is most seemly for him." Cicero *Offices* I. xxxi. 113.

honestly for the future, but I give them to others carefully and very liberally at the proper time and place,[21] and in this I defend my nobility of manners and character. Furthermore, if I did not concern myself with honest and legitimate gains, I would fall into obscure poverty, and so I could not do noble deeds, and my nobility of character would remain only an empty name, a kind of courtesy or nobility which men never put much faith in. Suppose a well-born man who was poor and needy should talk about generosity. The common people would say things like this about him, 'This man boasts of his generosity, because he has nothing he can give away; if he did have anything on earth, he ought to act toward men in accordance with his birth and nature. It comes naturally from the fact that he has nothing, that he pours out his generosity in lavish words.' If you [22] should object that I have enough money, I shall still defend honest gain for men of my class.

"The next thing you said—that every man should stay within the limits of his own class and not seek for love in a higher one—I cannot deny. But if I have cultivated a character excellent through and through, I think that puts me inside the walls of nobility and gives me the true virtue of rank, and so my character puts me among the nobles. It cannot be considered a presumption, therefore, if I seek a love from among the nobility, for any man's nobility is determined more by his character than by his birth. You said, too, that even if my words should win you over to stoop to my desire, my heart would not be able to endure such great things. A soldier is a fool who seeks to bear arms that his limbs are too weak to endure, and no one wants a horse that he is incapable of managing or guiding. Such people are laughing stocks for the crowd. Now I grant that the things I am asking for are very great, so if you consider that I am not competent to receive them, Your Grace should grant only what you can without having people know about it, and then, if you find me wholly unworthy, you may expose me to your

[21] Aristotle *Nicomachean Ethics* IV. I.

[22] The man here changes from the formal plural of address (the modern *vous*) to the more familiar singular (the modern *tu*).

own derision or that of anyone else. But I have complete confidence that the same greatness of heart that impels me to ask for such great things would, if Your Grace granted them to me, keep them as possessions for me forever.

"What you said about the kite and the buzzard is no objection, since it is their bravery alone that makes hawks, falcons, and merlins valuable. At times we see hawks of the lighter kind by their courage take great pheasants and partridges, for a boar is often held by a fairly small dog. On the other hand, we see many gerfalcons and peregrine falcons terrified by the commonest sparrows and put to flight by a buzzard. So if the kite or the buzzard proves to be hardy and bold, different from his parents, he deserves to be honored with the perch of the falcon or the hawk and to be carried on a warrior's left fist. So, then, if you find that I am unlike my parents, you should not call me by the disgraceful name 'kite,' but by the honorable one 'tercel.' And do not look down on worth, no matter in whom you find it, since we gather roses from the sharp thorns amid which they grow, and gold which we find in a vessel of cheap material cannot lose any of its value.

"It is clear from your answer that you did not understand me correctly when I said that no one should ask more than whether the person who seeks for love has been wounded by Love; it is the indefiniteness of the word that caused you the confusion. You should take my remark that a lover ought not ask as meaning that she whose love is sought ought not ask whether the man who seeks it comes of a noble or an ignoble family; she should ask only whether he has good habits and a good character. Therefore you may well say, 'Love at times carries an inequitable weight in his hand.' But although it is true that Love does carry at times unequal [23] weights, you cannot attribute it to his injustice, for it is sufficient if he touches one of the lovers with his dewy breath and from the fountain of his abundance sets him loving.

---

[23] The play on the two meanings of the word *inaequalis* (translated here as "inequitable" and "unequal") is difficult to render in English. The same play is implied also by the Biblical passages (see p. 47).

After he has struck one of the lovers with an arrow of love, he very properly leaves the other free to do as she chooses; so that if she does those things which Love finds pleasing, she may deserve to receive great rewards from him and to have her praise proclaimed among men, but if she goes counter to his desire, she may receive the contrary kind of rewards. Love therefore leaves it to the woman's choice, so that when she is loved she may love in return if she wishes to, but if she does not wish, she shall not be compelled to, since a person is thought to deserve greater rewards when he does well of his own accord than when he has done so under compulsion. And we believe that this is done after the example of the Heavenly King, who leaves each man to his own free choice after he has acquired knowledge of good and evil, promising unutterable rewards to those who do well, but threatening unbearable torments to those who do evil. Therefore a woman ought to inquire diligently whether the man who asks for her love is worthy of it, and if she finds that he is perfectly worthy, she ought by no means to refuse him her love unless she is obligated to love someone else. If, then, you are not obligated to anyone else, you have no reason not to love me."

The woman says: "You are trying to bolster up your errors with so much eloquence that it will not be easy for me to reply to your more-than-empty words, but I shall try by my argument to refute some of them. If, as you say, we find good character alone worthy of Love's rewards and that this makes people look upon a man as noble, then the order of nobility, discovered and set apart by such obvious marks of distinction, would long ago have been found to be useless, when it was clear that every man distinguished by character and worth would have to be called noble. And so we would have to say emphatically that those who founded the order of nobility wasted their efforts, and I shall not try to show you how absurd that is. Therefore I say firmly that no one should go beyond the bounds of his rank, but each worthy man should seek within it for the love of some worthy woman, and a man of the middle class should seek for the love of a woman of that same class, and then everybody's class would remain inviolate and each man would come away with a reward for his efforts. The fact that you engage in honorable business suitable to your station in life is no concern of mine, except for the fact that you are seeking a love from the noble class, while your mind is on business—an unseemly thing and one that will result in great bitterness and grief. As for the fact that you are generous in giving away what you make in business, this makes you very worthy of the love of a woman of your own class. But even if a falcon should sometimes be put to flight by a buzzard, still the falcon is classed with falcons, and the buzzard with buzzards—the one being called a worthless falcon, the other a very good buzzard. Similarly, your good character doesn't put you in the class with the nobles, but gets you the name of a good man of the middle class, worthy of the love of a good woman of that same class. That is perfectly clear and obvious, and even if I am not obligated to anyone else, I find you just as unworthy of my love as though I were a woman from another country."

The man says: "Although I would not like to dispute what you say, still I cannot see any reason why if a man of the middle class excels a nobleman in the excellence of his character he ought not receive a greater reward, since we are both descended from a common ancestor, Adam."

The woman says: "Gold is more appropriate on the king's table than in the home of a poor man or the hut of a peasant, and it is far more honorable to ride a thin horse that trots than a fat ass with the finest and gentlest of gaits. Therefore turn your back on your errors, and leave me for others."

The man says: "Although I am repulsed by what you say, still as long as I live I shall not give up the idea of your love, because even if I am never to get the result I hope for, the mere hope I have gained from the greatness of my heart will cause my body to lead a tranquil life, and ultimately, perhaps, God will put into your mind a cure for my pain."

The woman says: "May God give you a reward suited to your effort."

The man says: "That word alone shows me that my hope is bearing fruit, and I pray to God that you may always be interested in the care of my health and that my sails may find a quiet haven."

Third Dialogue

A man of the middle class speaks with a woman of the higher nobility

If a man of the middle class seeks the love of a woman of the higher nobility, he ought to have a most excellent character, for in order that a man of this class may prove worthy of the love of a woman of the higher nobility he must be a man with innumerable good things to his credit, one whom uncounted good deeds extol. It would seem a very great shame and a cause of reproach for a noblewoman to pass over the upper and the intermediate ranks and take a lover from the lower class unless good character in overwhelming quantity makes up for the lack of nobility. For it would not seem reasonable to any sensible people that one could find in the lowest class good and excellent men, worthy of the love of a woman of such high rank, while in the two upper classes no worthy man could be found, but all had to be rejected as of inferior quality. This is what you are told by the general rule of the logicians, which says, "If what appears more present is not present, neither will that which is believed less be." [24] A man of the middle class must therefore greatly excel in character all the men of the two noble classes in order to deserve the love of a woman of the higher nobility, for no matter how worthy any commoner may be, it seems very much out of place if a countess or a marchioness or any woman of the same or a higher rank gives her love to a man of the middle class, and even the lower classes look upon it as a lowering and a demeaning of herself. The first thing people will think is that she does it out of too great an abundance of passion (a thing which I shall show later is wholly reprehensible), unless the man's character is so well known as to remove the

[24] Aristotle *Topics* II. x; Boethius *Interpretation of the Topics of Aristotle* II. iv.

suspicion of that. Well, then, isn't it proper that a woman of the higher nobility should give her love to a commoner if she finds him excellent in every way? I answer that if she finds anyone in the classes above him who is more worthy or as worthy, she ought to prefer the love of that man; but if she doesn't find any such person in these classes, then she should not reject the commoner. But she ought to test his constancy by many trials before he deserves to have the hope of her love granted him, for that which is not in keeping with anyone's character is usually blown away by a light breeze and lasts but a brief moment. It is said that at times some are born among the buzzards who capture partridges by their courage or ferocity, but since we know that this is not in accord with their natures, this ferocity, men say, does not last in them for more than a year after their birth. Therefore a man of the middle class may be chosen in love by a woman of the higher nobility if after long probation he is found to be worthy; in that case they may make use of all the speeches that have already been given in the dialogue between the man of the middle class and the woman of the simple nobility, or the commoner may make use of this other speech.

"It doesn't seem at all profitable to dwell very much on the praise of your person, for your character and your beauty echo through widely separated parts of the world, and, furthermore, praise uttered in the presence of the person praised seems to have the appearance of clever flattery. For the present, then, it is my intention, and the principal object which brings me here to you, to offer you myself and my services and to beg earnestly that Your Grace may see fit to accept them. And I beseech God in heaven that of His grace He may grant me to do those things which are wholly pleasing to your desire. I have in my heart a firm and fixed desire, not only to offer you my services, but on your behalf to offer them to everybody and to serve with an humble and acceptable spirit, since I have a firm faith that my labor can never remain with you without the delightfulness of fruit. If my trouble should prove fruitless, I must, after many waves and tempests of death, suffer shipwreck unless my soul is guided by hope, even though it is a false one. For only a hope, even one granted with a deceitful mind, can keep the anchor of my support firmly fixed."

The woman says: "I have no intention of refusing your services or those of any other man or of not responding to gifts which I accept as suitable, for anyone who refuses to accept services when they are offered embarrasses the giver and shows that he himself is constrained by the vice of avarice. He, then, who freely gives his services to others receives from others fitting rewards. But you seem to be tending in another direction and hunting other game than you are worthy to take, for, as your remarks seem to indicate, you are asking to be loved by me. But I do not wish to love, particularly a man in a class two below my own, although you might under other circumstances be infinitely worthy. You say that if I will grant you only the hope of my love it will be enough to keep you from the perils of death. To this I answer that the mere fact that you accuse me of clever deceit and falsehood shows that you are infected with this same failing and that you keep one idea in your mind and speak another with your deceitful tongue. By rights, therefore, you should be repulsed from Love's bosom, because fickle and untruthful people ought not come under the sway of Love's court. Moreover, you appear to be urging me to neglect my good name, and this is a worse fault than the other, for nothing is more disgraceful for a noblewoman than not to keep her promises, to destroy a hope she has given, and to say things that belie her birth. This sort of thing seems more appropriate to those women who conduct themselves like harlots, who for the sake of money strive to subvert Love's mandates and to disgrace his service for the sake of gain. Your advice therefore seems unsound, since from it so many grave perils threaten."

The man says: "I admit that I ask to be loved, because to live in love is more pleasant than any other way of life in the world. But your remarks show clearly that you refuse to love me because of the humbleness of my inferior rank, although my character is of the very best. To these remarks I reply that my family, as represented by myself, is driven by its natural instincts and cannot be kept within the bounds of its own class. Since, then, nature did not wish me to remain fixed within the established bounds of my class and she did not wish to close to me the doors of the higher ones, on what grounds, since I have no bad qualities to bar me, do you presume to set up definite limits for me and impose upon me the yoke of a class? We find that from very ancient times this distinction of classes has been used only against those who prove themselves unworthy of the rank to which they have been assigned or those who keep to their own class but are not found at all worthy of a higher one. I say this because of the resemblance to that passage in Holy Writ which says that the law is not made for the just man, but for sinners.[25] This ancient distinction of classes does not forbid me to be enrolled in any of the higher ones or to ask the rewards of a higher class, provided, however, that no one may justly raise any objections to my character. Moreover, when I said that a hope, even though granted with the intent to deceive, was enough to keep me from death, I didn't say this with the desire of detracting from your glorious reputation or because I was conscious of any trace of fraud which would be to your disadvantage. I said it to give you a clear proof what affection I feel for you and how much I would prize the full grant of your love, so that when you recognized the immensity of my love for you, you in turn might the more easily incline your mind to me."

The woman says: "Although good character may ennoble a commoner, still it cannot change his rank to the extent of making him a lord or a vavasor unless this is done by the power of the prince, who may add nobility to the good character of any man he pleases, and so it is proper that you should be refused advancement to the love of a countess. Besides, the hope of attaining to her has deceived you too much, since you were not ashamed to utter falsehoods boldly in her presence. You

[25] I Tim. 1:9.

contend that you are renowned among the warriors, yet in you I see many things that are harmful or opposed to such service. For although soldiers ought naturally to have long, slender calves and a moderate-sized foot,[26] longer than it is broad and looking as though formed with some skill, I see that your calves are fat and roundly turned, ending abruptly, and your feet are huge and immensely spread out so that they are as broad as they are long."

The man says: "If we find any commoner who because of his habits and his character deserves to be ennobled by the prince, I do not see why he is not worthy of a noble love. For since it is character alone that makes a man worthy to be ennobled and we find that only nobility deserves the love of a noblewoman, properly then only good character is worthy of the crown of a noblewoman's love. And that objection you raised about my large, flabby legs and my big feet doesn't show much intelligence. Men say that in the further parts of Italy there lives a man of a line of counts [27] who has slender legs and is descended from the best of parents who enjoyed great privileges in the sacred palace; he himself is famous for every kind of beauty and is said to have immense wealth, and yet, so they say, he has no character at all—all good habits fear to adorn him, and in him everything bad has found a home. On the other hand, there is a king in Hungary [28] who has very fat, round legs, and long, broad feet and who is almost wholly destitute of beauty; yet because the worth of his character shines so bright, he deserved to receive the glory of the royal crown, and proclamations of his praise resound throughout almost the whole world.

---

[26] The mixture of singular and plural follows the Latin here.

[27] Arpad Steiner suggests (*Speculum*, XIII, 304) that the reference is to Count William I ("The Bad") of Sicily. In 1176 or 1177 his son William II had married Joanna, daughter of Queen Eleanor and of Henry II.

[28] Steiner suggests (in *Speculum*, IV, 92) that the verbs in this passage are historical presents and that the king referred to is King Coloman, who reigned from 1095 to 1116 (Steiner says 1114); he was one of the greatest of the Hungarian kings, but is described by the chroniclers as flabby and very ugly. Béla III, who reigned from 1163 to 1198, was a tall, handsome man.

You should not, therefore, inquire what my feet and legs are like, but what my character is like and what I have made of myself. When you receive gifts, you should not consider how beautiful the giver is, but how much he deserves because of his own merits. You should learn to base your objections on a man's character, not on his legs, because in objecting to legs you seem to be blaming divine nature."

The woman says: "You seem to have a reasonable defense, but what good deeds glorify you, what sort of character makes you worthy to obtain what you ask, I have never heard. For he who asks for the love of an honorable woman, especially one of the upper nobility, ought to be of great fame and of all courtliness; but of you lofty fame seems to be perfectly silent. First, therefore, you should strive to do such things as deserve the reward which you ask, so that your request may not be considered too impudent."

The man says: "The height of courtesy seems to be contained in your remarks, in which you are so clearly concerned that all my actions should be laudable. And so, since I see that you are thoroughly instructed in the art of love, I ask you to give me a lesson—that is, I ask that Your Grace may see fit to teach me those things that are specially demanded in love, those which make a man most worthy of being loved, because after I have been instructed I shall have no defense for any mistakes I make and no opportunity to excuse myself. Since all courtesy comes from the plentiful stream of Love and to this generous lord should be credited the beginning of all good deeds and the carrying out to the end of every good, and since I am still inexperienced in love and ignorant of the subject, it is no wonder that I know nothing of what he can do and that I urgently seek to be taught his precepts; because what anyone desires with all his mind he begs for vehemently and receives with eagerness."

The woman says: "You seem to be upsetting the natural order and course of things, since first you ask for love and then you show yourself in every way unworthy of it by asking like a raw recruit to be trained in the science of love. But since it would seem to set a shameful precedent, one prompted by avarice, if those who have experience were to deny their lessons to those who have not and ask to be taught, you will without a doubt obtain the grant of our instruction; and if you will pay careful attention to our words, before you leave you will be fully informed on the subjects you ask about.

"Well then, the man who would be considered worthy to serve in Love's army must not be in the least avaricious, but very generous; he must, in fact, give generously to as many people as he can. When he sees that money is needed, especially by noblemen and men of character, and when he thinks that his gifts would be helpful to anybody, he ought not wait to be urged, for a gift made in answer to a request seems dearly bought.[29] But if he cannot find a pressing opportunity of giving something under these circumstances, let him give something helpful to the man who does ask, and give it with such a spirit that it may seem more pleasing and acceptable to his feelings to give the thing to his friend than to keep possession of it himself. And also if he sees that the poor are hungry and gives them nourishment, that is considered very courteous and generous. And if he has a lord, he should offer him due respect. He should utter no word of blasphemy against God and His saints; he should show himself humble to all and should stand ready to serve everybody. He ought never speak a word in disparagement of any man, since those who speak evil may not remain within the threshold of courtesy. He ought not utter falsehood in praise of the wicked, but he should if possible make them better by secret reproofs. If he finds that they remain wholly incorrigible, he should consider them stiff-necked and banish them from his company lest he be considered, and rightly, a promoter and a sharer of the error. He ought never mock anyone, especially the wretched, and he should not be quarrelsome or ready to take part in disputes; but he should be, so

---

[29] Seneca *Benefits* II. i. Andreas may get the idea through the *Moral Philosophy* (i. 13) of Hildebert of Le Mans.

far as possible, a composer of differences. In the presence of women he should be moderate about his laughter, because, according to Solomon's saying,[30] too much laughter is a sign of foolishness; and clever women are in the habit of turning away fools and unwise men in contempt or of eluding them beautifully. Great prudence is necessary in the management of a love affair and diligence in all one does. He ought to frequent assemblies of great men and to visit great courts. He should be moderate about indulging in games of dice. He should gladly call to mind and take to heart the great deeds of the men of old. He ought to be courageous in battle and hardy against his enemies, wise, cautious, and clever. He should not be a lover of several women at the same time, but for the sake of one he should be a devoted servant of all. He should devote only a moderate amount of care to the adornment of his person and should show himself wise and tractable and pleasant to everybody, although some men have the idea that women like it very much if they utter foolish, almost crazy, remarks and act like madmen. He should be careful, too, not to utter falsehoods and should take care not to talk too much or to keep silent too much. He should not be too quick and sudden about making promises, because the man who is good-natured about making promises will be slow to keep them, and the man who is too ready to make them gets little credit. If any worthy man wants to give him some money, he should accept it with a look of joy and by no means refuse it unless the giver had the idea that he needed it, when he didn't. In that case he may decline it in this way: 'Since I have no need for this at present, I consider it as given to me, and I return it to you that you may make use of it in my name in any way you please.' He should never utter foul words and should avoid serious crimes, especially ones that are notorious. He should never cheat anyone with a false promise, because anybody can be rich in promises. If anybody has deceived him with a false promise or has been rude to him, he

---

[30] Apparently the verse he has in mind is Ecclesiasticus 21: 23, which some persons in the Middle Ages attributed to Solomon. See, for example, John of Salisbury *Policraticus* II. XXIX.

should never say anything to disparage the man, but on the contrary he should do good to him in return and serve him in every way, and thus prudently compel him to acknowledge his fault. He should offer hospitality freely to everybody. He should not utter harmful or shameful or mocking words against God's clergy or monks or any person connected with a religious house, but he should always and everywhere render them due honor with all his strength and with all his mind, for the sake of Him whose service they perform. He ought to go to church frequently and there listen gladly to those who are constantly celebrating the divine service, although some men very foolishly believe that the women like it if they despise everything connected with the Church. He ought to be truthful in everything he says and never envy any man's renown. I have presented to you briefly the main points. If you have listened attentively to them and will be careful to practice them, you will be found worthy to plead in the court of Love."

The man says: "I am impelled to give all sorts of thanks to Your Dignity for being willing to explain to me so industriously and so prudently the articles of love and to give me a conception of the subject. But still I shall not cease to ask continually that you may see fit to grant me the hope I seek, at least on condition that I try to do all those things that you have taught me. For the hope of the love I desire will always keep before my mind the determination to do good deeds, and what you said about mixing up the regular order will not raise any difficulties. For since love offers everybody in the world an incentive to do good, properly before everything else we ought to seek love as the root and principal cause of everything good."

The woman says: "It would be unseemly and discourteous to give anybody a hope of love in this fashion; one should wholly grant it or else wholly deny it, because even after it is granted the woman may draw back her hand and take away the hope that she has given. Strive, there-

fore, to do good deeds, that my words of instruction may seem to have
been profitable to you."

The man says: "It was with good reason that the Heavenly Majesty
put you in the class of the greater women, since you have been willing
so prudently to respond to all men according to their deserts and to
grant me more than I knew how to ask, and I pray God that He may
ever increase my determination to serve you and that He may incline
your mind toward me, and ever keep it so, to reward me to the extent
of my deserts."

Fourth Dialogue

A nobleman speaks with a woman of the middle class

If a nobleman prefers to select for his love a woman of the middle
class, he should woo her with a speech of this kind. First let him greet
her in his own fashion, and next he may, even without her permission,
choose a seat at her side, by virtue of the privileges his higher rank gives
him. For I tell you, Walter, it is the usual rule that when a man is considered to be of a more privileged rank than the woman, he may, if he
wishes, sit down beside her without asking permission. If they are of
the same rank he may ask permission to sit beside her, and if she grants
it he may sit down by her side, but not unless she does. But where the
man is of lower rank than the woman, he must not ask permission to
sit beside her, but he may ask to sit in a lower place. If, however, she
gives him permission to sit beside her, he may without fear oblige her.
Then he should begin talking in this fashion.

"To tell you the truth, I am an ambassador sent to you from the court
of Love to entrust to Your Prudence the solution of a certain doubt:
In which woman does a good character deserve more praise—in a
woman of noble blood, or in one who is known to have no nobility of
family?"

The woman says: "It doesn't seem very appropriate to leave it to me to make a final decision in such a matter, since the subject concerns me and everybody is forbidden to pass judgment on his own case; still, because I cannot refuse a task laid upon me by Love, I shall try to define my feeling on the subject. But first I want you to tell me something about the case, so that I may get my information from an excellent presentation of the facts and may not make any mistake about them. At first sight it would seem that excellence of birth deserves the more praise, for those things we come by naturally seem more to be desired than those which are external and come from without. Now in the case of women, a color that is natural is more admired than one that is applied, and words spoken by a man are more pleasing than the same words spoken by a parrot. Likewise the color of the brilliant scarlet dye looks better in English wool than in the wool of lambs from Champagne or Italy. So I suppose good character is more suited to noble blood than to a person descended from the middle class."

The man says: "I wonder whether you think and feel what your tongue seems to pronounce, for what you say cannot properly be proved by the examples you give; in every one of them it is human skill that we commend, and men prefer natural qualities to accidents. But character in a plebeian woman arises only from the innate qualities of her soul and the admirable ordering of her mind, and so we may consider it natural. Therefore your illustrations cannot support your contention, and I believe we should properly say that good character deserves more praise in a plebeian than in a noblewoman. We value more highly a pheasant captured by a sparrow hawk than one taken by a falcon, and a man who pays more than he owes deserves greater credit than one who offers only what he is bound to. Again we think more of the skill of an artisan who is able to make a good boat out of poor timbers than of that of a man who builds it of very good, well-fitted ones. And is it not considered better and more laudable if a man acquires some admirable craft all by himself than if he learns it from some other craftsman?

That, at any rate, is certainly true if you would but admit it. It is quite proper, then, that in this case we should give the decision against the woman who is of noble descent."

The woman says: "It seems to me there is a good deal of doubt of your good sense, since you are so clearly trying to speak against yourself. Although you are of noble blood and well-born, you are openly trying to belittle nobility and to plead against your own rights. And you make such a reasonable defense of your position that I am inclined to believe we should consider that good character deserves more credit in a plebeian than in a noblewoman, because no one has any doubt that the rarer any good thing is the more dearly is it prized."

The man says: "I consider your opinion very just and think it quite correct, and so of necessity I am forced to admit that one ought to seek the love of a plebeian woman with an excellent character rather than that of a noblewoman with a very good one. Therefore, since in you the plebeian class has been exalted by reason of your good character, I have quite properly chosen you, out of all the women in the world, as my lady, and I have determined to do all my good deeds for the sake of you alone. And therefore I pray God unceasingly to keep always firmly fixed in your heart the idea of accepting my services without delay, that my soul may daily increase in well-doing and thereby I may worthily attain to the rewards I desire."

The woman says: "It does not seem very appropriate to your nobility to condescend to a woman of the plebeian class or to seek for love from her, nor do you seem to have obtained the name 'nobleman' through your merits, because you have not been worthy of the love of any woman of your own class. He who has not proved himself a good soldier in his own class does not do well, I believe, when he serves in some other one. Seek, therefore, a love within your own class and do not try to attack a woman in another one, lest you meet with a well-deserved rebuke for your presumption."

The man says: "You seem to have very little experience in the art of love, since you show that you are ignorant of what is clear to everybody else. For it seems to be 'known to all the half-blind and the barbers' [31] that neither excellence of birth nor beauty of person has much to do with the loosing of Love's arrow, but it is love alone that impels men's hearts to love, and very often it strongly compels lovers to claim the love of a stranger woman—that is, to throw aside all equality of rank and beauty. For love often makes a man think that a base and ugly woman is noble and beautiful and makes him class her above all other women in nobility and beauty. For when a man has seen fit to love a woman honorably, her beauty is always very pleasing to him even though others find her misshapen and spiritless. Compared to her, all other women seem to him plain. Therefore you should not wonder that although you are of humble birth I persist in loving you with all my might because of your dazzling beauty and the fame of your excellent character. I do not seek for these things like a man who has been rejected by the women of his own class; but Love compels me to love as I do, and your worth and your nobility have pleased me more than those of any other women. From all these things it should be clear enough to Your Prudence that you should by no means reject my love if you find that my character corresponds with my birth."

The woman says: "Even if what you say rested upon clear truth, still I could derive from your own words another just reason for refusing you, since the opinion I advanced and you approved of a little while ago seems to imply that good character deserves more praise in a plebeian than in a noblewoman. From these words you have drawn the conclusion that any man should choose for his love an excellent plebeian rather than a noblewoman of great worth. Why, then, shouldn't I choose for my lover a plebeian of perfect character rather than a man of great nobility? Answer me that, if you please."

[31] Horace *Satires* I. vii. 3.

The man says: "Although I did say in so many words that the love of
an excellent plebeian was more to be preferred than that of a suitable
noblewoman, still you must not get the idea that the love of a noblewoman is not a praiseworthy thing and very desirable. In fact the love
of the noblewoman is to be preferred if her character is better than that
of the plebeian. When I used the word 'more' I meant that if we find
a plebeian woman more worthy than the noblewoman she is to be preferred to her; if we see that in character they go along together side
by side, one is free to choose either of them, according to the opinion
of Queen Eleanor of England.[32] But I say that when they are equal in
this respect the one of lower rank is preferable and should be chosen.
But if the adverb 'more' should be interpreted otherwise than as I have
tried to explain it to you, it would lead to great absurdity and great
harm, for it seems that belonging to a good family would bring a man
intolerable loss rather than any advantage if a more worthy noblewoman were placed below a less worthy plebeian. If, then, you should
find a plebeian in whom you know there is a better character than there
is in me, and if you give him your love, I will not urge that this idea
of yours is improper, because, according to what we have already said,
it seems that you are permitted to do this. Therefore let Your Prudence
make a careful investigation and accept the love of the more worthy
man."

The woman says: "In your remarks you seem to be going backward,
the way a crab walks, because now you are trying to deny what you
asserted so firmly and boldly when you were praising me. But it doesn't
seem like a man of sense to go so shamelessly against his own opinion
in order to agree with any sort of opinion that a prudent woman utters
and to deny now what a little while ago he admitted so plainly. However, since it is right for anyone to depart from his error and come to
his senses in a matter in which he now feels that he was wrong, if you

---

[32] Eleanor of Aquitaine, divorced wife of King Louis VII of France, and mother of
Countess Marie of Champagne, married Prince Henry, later King Henry II of England, in 1152.

want to correct your unconsidered and unqualified statement you will deserve a great deal of praise for this and you ought to be commended by the good sense of everyone. I am greatly pleased by the interpretation of your words by which you allow me to consider which lover I should select as preferable, because I guard that gate of Love's palace which neither refuses to let anybody into the palace nor permits everybody to enter who asks, but admits only the man who gets in on the strength of his own good character after we have consulted long and deliberated carefully.[33] Therefore after I have thought the matter over and carefully weighed the considerations, I shall try to admit the better man."

The man says: "If there weren't a snake here hidden in the grass, and if you were not asking for a chance to think the matter over only as a clever pretext, such a deliberation would be very sweet and pleasant to me. But because I am very much afraid that this comes at bottom from a desire to put things off, it doesn't seem to me safe to give my assent to this deliberation. For to me the matter is a very serious one and it looks like the death of me if you let me go away without granting me the hope of your love. Such a capricious putting things off is usually a sign that love is departing, and with a little delay the chance of fortune usually changes. If, then, you send me away without the hope of your love, you will drive me to an early death, after which none of your remedies will do any good, and so you may be called a homicide."

The woman says: "I have no desire to commit a homicide, but you can have no reason to deny me a chance to deliberate, because according to the saying of a certain wise man whatever is done after deliberation does not need to be repented of in shame, but stands forever."

The man says: "I cannot refuse you the chance to deliberate, but I shall never cease to pray God earnestly to make you love the man you should."

[33] See page 73.

The woman says: "If I should choose to devote myself to love, you may know of a certainty that I will try, so far as I can, to choose the solaces of the man who is preferable."

The man says: "There is no doubt that you have a free right to choose which one you will love, but I shall never cease to serve you, and on your account to offer to do everything I can for everybody."

The woman says: "If you really intend to do what you say you propose to, it can hardly be that you will not be abundantly rewarded, either by me or by some other woman."

The man says: "God grant that your words express what you really feel; I may seem to depart from you in the body, but in my heart I shall always be bound to you."

Fifth Dialogue

A nobleman speaks with a noblewoman

If any nobleman seeks the love of a noblewoman, let him try to attract her with these words. After he has got the conversation started, he should open his heart in this fashion:

"So much nobility is apparent in you, and you are distinguished by so much courtesy, that I believe in the presence of Your Prudence I may without fear of censure say all those things that are lying in my heart waiting to be said. For if men were not permitted to reveal to ladies, when they wished, the secrets of their hearts, then love, which men say is the fountain head and source of all good things, would already have perished utterly, and no man would be able to help another, and all works of courtesy would be unknown to mankind."

The woman says: "You are right, and it pleases me greatly to hear you say it."

The man says: "Although in the flesh I rarely come into your presence, in heart and in spirit I never depart from it, for the continual thought which I have of you makes me present with you very often and makes me see constantly with the eyes of the heart that treasure about which all my attention turns, and it brings me both pains and many solaces. For what a man desires with all his heart he is always afraid some unfavorable happening may interfere with. How faithful I am to you and with what devotion I am drawn to you no words of mine can tell. For it seems that if the fidelities of every living soul could be gathered together in a single person, the total would not be so great, by far, as the faith that prompts me to serve you, and there is nothing so unalterable in my heart as the intention of serving your glory; that would be glorious to me beyond all else, and I would consider it a great victory if I could do anything that would be pleasing to you and remain acceptable to Your Grace. Therefore, while I can see you no pain can touch me, nobody's plottings can disturb me, just the bare sight of the places which you seem to inhabit, when reflected in the air, provides me with powerful incentives for living and with many solaces for a lover. But when I cannot see you with my bodily eye or breathe the air about you, all the elements round about begin to rise up against me, and all kinds of torments begin to afflict me, and I can find no pleasure in any solaces except those deceitful visions that the drowsiness of slumber brings before me when I am asleep. But although sleep deceives me at times with a false gift, yet I am exceedingly grateful to him because he did see fit to deceive me with such a sweet and noble misrepresentation. For this drowsy gift furnishes me a way and a means for keeping alive and preserves me from the wrath of death; this seems to me a very great and special boon, for there is no use giving medicine to a dead man. But so long as I retain life, even though it may be a painful one, the light air can drench me with a shower of release or cover me with the waters of gladness. For I believe and have firm confidence that such a noble and worthy woman will not long permit me to endure such heavy pains, but will raise me up out of all my difficulties."

The woman says: "Truly in your person good sense has been ennobled and gentle words have found a home, since you can so thoughtfully and so prudently put forward your claims. I am properly grateful that you desire to think of me when I am absent and are determined to be of service to me in every way you can, and I, too, for my part will gladly think of you when you are absent, and I shall not refuse to accept your services at the proper time and place, since you are so great and so eminent a man of worth that it would be considered no honor to any woman to refuse them. Nay more, I do not wish you to be content with merely looking at the air, but you can have sight of me with your corporeal vision and look into my face. For I would rather exert myself to give you directions for keeping alive than offer you cause for death or incur the crime of homicide."

The man says: "Although in summertime the life of the crops may be prolonged by light showers, they are not saved from the danger of drying up unless they are drenched with rain. You can, in the way you mention, prolong the life of your lover, but cannot free him from serious danger of death. For a relapse seems more serious than the original disease and makes a man die a harder death, and it is worse to do without what we have been given some hope of attaining than what the wish alone prompts us to hope for. Therefore I would rather perish instantly than suffer the perils of death after many agonies. Therefore let Your Prudence consider and examine carefully which seems more to your credit—to give hope to a lover and so save him from the wrath of death and open up to him the road, which he does not know, to all good deeds, or by denying him this hope to close the road to all good deeds and open up the way of death."

The woman says: "Such aid as I can offer you—that is, that you may see me daily with your bodily eye—I have promised you freely, but what you are asking for you can never obtain by any amount of prayers or efforts, for I am firmly resolved with all my heart never to subject myself to the servitude of Venus or endure the torments of lovers. No one can know, unless he has experienced them, how many troubles lovers undergo, for they are exposed to so many pains and wearinesses that no one could learn them except from experience. But although I shall try by every means to avoid falling into Love's snares, I shall never refuse to you, or to any other man who wishes to serve me, the favor of doing so."

The man says: "My lady, God forbid that you [34] should persist in this terrible error, for only those women who are known to have joined Love's army are considered worthy of true praise among men and deserve to be mentioned for their worth in the courts of all rulers. What good in the world it does to have anyone do any good deeds unless they take their origin from love I cannot see. Therefore let such beauty and such worth of character as yours tread the paths of love and try its fortunes, for neither the nature nor the character of a thing can be truthfully understood until it has been tried. Only after you have tried it is it proper for you to reject it."

The woman says: "Men find it easy enough to get into Love's court, but difficult to stay there, because of the pains that threaten lovers; while to get out is, because of the desirable acts of love, impossible or nearly so. For after a lover has really entered into the court of Love he has no will either to do or not to do anything except what Love's table sets before him or what may be pleasing to the other lover. Therefore we ought not seek a court of this kind, for one should by all means avoid entering a place which he cannot freely leave. Such a place may be compared to the court of hell, for although the door of hell stands open for all who wish to enter, there is no way of getting out after you are once in. I would rather, therefore, stay in France and be content with a few coppers and have freedom to go where I would, than to be subject to a foreign power, even though I were loaded down with

[34] The man here uses the familiar singular form, then returns to the more formal plural.

Hungarian silver,[35] because to have so much is to have nothing. I have therefore good reason to hate the palace of Love, so you must look elsewhere for love, brother."

The man says: "No one can have a freer choice than not to wish to be separated from that which he desires with all his heart, for anybody ought to be pleased if he cannot help wishing what he desires with all his might, provided only that the thing is one that may be desired. But one can find nothing in the world more desirable than love, since from it comes the doing of every good thing and without it no one would do anything good in the world. It seems, therefore, that you ought to embrace Love's court with both arms, and his palace should not be at all hateful to you."

The woman says: "To fight under Love's protection may seem to anybody else liberty and a thing to lay hold of, but to me it seems the worst kind of servitude, a thing to be avoided at all costs. You are therefore laboring in vain, since the whole world could not move me from my position."

The man says: "If you choose to walk that path, unbearable torments will follow you, the like of which cannot be found and which it would be difficult to tell about."

The woman says: "I pray you tell me what these torments are which seem to threaten me because of this, so that if I forsee them they may hurt me less, since men say if you see an arrow coming, it doesn't strike so deep." [36]

[35] Marguerite, daughter of King Louis VII and half sister of the Countess Marie, was married to King Béla III of Hungary in 1185 or 1186. In 1184 King Béla sent to Paris a detailed report showing that his yearly revenue amounted to the equivalent of one million six hundred thousand dollars today (*Speculum*, XIII, 308). At the time this passage was written the negotiations for the marriage had evidently been begun but had not progressed far.

[36] John of Salisbury (*Policraticus* III. xi) records the same belief. "Just as spears which are seen before they strike inflict less severe wounds, but those which are entirely unexpected inflict deeper wounds . . ."

The man says: "If you saw these coming a long way off, they would strike you just as deep—unless you take care to rid yourself of this error we have been speaking of. Nevertheless, if you wish, you may hear about these torments. But first I wish to beg Your Grace to be so good as to tell me what place in Love's palace is reserved for you.

"Now men say, and it is true, that in the middle of the world there is built a palace with four very splendid façades, and in each of these is a marvellously beautiful door. The only people entitled to live in this palace are Love and certain communities of ladies. The eastern gate the God of Love has reserved for himself alone, but the other three are assigned to three definite classes of ladies. The ladies at the southern gate always linger around the open door, and you can always find them at the entrance. The ladies at the western gate do the same, except that you can always find them roaming around outside the entrance. But those who have been assigned to the care of the northern gate always keep the door shut and never look at anything outside the palace walls. With which of these groups do you say that you keep company?"

The woman says: "These things are too obscure for me, and your words are too allegorical; you will have to explain what you mean."

The man says: "Those who always linger around the open gate and are always to be found at the entrance are those women and ladies who, when anybody asks for admittance, learn by diligent inquiry what he deserves who seeks to come in by the open door and how good a character he has; and after they are fully convinced of a man's worth they admit the worthy ones with all honor, but drive the unworthy ones away from Love's palace. Those who claim the place at the western gate are those common women who never refuse any man, but admit everybody without distinction and are subject to the passions of everyone. But those who have the watch in the north and always keep their doors closed are those women who never open to anybody who knocks, but deny to everyone an entrance into Love's palace. Those at the south, then, are those women who wish to love and do not reject worthy lovers; this is proper since, being all in the south, they are worthy to be illumined by a ray from Love himself who lives in the east. Those of the west are loose women who seldom love anybody and are never loved by any good man; this is proper because, since their dwelling is in the west, the fiery ray of Love cannot reach to them from the east. Those of the north are those who refuse to love, although they may be loved by many; and this is proper, too, since the god has no consideration for those placed upon his left hand, because they are cursed.[37] Now from what I have said the arrangement of the palace of Love is clear."

The woman says: "Within the northern gate I maintain that I will be safe, not cursed."

The man says: "Listen, then, to the endless torments that are prepared for you.

"While I was attending as squire upon my lord, a certain very noble Robert,[38] on one very hot summer day I was riding with him and many other noble knights through the royal forest of France, and the woodland path led us to a most pleasant and delightful place. It was a grassy spot, surrounded on all sides by the trees of the forest. Here we all dismounted and turned our horses loose to graze; then after we had refreshed ourselves with a little nap we roused up and quickly saddled the wandering horses. But as my own horse had wandered a little farther in the pasture than the others, getting him ready took me so long that I found myself left alone in the glade. Not knowing the way, I was wandering around at a loss and looking carefully in all directions, when I spied an infinite number of mounted folk riding along at a walk near the edge of the wood. Believing firmly that my lord was riding

---

[37] Matt. 25:41.

[38] There were so many noble Roberts at the time that it is difficult to tell which is meant; perhaps the best guess is that it is Count Robert of Dreux, brother of King Louis VII, or his son Robert II, who reigned from 1184 to 1218. As a cousin of Countess Marie he would of course have been well known to her, but he might be "a certain very noble Robert" to the lady whom the knight was addressing.

among them, I was very glad and tried as hard as I could to ride up to them. But although I looked carefully I could not see him, since he was not among them. As I drew near and looked more carefully at the handsome throng, I saw a man riding in front of them, seated on a very beautiful horse, well worth looking at, and crowned with a golden diadem. Close after him followed a large and charming band of women, each of whom was mounted on a fair, fat horse with a gentle gait. Each woman was dressed in costly, many-colored garments with a gold-embroidered cloak and was accompanied by knights, one on the right hand and another on the left, while a third walked before her like a servant, holding her bridle in his hand all the time so that she rode gently forward on her horse without the least annoyance. Such was the dress and such the manner of riding of each woman in the first group. After them followed an unnumbered host of finely dressed knights who kept them from the clattering of those who followed them and from being annoyed by these people. Next to these there came a great multitude of women with various kinds of men, on foot and on horseback, pressing forward to serve them; but so great was the clatter of those who wished to be of service and so annoying was the crowd, that the women could not accept any services, nor could those who were ready to serve do so conveniently; and so the multitude of servants resulted in a great lack and deficiency of service, and the women would have considered it a great comfort, indeed, if they had been left to serve themselves.

"Then in the third group there followed a mean and abject troop of women. They were certainly very beautiful, but they were dressed in the most filthy clothes, wholly unsuited to the weather, for although they were in the burning heat of summer, they wore unwillingly garments of fox skins; besides that, they were very dirty and rode unbecomingly upon unsightly horses—that is, very lean ones that trotted heavily and had neither saddles nor bridles and went along with halting steps. No one tried to aid these women, who were without assistance from anyone, and besides, those on horseback and on foot who had gone ahead of them stirred up such a cloud of dust with their feet that the women could barely see each other, because the dust filled their eyes and clogged their lips.[39]

"When I had carefully observed all these people and had commenced to wonder greatly what it all meant, a lady with a calm, dignified face, who after all the others had gone by followed them on a very thin and dirty horse that halted on three feet, called me by name and bade me come to her. When I approached and saw her charming and beautiful face and that she was sitting on such a dirty horse, I at once offered her mine. But she declined it and said to me, 'You are looking for your lord, but you cannot find him here, because you have wandered rather far from his course.'

"I answered, 'My lady, I beg you, please deign to show me the right way,' to which she replied, 'Until you have seen these troops established in their own camps I cannot show you a safe road.' Then I replied, 'Then I ask you to explain to me, if you will, whose army this is that I see, and why so beautiful a woman has chosen to ride such a common horse and to wear such mean clothes.'

"To this the woman replied, 'This army which you see is that of the dead.' When I heard that, my soul was immediately troubled beyond measure, and my color changed, and all my bones began to loosen in their joints. Trembling and greatly terrified, I would gladly have left the company, but she began at once to speak comforting words to me and promised to keep me unharmed from every peril. She said, 'You will be safer and more secure here than in your father's house.' When I heard this I regained the quickening spirit I had nearly lost, and, coming closer to her, I began to ask diligently about all these things. She answered all my questions in order, saying,

" 'That knight whom you see crowned with a golden diadem, going before all the people, is the God of Love, who joins this army one day in every week, and in a marvellous fashion gives to each one his

---

[39] Much the same story is told in the almost contemporary *Lai du Trot*. Apparently neither author borrowed from the other, but Trojel (*De Amore*, xiv) conjectures that both heard the tale at the court of Troyes; see also E. M. Grimes in *Romanic Review*, XXVI (1935), 313–21, and W. A. Neilson in *Romania*, XXIX (1900), 86.

deserts, according as he has done good or evil in life. And those women, so beautiful and so honored, who follow after him in the first rank, are those most blessed of women who while they were alive knew how to conduct themselves wisely toward the soldiers of love, to show every favor to those who wished to love, and to give appropriate answers to those who under pretense of love sought love falsely; for this reason these women now have their full reward and are honored with innumerable gifts. Those women who follow in the second group and are so pestered by the services of so many men are those shameless women who while they lived did not fear to subject themselves to the pleasure of every man, but assented to the lust of any man who asked them and denied entrance within their gates to no man who sought it. And in this court they have earned this kind of reward. In return for their excessive giving of themselves and their indiscriminate acceptance of men they are unceasingly wearied by the indiscriminate services of innumerable people, and for them such services are converted into their harmful opposites and cause them great annoyance and shame. Then those women who follow in the last group, so meanly equipped, going along with downcast faces, without help from anybody and wearied by discomforts of all kinds, as you can plainly see with your own eyes (in which group I find a place), are those most wretched of all women who while they lived closed the palace of Love to all who wished to enter it and would not give a fitting answer to any man who did good deeds or who asked of them a cause and approval of well-doing; they rejected all who asked to serve in Love's army and drove them away just as though they hated them, not at all considering what sort of person is this God of Love whom those who were asking for love sought to serve. So now we suffer these well-deserved punishments and receive from the King of Love, through whom the whole world is ruled and without whom no one does anything good in this world, payment appropriate to our sins. We are, besides these, subjected to so many other kinds of punishments which no one could know about unless he learned by experience, that it would be impossible for me to tell you about them and very difficult for you to listen to the account. Therefore let those women who are still living in the world take care lest they join us in these torments, since after they are dead no penance can be of any use to them.'

"I answered the woman, 'As I see and understand it, he who has chosen to do the things well pleasing to Love shall receive his reward a hundredfold, while the god cannot pass over the sin of one who has dared offend him, but, it seems to me, will avenge more than a thousandfold the crime committed against him. It is unsafe, therefore, to offend such a god,[40] and it is safest to serve in all things him who can reward his own with such gifts and afflict with such heavy torments those who scorn him. Therefore, my lady, I ask and beseech you with all my might to give me permission to leave, so that I may tell the ladies what I have seen.'

"She answered, 'You may not have leave to go until you have learned of the heavier and harder torments that we suffer and have seen the greater joy and beatitude of the other ladies.'

"While we were talking thus we had gone a good distance and had come to a most delightful spot, where the meadows were very beautiful and more finely laid out than mortal had ever seen. The place was closed in on all sides by every kind of fruitful and fragrant trees, each bearing marvellous fruits according to its kind. It was also divided concentrically into three distinct parts. The first of these, the central one, was separated from the next part and surrounded on all sides by it, while the third, on the outside, was completely walled off from the first by the intervening part. Now in the middle of the first and innermost part stood a marvellously tall tree, bearing abundantly all sorts of fruits, and its branches extended as far as the edge of the interior part. At the roots of the tree gushed forth a wonderful spring of the clearest water, which to those who drank of it tasted of the sweetest nectar, and in this spring one saw all sorts of little fishes. Beside the spring, on a throne made of gold and every sort of precious stones, sat

[40] Ovid *Heroides* IV. II.

the Queen of Love, wearing a gorgeous crown on her head, dressed in very costly robes, and holding a golden scepter in her hand. At her right hand was prepared a seat that glowed with everything costly and bright, but no one was sitting on it. This section, the inner one, was called 'Delightfulness,' because in it every sort of pleasant and delightful thing was to be found. And in this inner part were prepared a great many couches, marvellously decorated and completely covered with silken coverlets and purple decorations. From the spring I have mentioned many brooks and rivulets flowed out in all directions, watering the whole of Delightfulness, and every couch had a rivulet by it.

"The second part was called 'Humidity' and was arranged in this fashion: the brooks which stayed within their channels and watered Delightfulness, in this second part grew too large and overflowed all of Humidity so that you could see grass mixed with water just as you can in the fields in the rainy days of spring. And the water, after it flowed into this section, became so cold that no living being could bear to touch it, while from above the sun poured down an intolerable heat, for there wasn't a single tree to shade the place. But the water did not extend beyond the bounds of this part.

"The third and last part was called 'Aridity,' and with good reason for water was completely lacking, the whole place was arid, and the heat of the sun's rays was intense, almost like fire, and the surface of the earth was like the bottom of a heated oven. All about the place were innumerable bundles of thorns, each with a pole through the middle which stuck out a distance of two cubits at each end, and at either end of the pole stood a very strong man, holding the end of the pole in his hands. But there was a very beautiful road passing through Aridity and Humidity, leading to Delightfulness, and in it no one of these discomforts was felt in the least.

"When we came to this place, the King of Love entered first; and the Queen of Love received him with an embrace, and with her help he sat down on the throne prepared for him, holding a crystalline scepter in his hand, and after him, by the same road, followed all the first band of women and knights. For each of the women there was prepared a most beautiful couch on which to sit, and the knights chose for themselves the seats they preferred. No human tongue could tell how great was the blessedness and the glory of these people, for the whole place of Delightfulness was appointed for their pleasure, and before them jugglers of every kind sported and sang, and men played all kinds of musical instruments there.

"Next, through the same road came the whole crowd of common women who had been following them, and the crowd of men who had been trying to serve these women. They came as far as the edge of Delightfulness, and when they could not pass beyond they began to slacken rein in Humidity and to find what comfort they could there, since this was the place appointed for them by the court of Love. And what noises and lamentings there were would be most difficult to tell! And the torments of these women were greatly increased by the glory which they saw of those who were in Delightfulness. Then, at the same place entered the third and last throng of women—those who would not have pity on the soldiers of Love—and they came as far as the edge of Humidity; but when they found no entrance, they commenced to spread out all through Aridity, since that was the place prepared for them from of old. And there was a seat on a bundle of thorns prepared for each of the women, and the men assigned to each, as I mentioned, kept shaking the bundle so that the women were very severely torn by the sharp thorns; and their bare feet rested on the burning ground. So great was the grief and suffering there that I believe the like is scarcely to be found among the infernal powers themselves.

"When I had seen these things I asked for permission to depart, and she said, 'I cannot give you permission, but leave your horse here and go quickly to the King of Love, along the way by which he entered, and ask permission of him as though he were your lord and pay careful attention to what he bids you do. And do not forget to intercede for me.' As soon as I had heard this I took the designated road and came before the King of Love and said to him, 'Mighty and glorious king, I render you all gratitude for deigning to reveal to me your mighty works and the wondrous secrets of your realm. Therefore I pray unceasingly to Your Grace to deign to bid me, your servant, do those things that are pleasing to you, and to indicate truly what are the chief rules in love, and at my intercession graciously to free from the heavier punishments that woman through whose beneficence I have been blessed with a sight like this, and in your mercy to give her a place here in Delightfulness with those women whom I see here in such honor, and finally, if you please, to give me leave to depart.'

"To my request he answered, 'You have been permitted to see our mighty works that through you our glory may be revealed to those who know it not, and that this sight which you now see may be a means of salvation for many ladies. We therefore command and firmly enjoin upon you that wherever you find a lady of any worth departing from our pathway by refusing to submit herself to love's engagements, you shall take care to relate to her what you have seen here and shall cause her to leave her erroneous ideas so that she may escape such very heavy torments and find a place here in glory. Know, then, that the chief rules in love are these twelve that follow:

I. Thou shalt avoid avarice like the deadly pestilence and shalt embrace its opposite.

II. Thou shalt keep thyself chaste for the sake of her whom thou lovest.

III. Thou shalt not knowingly strive to break up a correct love affair that someone else is engaged in.

IV. Thou shalt not choose for thy love anyone whom a natural sense of shame forbids thee to marry.

V. Be mindful completely to avoid falsehood.

VI. Thou shalt not have many who know of thy love affair.

VII. Being obedient in all things to the commands of ladies, thou shalt ever strive to ally thyself to the service of Love.

VIII. In giving and receiving love's solaces let modesty be ever present.

IX. Thou shalt speak no evil.

X. Thou shalt not be a revealer of love affairs.

XI. Thou shalt be in all things polite and courteous.

XII. In practicing the solaces of love thou shalt not exceed the desires of thy lover.

There are also other lesser precepts of love which it would not profit you to hear, since you can find them in the book written to Walter.

" 'As for that woman for whom you pleaded, she may not find a place here within the bounds of Delightfulness, as you ask, because her own deeds have made it impossible for her to remain in so glorious an abode. However, in answer to your plea we grant her a fat and gentle horse with a saddle and bridle and that she may have no attendants to shake her bundle of thorns; and with our permission she may have a cold stone under her feet. Take now this crystalline staff, and with our grace-depart; but throw the staff into the first stream you find.'

"I took my way back and returned to the lady who had led me there, and I found her sitting on a bundle without any attendants, resting her feet very comfortably upon a stone newly placed there, having a fat horse with fine trappings by her side, and feeling very little pain. She thanked me effusively and added, 'Depart now with the favor of heaven, my friend, since you may not see more of the affairs of this court. For the others have a glory and we a torment twice as great as those you see, but it is not granted to any living person to behold them.' When she had finished speaking I mounted my own horse, and in the twinkling of an eye I was led through the waters that surrounded the place. Into them I threw the crystalline staff and returned unharmed to my own home.

"Behold then, my lady, how great is the affliction of those who will not love—to what torments they are subjected, and what glory and honor those have earned who did not close the gates of Love to those who desired to enter—so that you may lay aside your erroneous opinion and be worthy to receive the rewards and to escape the torments I have told you about. For it would be unseemly and a desperate evil were a woman so wise and so beautiful as you to be subjected to such heavy torments or to endure so many perils. Now so far as you are concerned I am free from the task appointed me by Love; but you must be attentive and harken to his precepts that you may be worthy to enter into the glory of his beatitude."

The woman says: "If those things which you say are true, it is a glorious thing to take part in the services of Love and very dangerous to reject his mandates. But whether what you say is true or false, the story of these terrible punishments frightens me so that I do not wish to be a stranger to Love's service; but I would be reckoned among his fellowship and would find myself a dwelling at the southern gate. I must therefore follow in every respect the custom of the ladies at the southern gate and neither reject everybody nor admit everybody who knocks at Love's gate. I shall try, therefore, to find out who is worthy to enter, and having tried him and known him I shall receive him in good faith."

The man says: "I give thanks to the most mighty King of Love who has seen fit to change your intention and to banish your dire error. But your statement that you wish to consider whether I should be admitted when I cry at the door of Love's palace seems to me a bitter thing, and your word seems rather harsh; for if you have decided about the worth of my character, you can have no real cause for further deliberation. Yet since it is not easy for all a man's good deeds to become known to everybody, it may be that mine are unknown to you, and so perhaps in view of the state of your knowledge this time for consideration for which you ask would be reasonable. But I have so much confidence in the worthy things I have done and in the justice of Your Nobility, that although the gift I ask for may be delayed, I do not believe that services can long be deprived of their rewards. Therefore may God wish me to feel that my hope is bearing fruit, and may the Divine Power make you think of me when I leave, just as I shall retain in my absence the constant thought of you."

Sixth Dialogue

A man of the higher nobility speaks with a woman of the middle class

If a man of the higher nobility should seek the love of a woman of the middle class, he may keep the same style of address that a man of the simple nobility uses when he talks with a woman of this class, or else he may conveniently proceed in this fashion:

"For a long time past I have been looking forward to this day, fully determined to tell you my thought and intention and how great is my continual thought of you, but until now I have found no fitting occasion to speak of love. You should know, however, that I have put all the thought and the reliance of my mind on you, and that nothing in the world can make me happy except the most precious treasure of your person. Without this I seem to have nothing in the world, and I look upon the abundance of my worldly goods as the deepest poverty. Your love alone can crown me with the diadem of a king and make me revel in wealth even if I am in direst poverty. The hope of your love keeps me alive in the world, and if I lose this hope I must die. May Your Grace, therefore, deign to retain me in your service and not reject the love of a count, for only a count or one of still higher rank is worthy of a love such as yours. God forbid that one so beautiful and of such an excellent character should ever care to select a lover from the middle class. May Your Prudence, therefore, consider the faith and devotion of the count who is speaking and give him an answer appropriate to his deserts."

The woman says: "A woman of the middle class who found herself worthy of the love of a count would be truly blessed; but you should consider carefully what praise or what reward a count or a marquis would deserve if he asked a woman of the middle class for her love. What a strange tercel would we consider one who would leave the partridges, cranes, and pheasants and seek his quarry among the wretched sparrows or the sons of the hens. I am glad, of course, that a count finds me worthy of his love, but nevertheless I am afraid to accept a man of such a lofty and grand family who asks for the love of such a humble woman. It seems to me that he does so only out of the meanness of his spirit, for only the great-spirited deserve to know the secrets of ladies and to have their love. So if I should give you my love and then find in your person a lack of those things that one demands in love (and I might not have them either, because they are not natural to my class) then our love could not long be managed as it should be. It is better, then, to refrain from entering into such an affair than to suffer so much that we have to end it after it has been begun."

The man says: "Every man ought to ask for love where love's persuasion impels him; for that love is excellent which in any class arises solely from pleasure and delight in the beauty of some woman and is not sought after because of the privileges of rank alone. Therefore I do not violate Love's precepts if I choose my love from a lower class, but rather do I seem by so doing to follow them. For this is the precept of Love: He who desires true love must not dare to go beyond the bounds of his own desires or to make distinctions of classes under Love, who desires to adorn his palace from every class and to have everyone in his court serve on equal terms with no special privileges of rank. Therefore a woman of the middle class deserves to rank in Love's court on an equal footing with a count or a countess. As my whole heart's desire is directed toward you, I may choose you without the least blame, and men will not think that I am aiming at mean things, but at very great ones. For since you are worthy of the honorable court of Love and my will impels me to love you, Your Prudence ought to reckon me among the great-souled. You must not, therefore, refrain from loving me unless you see that I lack good character and am a stranger to good deeds. Besides, a tercel flies better when it takes a resourceful lark than when it takes a fat quail that flies in a straight line."

The woman says: "Even though you might, by these arguments, compel me to love you, there is another reason which necessarily keeps me from doing so. Suppose everything did turn out prosperously for our embraces, if the affair came to the ears of the common people they would ruin my good name by blaming me openly on the ground that I had gone far outside my natural limits. Besides, it is not usual for a man of higher rank to love faithfully a woman of a lower one, and if he does he soon comes to loathe her love, and he despises her on slight provocation. It is easy to see that this is contrary to the mandates of Love, in whose court there is no place for distinctions of rank; lovers of whatever rank serve on equal terms in his palace, and no one enjoys any privileges because of his higher station. I have therefore a just cause for opposing you, since our inequality of rank might prevent what you propose."

The man says: "It is marvellous how Your Prudence seeks to defend yourself with so short-sighted an argument. For what sort of love would that be which is perfected in the presence of the people and torn to pieces by the remarks of the crowd? Does not Love's precept say that you must not confide your love to many people? Besides, a woman of any strength of character ought not to love anyone with the idea that after she has entered upon the path of love she will draw back because of the usual empty chatter of the crowd or the suspicions rumored abroad by spies, and so bring to pass the desire of evil men. For, as you well know, the false have the idea and the intention, plain to everybody, of interfering with the actions of good men wherever possible and of opposing the solaces of lovers. Your Serenity should therefore learn to despise the deceitful slander of bad men and to avoid their snares, so that the deeds of the wicked may not prove a hindrance to the good. For evil men can never be better rewarded than by seeing that their frauds have made harder the path of good men.

"But neither I nor anyone else can fully convince you of the good faith and lawfulness of my love, because God Himself is the only searcher and beholder of the human heart; to Him alone is the thought of man apparent. A wise woman should therefore judge the inward thought by the deeds and the outward works. If, then, my deeds or my works make me unworthy of your love or give you just cause to suspect me, I beg you to show me no mercy. But if you should discover that my deeds cannot rightly do me any harm, with full confidence in myself I beg of you not to let your decision do me any injury. But since no man can make his good faith absolutely convincing to any woman, by the same reasoning that you use any woman might reject any man. Therefore may Your Prudence make long and careful investigation as to what answer you ought to make to my proposals. For, as you yourself have well said already, no matter how much nobler one of the lovers is than the other, after they have begun to love they should walk in Love's court with equal steps."

The woman says: "Although it is not proper that the course of good men should be impeded by the snares of the wicked, still it does not follow that the anchor of good men should always find bottom. For it is left to the decision of every woman, when asked for her love, to refuse it if she will, and no one has a right to be injured thereby, as you have asserted in what you said. For what sort of injury can it be if a person declines to give something to someone who asks for it?"

The man says: "Of course I admit that a woman has the right to give her love to a man who asks for it if she wishes to, and if she does not give it, it would seem that she does him no injury. Yet without a doubt injury is done to a lover when he, a good man, is defrauded of his deserts because of what bad men have done, or when because of an idle suspicion his efforts cannot be properly rewarded. A woman whose love is sought should either promise it to her suitor or deny it outright, or if she is in doubt about the character of the man who asks she may say, 'Do good deeds before you seek the reward of good deeds.' For a faithful lover should not be rejected on the excuse that some only pretend to love, since it seems very wrong that one man should suffer for another's sin."

The woman says: "Since you would rather have love denied you outright than be left in doubt by a 'perhaps,' I shall try to humor you and I shall refuse to love you."

The man says: "I beg Your Prudence to inform me whether, in your heart, you are disposed to love anyone else."

The woman says: "Neither the law of Love nor the custom of lovers requires me to inform you of the state of my heart. For even if I were inclined to love someone else, it would not be proper for you to ask or for me to tell you about it."

The man says: "Then in the present case there is no help left for me but to argue with you at length and by discussing the matter find out whether or not it is proper for you to deny me your love if you haven't given it to any other lover. Now I shall prove to you that you cannot properly deprive me of your love. Loving is either a good thing or a bad thing. It is not safe to say that it is a bad thing, because all men are clearly agreed and the rule of Love shows us that neither woman nor man in this world can be considered happy or well-bred, nor can he do anything good, unless love inspires him. Wherefore you must needs conclude that loving is a good thing and a desirable one. Therefore if a person of either sex desires to be considered good or praiseworthy in the world, he or she is bound to love. But if you are bound to love you must love either bad men or worthy ones. But certainly you cannot love bad men, because Love's precept forbids that; it follows then that you must give your love only to good men. Therefore if you find that my character is good you do wrong in denying me your love."

The woman says: "I admit that loving is a good thing and that we must give our love only to the good, but you are trying to deprive me of the freedom that Love has given to every lover. One cannot give love to every man who asks for it; so, supported by Love's teaching, I may without blame refuse my love to you and give it to some other man who asks for it."

The man says: "The freedom to love which is granted you cannot deprive you of your free choice, but your choice should be a just one so that you will be careful to love what you should. Love did not wish to give you this freedom of choice for you to abuse the privilege granted you, but that you might deserve from him greater rewards by being careful to choose, for his sake, the way of service when you are placed at such a parting of the ways; but if you go astray on the other path, you may be sure he will be greatly offended. Nor can you defend yourself by giving your love to some man who asked for it after I did, for it is dishonorable to deny one's love to the first worthy man who asks for it and not very honorable to give it to a later suitor, since Love does not want one of his servants to be benefited at the expense of another. I beg you, therefore, do not pay to one man what properly you owe to another."

The woman says: "What you say is reasonable enough if my heart would submit to my will. It would be my will to do what you propose, but my heart absolutely forbids and wholly dissuades me from doing what I desire with all my will. Therefore, since my heart forbids me to love, tell me, I pray you, which I should follow—my heart or my head."

The man says: "I do not recall ever having heard before this of such a disagreement as that the heart should desire one thing and the will another. But if things are as you say, you ought to choose the side that is supported by justice and truth."

The woman says: "What you say cannot stand, because no one likes forced services or considers that they deserve a reward. Why then should I serve Love if I am not to receive the rewards of love? Besides what sort of love can it be that is undertaken against the desire of the heart? Only that which is first desired by the heart and the will should have the rewards of love, but I do not see how I can love what I do not desire with my heart. You said, too, that I cannot properly give my love to one man if another one has previously asked for it. But doesn't a wild beast who has been wounded by the spear of one hunter and then is later taken by another, belong to the man who got her? Most assuredly she does; and so in love the second lover ought to get the rewards rather than the first."

The man says: "Even though we cannot render to a king services that please him, we ought not to offend him; for he who is offended by the mere withholding of service is much more provoked to wrath if he is injured. But Love is injured when honor which is due to one of his knights is given to another. Therefore if I was the first to ask you for your love, you ought not be in too great haste to give it to some other man, even if your soul does not incline toward me, because, 'The hour that we did not hope for is pleasing when it comes.' [41] The King of Love can in a short time rain a shower of pity over your mind and bring me the fruit of your love that I have despaired of; but this could not happen if you had already granted it to some other man. What you said about hunting cannot stand in my way, because we know that this applies to a particular practice, unfair enough, of certain people. But the usual rule throughout the world is that if anyone starts a wild beast from her lair and follows her, even though someone else takes her, custom reserves her for the first man. Therefore, since my suit came before that of the other man, you cannot with justice deprive me of your love."

The woman says: "It seems very discourteous and an open breach of good manners for a man to want to deny to some other person a good thing that he cannot have for himself. Therefore, since you cannot have my love because I have no fondness or affection in my heart for you, you ought not close the way for others to love me. For since Love did not want me to fall ardently in love with you, but did inspire me with love for someone else, I may without any blame love the other man. However, in order to take away from you any ground for a complaint

---

[41] Horace *Epistles* I. iv. 14.

against me, I shall not take the trouble to devote myself to love, and I shall see whether 'a sinful maiden has conceived and a gentle hen given birth to a serpent.' " [42]

The man says: "Although your words seem pleasant to human ears, if one looks at them with the searching eye of truth they are cloaked in sophistry. Shall a sinner remain excused of God because God has not poured grace upon him? By no means; he shall be delivered over to everlasting torments. Therefore, if you wish to escape Love's wrath and desire to be inflamed by his breath, you must render yourself fit and worthy to receive Love's grace."

The woman says: "No matter how much good any man does in this world, it is of no profit to him in attaining the rewards of eternal blessedness unless he is prompted by love.[43] For the same reason, no matter how much I may strive to serve the King of Love by my deeds and my works, unless these proceed from the affection of the heart and are derived from the impulse of love, they cannot profit me toward obtaining the rewards of love. Therefore until Love's arrow strikes me you cannot obtain the grant of my love."

The man says: "And I shall ever pray to God on bended knees to make you love what you should and what will clearly profit Your Highness."

Seventh Dialogue

A man of the higher nobility speaks with a woman of the simple nobility

When a man of the higher nobility addresses a woman of the simple nobility, let him use the same speeches that a nobleman and a man of the higher nobility use with a woman of the middle class, except that part dealing with the commendation of birth, and he must not boast

---

[42] This is among the portents listed in Walter of Châtillon's *Alexandreis*, Bk. x.
[43] I Cor., chap. 13.

very much of the fact that he is noble. In addition he might begin with this formula:

"I ought to give God greater thanks than any other living man in the whole world because it is now granted me to see with my eyes what my soul has desired above all else to see, and I believe that God has granted it to me because of my great longing and because He has seen fit to hear the prayers of my importunate supplication. For not an hour of the day or night could pass that I did not earnestly pray God to grant me the boon of seeing you near me in the flesh. It is no wonder that I was driven by so great an impulse to see you and was tormented by so great a desire, since the whole world extols your virtue and your wisdom, and in the farthest parts of the world courts are fed upon the tale of your goodness just as though it were a sort of tangible food. And now I know in very truth that a human tongue is not able to tell the tale of your beauty and your prudence or a human mind to imagine it. And so the mighty desire, which I already had, of seeing you and serving you has greatly increased and will increase still more, because it is perfectly clear and manifest to me that merely to serve you is to reign over everything in this life and that without this no man in the world can do anything worthy of praise. Indeed I pray to God in heaven that of His grace He grant me only that I may always do what is wholly pleasing to Your Excellency, for if I do, no adversity can trouble me or evil chance of fortune embarrass me. And I wish ever to dedicate to your praise all the good deeds that I do and to serve your reputation in every way. For whatever good I may do, you may know that it is done with you in mind and with the constant thought of you."

The woman says: "I am bound to give you many thanks for lauding me with such commendations and exalting me with such high praise. You should know that because of all this your coming gives me joy and your presence is pleasing enough to me, since you tell me that being able to see me in the flesh is a sovereign remedy to you. I am happy, too, if I may be found worthy of such great blessedness as to be the cause or occasion of well-doing by you or any other men. But I want to warn you of one thing in particular: you must never praise anyone so highly that you may afterward be ashamed to qualify this praise by a word of disparagement, and you must not disparage anyone so much that you cannot afterward praise him without shame. Furthermore, you must never praise one woman so effusively that what you say detracts from the worth of any other woman. But saying that merely to be of service to me is to reign in this life seems to be an insult to all other ladies, to serve whom may perhaps be as praiseworthy as to serve me, or even more so. It would not be proper for you to refuse your services to any woman, because, it seems clear, you are a man of excellent character, famous for your great courtesy and noted for your generosity. Therefore you do well if you strive to do the things that are in keeping with your birth and character. For men of the higher nobility are bound to have more noble manners than other men, and they do more harm to their reputations by a little boorishness or by refraining from doing good than men of low birth and common breeding do to theirs by committing rather grave offenses. I am therefore glad if I am to you a cause and origin of good deeds, and so far as I am able I shall always and in all things give you my approval when you do well."

The man says: "I now see for myself very clearly that all the things that are told about you throughout the world are true. It is clear from your answer how wise you are and how fine your character. Your Prudence has therefore taken the pains to warn me to try to keep to moderation in praising or blaming anyone, and in this the fulness of your wisdom is manifest. God forbid that I should ever be so clearly taken in a falsehood as to say things that cast a shadow over what all men praise, for if we find anyone saying things in detraction of the fame of either bad men or good men, it can make no difference, among prudent men, in the reputation of the man about whom they are spoken; but we know that what the man says hurts his own reputation. Therefore whatever you may wish to say or do to me you may do safely without fear that I will tell evil tales about it. Yet you must be very careful in this affair because if you do good things nobody's mouth will refrain from praising your person; but if you do bad things, even though I may keep silent concerning the misdeeds you have done, since no man of character should relate bad things about anybody, I shall cease to sing your praises. Then the slanderers who know no moderation in their evil speaking, and whose meat and drink it is to ruin other people's reputations in their wicked fashion, will in their usual way never stop talking about the bad things you have done. As for my remark that merely to serve you is to reign in this life, I don't think there can be any harm to the other ladies in this, because I could not make my services more valuable to you were I to refuse them to the other ladies, while by obeying their wishes I believe I am continually doing what you want, especially when the services are done to other ladies for your sake. Moreover, your sweet and pleasing instruction has impressed upon me the fact that I should strive to do those things that are suitable to my birth and thoroughly in keeping with my character, advice which you know I am very eager to accept and wholly ready to follow, for no man who has any reputation for goodness should do things that depart from the way of good men, as what you have just said makes very clear. In the same way it seems to be in keeping with your character for you to be careful to act in accordance with the nature of the stock from which obviously you are descended. It is clear that nothing is more in keeping with your nobility than to attempt to act in such a way that those who look to you may always increase in their determination to do good and may be kept in the mood for it. But I know that if there is any man in the world who by the purity of his faith and his ready inclination to serve you is found worthy to be promised your solaces and by his merits to obtain your grace, I deserve to be honored by you before all the others and with greater rewards than anyone else. For by the best election I have chosen you from among all women to be my mighty lady, to whose services I wish ever to devote myself and to whose credit I wish to set down all my good deeds. From the bottom of my heart I ask your mercy, that you may look upon me as your particular man, just as I have devoted myself particularly to serve you, and that my deeds may obtain from you the reward I desire."

The woman says: "There is nothing in the world that my soul so eagerly desires as that men may know me to be one who does what is worthy of praise and reward, and I have full confidence in God the Father that so long as He preserves unharmed the disposition He has given me I shall never try to do anything that is not open to every criticism. But it seems to me impossible wholly to escape the detractions of the wicked and difficult to curb them, for it would be much easier to take a stream that is flowing naturally down hill and lead it through the same channel swiftly back to its source than it would be to stop the mouths of slanderers or to keep them from plotting. Therefore I think we should leave them to their own devices instead of trying to correct those whose very nature makes it impossible for them to keep from speaking evil. We should merely despise their empty prattle and have no speech with them, because, no matter what good men may really do, if slanderers speak about them they always put an evil interpretation upon it. Therefore it is enough for any honest man to have a clear conscience and a good reputation among good men. As for the other matter, I admit it is true that by serving the desires of other ladies you seem to be serving me, but as for crediting me with all the good deeds done in the world, that seems to me unjustified and very unfair, since there may be many other women of as good or better character who are more worthy of the honor. Moreover it is my desire to use my nobility with such moderation that you, or any other man in the world who does good deeds for my sake, may always increase in the determination to do good and may be kept quite in the mood for it. Now you say that in everything you are devoted to my service and that you deserve greater rewards from me than any other man does, because of your great desire to serve me and because, as you say, you have chosen me as your particular lady. God forbid that any service done me, by you or anybody else, should long go unrewarded if it comes to my attention in any way. But your request that I should consider you as my particular man, just as you are particularly devoted to my service, and that I should give you the reward you hope for, I do not see how I can grant, since such partiality might be to the disadvantage of others who have as much desire to serve me as you have, or perhaps even more. Besides I am not perfectly clear as to what the reward is that you expect from me; you must explain yourself more clearly."

The man says: "What I said to you about evil speakers was not said with the idea of putting on you the burden of holding in check the inclinations of evil men, but that your well-considered deeds may show you to be of such a character that the envy of the wicked will always keep on increasing and the opinion of good men will guard you from their plots, as your judgment has already most prudently indicated, for among good men it is enough for anyone to have a clear conscience. As for what you said about doing an injustice to other women if I credit all my good deeds to your praise, there seems to be nothing in that to wrong anybody or to give offense; although a woman ought to approve of a good deed done by anyone, every praiseworthy man should do all his good deeds to the special praise of one woman, and every woman of good sense, although she ought to be pleased by the good deeds of anyone, can laudably approve the acts of only one man, and she should consider them done to her special praise. No one is injured if I have devoted myself and my deeds, each and all, to your service and have acknowledged you as my special mistress. It is enough for the other women to be honored by the special services of other men; it wouldn't seem to do them any good for you to vex yourself with looking out for them, since my will is fixed on serving you in everything and the will cannot be controlled, as the teaching of the most learned Donatus [44] will show you, for the human will is so very

---

[44] Trojel was unable to find this statement in the works of Donatus the Grammarian (Aelius Donatus); I have not found it in the work of Donatus the Commentator (Tiberius Claudius Donatus). The Donatist heresy was sometimes credited to Donatus, but this heresy was not concerned with free will.

free that no one's efforts can divert it from a purpose firmly formed. Therefore the other ladies can ask me nothing as their due except that, with an eye to your contemplation, I grant them such services as are acceptable to them and that I keep discreetly silent as to the source of these services; but by the obligation I owe you I am bound to be worthy of praise in all that I do and to avoid all stain of depravity. And you owe it to me, as you yourself have agreed, to see that the services I do for you shall not long go without their reward. You said too, that if Your Ladyship were to show me special good will it would be to the disadvantage of others who perhaps have a greater desire to serve you than I have, or as great a one. To this I answer that if any man has a greater determination to serve you than I have, or as great a one, I ask that I may get no aid from you, nor may any laws of reason protect me. You said also that you did not fully understand what the reward was that I was hoping for, toward which all my attention was directed. I desire Your Clemency to be informed that the reward I ask you to promise to give me is one which it is unbearable agony to be without, while to have it is to abound in all riches. It is that you should be pleasant to me unless your desire is opposed to me. It is your love which I seek, in order to restore my health, and which I desire to get by my hunting."

The woman says: "You seem to be wandering a long way from the straight path of love and to be violating the best custom of lovers, because you are in such haste to ask for love. For the wise and well-taught lover, when conversing for the first time with a lady whom he has not previously known, should not ask in specific words for the gifts of love, but he should try hard to give a hint to the lady he loves, and should show himself pleasant and courteous in all that he says; then he should be careful to act in such a way that his deeds praise him truly to his love, even when he is absent. Then as the third step he may with more assurance come to the request for love. But you have upset this order by a clear violation, and I believe you have done so because you think that

I will be only too ready to grant what you ask, or because you are not experienced in the art of love. Therefore there is good cause to be suspicious of your love."

The man says: "If it is true that I have mixed up the order of love, it seems I have done so with your approval. For although my intention might have been guessed from what I said cautiously and in a round-about way, you asked me to explain to you more clearly what I wanted, as though you did not understand. I did not, therefore, make my request with any idea that you would be too ready to grant it, nor was I asking for a too hasty gift of your love; I merely desired to make my intention clear to you as you asked me to. Besides, although the order you mention ought to be followed, it may be changed where there is sufficient reason for so doing. If my feelings are too strong to resist, and if I bear an inward wound of love, I may plead necessity as a defense against the charge of unworthiness, for urgent necessity can be bound by no rules of law. Besides, if I have any lack of judgment in love, I must necessarily seek the love of a woman of great wisdom and worth so that my inexperience may thereby be remedied and I may learn all the doctrine of love. If an inexperienced man should ask for the love of an inexperienced woman, their love could not develop properly or long endure in the proper condition. For even though a favorable breeze springs up after a ship has been exposed to unfavorable conditions at sea and has been subjected to tempests, if a moderate gust strikes it, it will sink and go to the bottom unless it has a trained steersman and rowers. Both of your arguments are therefore silenced by the best of answers and can in no way oppose my proposal."

The woman says: "Even though I found you in every respect worthy of love, still we are separated by too wide and too rough an expanse of country to be able to offer each other love's solaces or to find proper opportunities for meeting. Lovers who live near together can cure each other of the torments that come from love, can help each other in their common sufferings, and can nourish their love by mutual exchanges and efforts; those, however, who are far apart cannot perceive each other's pains, but each one has to relieve his own trouble and cure his own torments. So it seems that our love should go no further, because Love's rule teaches us that the daily sight of each other makes lovers love more ardently, while I can see on the other hand that by reason of distance love decreases and fails, and therefore everybody should try to find a lover who lives near by."

The man says: "You are troubling yourself to say what seems to be against all reason, for all men know that if one gets easily what he desires he holds it cheap and what formerly he longed for with his whole heart he now considers worthless. On the other hand, whenever the possession of some good thing is postponed by the difficulty of getting it, we desire it more eagerly and put forth a greater effort to keep it. Therefore if one has difficulty in obtaining the embraces of one's lover and obtains them rarely, the lovers are bound to each other in more ardent chains of love and their souls are linked together in heavier and closer bonds of affection. For constancy is made perfect amid the waves that buffet it, and perseverance is clearly seen in adversities. Rest seems sweeter to a man who is wearied by many labors than to one who lives in continual idleness, and a new-found shade seems to offer more to one who is burdened by the heat than to one who has been constantly in air of a moderate temperature. It is not one of Love's rules, as you said it was, that when lovers seldom meet the strength of their love is weakened, since we find it false and misleading. Therefore you cannot properly refuse me your love with the excuse of the long and difficult distance between us, but you should gratify me rather than someone who lives near by; besides it is easier to conceal a love affair when the lovers do not meet than when they converse frequently with each other."

The woman says: "So far as hiding one's love goes, I do not think there is any choice between a distant lover and one who is present. If the lover proves to be wise and clever it doesn't matter whether he is far from his beloved or near her, he will so govern his actions and his will that no one can guess the secrets of their love; on the other hand a foolish lover, whether far or near, can never conceal the secrets of his love. Your argument must therefore fall before this most obvious one on the other side. Besides there is another fact, by no means trivial, which keeps me from loving you. I have a husband who is greatly distinguished by his nobility, his good breeding, and his good character, and it would be wicked for me to violate his bed or submit to the embraces of any other man, since I know that he loves me with his whole heart and I am bound to him with all the devotion of mine. The laws themselves bid me refrain from loving another man when I am blessed with such a reward for my love."

The man says: "I admit it is true that your husband is a very worthy man and that he is more blest than any man in the world because he has been worthy to have the joy of embracing Your Highness. But I am greatly surprised that you wish to misapply the term 'love' to that marital affection which husband and wife are expected to feel for each other after marriage, since everybody knows that love can have no place between husband and wife. They may be bound to each other by a great and immoderate affection, but their feeling cannot take the place of love, because it cannot fit under the true definition of love. For what is love but an inordinate desire to receive passionately a furtive and hidden embrace? But what embrace between husband and wife can be furtive, I ask you, since they may be said to belong to each other and may satisfy all of each other's desires without fear that anybody will object? Besides, that most excellent doctrine of princes shows that nobody can make furtive use of what belongs to him. Do not let what I have said seem absurd to you, for husband and wife may be joined together by every sort of affection, but this feeling cannot take the place of love. In friendship we see the same thing. Father and son may feel every sort of affection for each other, but there is no true friendship between them, because, as Cicero tells us, the feeling that offspring of the blood have for each other is affection.[45] It is clear then that there is just as much difference between every kind of affection of husband and wife and the obligation of lovers as there is between the mutual affection of father and son and the strongest friendship between two men, so that in the one case we say there is no love, just as in the other we say friendship is lacking. So then you see clearly that love can by no means exercise its functions between husband and wife, but has wished to withdraw its privileges completely.

"But there is another reason why husband and wife cannot love each other and that is that the very substance of love, without which true love cannot exist—I mean jealousy—is in such a case very much frowned upon and they should avoid it like the pestilence; but lovers should always welcome it as the mother and the nurse of love. From this you may see clearly that love cannot possibly flourish between you and your husband. Therefore, since every woman of character ought to love, prudently, you can without doing yourself any harm accept the prayers of a suppliant and endow your suitor with your love."

The woman says: "You are trying to take under your protection what all men from early times down have agreed to consider very reprehensible and to reject as hateful. For who can rightly commend envious jealousy or speak in favor of it, since jealousy is nothing but a shameful and evil suspicion of a woman? God forbid, therefore, that any worthy man should feel jealous about anyone, since this proves hostile to every prudent person and throughout the world is hated by everybody good. You are trying also, under cover of defining love, to condemn love between husband and wife, saying that their embraces cannot be furtive, since without fear that anyone may object they can fulfill each other's desires. But if you understood the definition correctly it could not interfere with love between husband and wife, for the expression 'hidden embraces' is simply an explanation in different

---

[45] This is not the idea that Cicero presents in *Friendship*, sect. 27, although the idea might possibly have been extracted from the sentence out of its context.

words of the preceding one, and there seems to be no impossibility in husband and wife giving each other hidden embraces, even though they can do so without the least fear that anybody may raise an objection. Everyone should choose that love which may be fostered by security for continual embraces and, what is more, can be practiced every day without any sin. I ought therefore to choose a man to enjoy my embraces who can be to me both husband and lover, because, no matter what the definition of love may say, love seems to be nothing but a great desire to enjoy carnal pleasure with someone, and nothing prevents this feeling existing between husband and wife."

The man says: "If the theory of love were perfectly clear to you and Love's dart had ever touched you, your own feelings would have shown you that love cannot exist without jealousy, because, as I have already told you in more detail, jealousy between lovers is commended by every man who is experienced in love, while between husband and wife it is condemned throughout the world; the reason for this will be perfectly clear from a description of jealousy. Now jealousy is a true emotion whereby we greatly fear that the substance of our love may be weakened by some defect in serving the desires of our beloved, and it is an anxiety lest our love may not be returned, and it is a suspicion of the beloved, but without any shameful thought. From this it is clear that there are three aspects of jealousy. A truly jealous man is always afraid that his services may not be sufficient to retain the love of the woman he loves, and he is afraid that she may not love him as he loves her, and he is so tormented with anxiety that he wonders whether she doesn't have another lover, although he believes that this cannot possibly be. But that this last aspect of jealousy is not proper for a married man is clearly apparent, for a husband cannot suspect his wife without the thought that such conduct on her part is shameful. Pure jealousy, in the case of a husband, takes a stain from the defect of its subject and ceases to be what it was. Water likewise may be beautifully clear, but if it begins to run over a sandy bed it becomes cloudy from the sand and loses its natural clearness; so charity, although by nature it deserves the reward of eternal blessedness, if given to the poor by a hypocrite or out of desire for empty glory loses its efficacy and causes the man to forfeit both what he gives and his reward for giving it. It is therefore plain enough that we have clearly demonstrated that jealousy cannot have its natural place between husband and wife and that therefore love between them must necessarily cease, because these two things always go together. But between lovers this jealousy is said to be preservative of love, because all three aspects which we have attributed to it are necessary to a lover; therefore jealousy between lovers is not condemned. We find many, however, who are deceived in this matter and say falsely that a shameful suspicion is jealousy, just as many often make the mistake of saying that an alloy of silver and lead is the finest silver. Wherefore not a few, being ignorant of the origin and description of jealousy, are often deceived and led into the gravest error. For even between persons who are not married this false jealousy may find a place and then they are no longer called 'lovers' but 'gentleman friend' and 'lady friend.' As for what you tried to prove by your answer —that the love which can be practiced without sin is far preferable— that, apparently, cannot stand. For whatever solaces married people extend to each other beyond what are inspired by the desire for offspring or the payment of the marriage debt,[46] cannot be free from sin, and the punishment is always greater when the use of a holy thing is perverted by misuse than if we practice the ordinary abuses. It is a more serious offense in a wife than in another woman, for the too ardent lover, as we are taught by the apostolic law, is considered an adulterer with his own wife.[47] But it seems that no one should approve your

[46] The Jews looked upon the conjugal act as a duty to be performed, under ordinary circumstances, once each day (*Babylonian Talmud*, Order Nashim, Tractate Kethuboth, sec. 61b). Most churchmen accepted this on the authority of I Corinthians 7: 3 (although St. Jerome *Against Jovinian* I. 7 considered that this precept was practically nullified by Paul's further injunction to "pray always"), but they frowned upon attempts to emulate Ovid (*Amours* III, vii. 26) or Catullus (XXXII. 8).

[47] Alanus de Insulis (*Epitome of the Art of Preaching*, chap. xlv) quotes the saying, "An ardent lover of his wife is an adulterer." Jerome (*op. cit.*, I. 49) and Peter Lombard (*Sentences* IV. xxxi) have the same but with *ardentior* instead of *vehemens*, which

interpretation, which you draw from the definition of love, for all the greater authors have told us that explanatory words must not be used in the actual definitions of things. From this everybody can see clearly that I have taken all the force out of your explanation, because that seems to be contrary to the meaning of the definition. But neither does your definition, which I admit you took from Love, have any reason back of it, for it includes the blind and the insane who, as the teaching of Andreas the Lover, chaplain of the royal court, shows us clearly, are to be completely banished from the court of Love. Since, therefore, you cannot raise a reasonable objection to my application, no man will consider it to your credit if you make me languish for love of you and suffer so many torments on your account."

The woman says: "You haven't advanced any argument, so far as I can see, that would weaken my opinion or properly compel me to assent to your desire. However, since those duties you impose on me look so very much as though they were real ones, in order to deprive you of any opportunity to make a charge against me I shall not refuse to have the decision given by any lady or any man of character whom you may select, on the points at issue between us: namely, whether love can have any place between husband and wife and whether jealousy between lovers may properly be praised, for it seems to me that we can never settle this discussion or bring it a proper end."

The man says: "I do not care to seek the decision of anybody else in this case if you will only examine properly what you yourself have said."

The woman says: "The world never heard of anyone passing judgment on his own case, so I refuse to have anything to do with the matter, and I leave it to be entrusted to someone else."

The man says: "I give you full power to appoint the arbiter in this dispute; however, I want to be judged by a woman, not by a man."

Alanus and Andreas use. Clement of Alexandria (*Pedagogue* II. x) expresses the same idea; it seems to have been a commonplace of medieval theology, and appears again after the time of Andreas.

The woman says: "If it suits you, it seems to me that the Countess of Champagne ought to be honored in this affair and should settle the disagreement."

The man says: "I promise forever to abide by her decision in every respect and to keep it absolutely inviolate, because no one could ever have any reason to raise a question about her wisdom or the fairness of her decision. Let us then by common consent and desire write a letter showing the nature of our disagreement and the pledge we have made to abide by her decision. Let us do it in this fashion:

The letter sent to the Countess of Champagne

To the illustrious and wise woman M., Countess of Champagne,[48] the noble woman A. and Count G. send greeting and whatever in the world is more pleasing.

Ancient custom shows us plainly, and the way of life of the ancients demands, that if we are to have justice done we should seek first of all in the place where Wisdom is clearly known to have found a home for herself and that we should seek for the truth of reason at its source, where it is abundant, rather than beg for its decisions where it flows scantily in small streams. For a great poverty of possessions can scarcely offer to anyone a wealth of good things or distribute an abundance of fertility. Where the master is oppressed by great want it is wholly impossible for the vassal to abound in wealth.

"Now on a certain day, as we sat under the shade of a pine tree of marvellous height and great breadth of spread, devoted wholly to love's idleness and striving to investigate Love's mandates in a good-tempered and spirited debate, we began to discern a twofold doubt, and we wearied ourselves with laborious arguments as to whether true love can find any place between husband and wife and whether jealousy flourishing between two lovers ought to be approved of. After we had argued the matter back and forth and each of us seemed to bolster up his position with reasonable arguments, neither one would give in to

[48] See Introduction, p. 13.

the other or agree with the arguments he brought forward. We ask you to settle this dispute, and we have sent you both sides of the question in detail, so that after you have carefully examined the truth of it our disagreement may be brought to a satisfactory end and settled by a fair decision. For knowing clearly and in manifest truth that you have a great abundance of wisdom and that you would not want to deprive anyone of justice, we believe that we will in no wise be deprived of it; we most urgently implore Your Excellency's decision, and we desire with all our hearts, begging you most humbly by our present address, that you will give continued attention to our case and that Your Prudence will render a fair decision in the matter without making any delay in giving the verdict."

The Letter sent back by the Countess of Champagne

"To the prudent and noble woman A. and the illustrious and famous Count G., M., Countess of Champagne, sends greeting.

"Since we are bound to hear the just petitions of everybody, and since it is not seemly to deny our help to those who ask what is proper, especially when those who go wrong on questions of love ask to be set right by our decision—which is what the tenor of your letter indicates —we have tried diligently and carefully to carry this out without any extended delay.

"Now your letter has shown that this is the doubt that has arisen between you: whether love can have any place between husband and wife and whether between lovers jealousy is blameworthy; in both questions each of you falls back on his own opinion and opposes that of the other, and you want us to give our opinion which side properly should get the decision. We have therefore examined carefully the statements of both sides and have in very truth inquired into the matter by every possible means, and we wish to end the case with this decision. We declare and we hold as firmly established that love cannot exert its powers between two people who are married to each other. For lovers give each other everything freely, under no compulsion of necessity, but married people are in duty bound to give in to each other's desires and deny themselves to each other in nothing. Besides, how does it increase a husband's honor if after the manner of lovers he enjoys the embraces of his wife, since the worth of character of neither can be increased thereby, and they seem to have nothing more than they already had a right to? And we say the same thing for still another reason, which is that a precept of love tells us that no woman, even if she is married, can be crowned with the reward of the King of Love unless she is seen to be enlisted in the service of Love himself outside the bonds of wedlock. But another rule of Love teaches that no one can be in love with two men. Rightly, therefore, Love cannot acknowledge any rights of his between husband and wife. But there is still another argument that seems to stand in the way of this, which is that between them there can be no true jealousy, and without it true love may not exist, according to the rule of Love himself, which says, 'He who is not jealous cannot love.' [49]

"Therefore let this our verdict, pronounced with great moderation and supported by the opinion of a great many ladies, be to you firm and indubitable truth.

"The first day of May, in the year 1174, the seventh of the indiction."

Eighth Dialogue

A man of the higher nobility speaks with a woman of the same class

If a man of the higher nobility should seek the love of a woman of the same class, he should first above all things follow the rule to use soft and gentle words, and he should take care not to say anything that would seem to deserve a reproof. For a noblewoman or a woman of the higher nobility is found to be very ready and bold in censuring the deeds or the words of a man of the higher nobility, and she is very glad if she has a good opportunity to say something to ridicule him.

[49] Page 184.

The present section might be adapted to much of what has gone before, as the careful reader can easily notice, but one may also speak in this fashion:

"Indeed I believe it is true that God has inclined all good men in this life to serve your desires and those of other ladies, and it seems to me that this is for the very clear reason that men cannot amount to anything or taste of the fountain of goodness unless they do this under the persuasion of ladies. But although all good things seem to proceed from women, and although God has given them a great privilege and we say that they are the cause and origin of everything good, still they are clearly under the necessity of so conducting themselves toward those who do good deeds that by their approval the good character of these men may seem in every respect to increase from strength to strength. For if their brightness were not to give light to anyone, it would be like a candle hidden under a bushel,[50] whose beam is not able to drive away anybody's darkness or shine to anybody's profit. Therefore it is clear that every man should strive with all his might to be of service to ladies so that he may shine by their grace. But the ladies are greatly obligated to be attentive to keeping the hearts of good men set upon doing good deeds and to honor every man according to his deserts. For whatever good things living men may say or do, they generally credit them all to the praise of women, and by serving these they so act that they may pride themselves on the rewards they receive from them, and without these rewards no man can be of use in this life or be considered worthy of any praise. Now I know many men who are sure they have been given perfect love, and I know others who are maintained only by the milk of nourishing hope; but I, who have neither perfect love nor the gift of hope, am more sustained merely by the pure thought of you, which I do have, than all other lovers are by unnumbered solaces. May your pity therefore turn and regard my solitary thought and give it a little increase. And truly I beg you most earnestly not to try to keep away from Love's court, for those who stay away

[50] Matt. 5: 15; Mark 4: 21; Luke 11: 33.

from the palace of Love live for themselves alone, and no one gets any profit from their lives; as they have no desire to be of any use, they are looked upon as dead to the world, and their reputation is in no wise worth speaking of, but ought by all means to be buried under the weight of silence. But those who desire to enjoy the solaces of love seem to be trying to increase their own good character and to be profitable to others. Therefore with good reason they are considered worthy of the greatest honor, and all men try to exalt their fame. But you must not believe that I am saying these things to you with the idea that I am trying by my remarks to spur you on to do these good deeds, for I believe with all my heart and am fully confident that nothing that might happen could divert you from doing what is good. But you should know that I have taken the trouble to advise you in this matter because things that are more often repeated are pleasing, become more firmly fixed, and are better remembered, and then, when the opportunity comes, they are carried out."

The woman says: "Although your words are too deep and profound and reach to the walls of Love's subtlety, I shall try, so far as I am able, to give them a fitting answer. And because the experience of Cicero tells us that the things which are said last in a discourse are more readily retained in the memory,[51] I shall try to answer your last remarks first. Now your urging me to strive to do what might increase my good character and that of others was pleasing and acceptable enough to me, because I had it in my heart to do that without advice from anyone. I know that women should, as you have asserted, be the cause and origin of good things, that they should, of course, receive everybody with a joyful face and give him a courteous reception, and that they should speak to each one words appropriate to his condition and should clearly persuade every man to do courteous deeds and to avoid everything that has the appearance of boorishness and not to be so tenacious of his own property as to blacken his good name. But to show love is gravely to offend God and to prepare for many the

---

[51] [Pseudo-]Cicero *Rhetoric to Herennius* III. x.

perils of death. And besides it seems to bring innumerable pains to the lovers themselves and to cause them constant torments every day. So what good can there be in a deed by which the Heavenly Bridegroom is offended and one's neighbor is injured, while we see that those who do such deeds undergo deadly perils and are tormented with continual pains? Therefore, although love impels all men to be courteous and makes them strangers to every sort of boorishness, still it seems a thing to be feared because of the great inconveniences that follow it and the terrible torments that threaten, a thing which no wise man should choose and which should be especially hated by soldiers. For those who seem to be every day in peril of death from some chance of battle ought to be especially careful not to do anything that might be considered offensive to the King of the Heavenly Country. It seems expedient for us, therefore, to keep clear of love and to avoid the laborious difficulties of lovers. For not only are lovers worn out by various wearisome pains when they are awake, but even when they are asleep they are tormented in a great many ways. So those tell us who are harassed by love's labor and who daily frequent Love's palace; I myself have had no experience in love and so naturally I can tell you nothing about its nature except so far as I have learned about it from what others tell me."

The man says: "You talk like a person who wants to make her friends rich on words alone, but who intends to deprive them completely of anything substantial. For to receive anyone with a joyful face when he comes, to give him soft answers, and then when the danger of poverty threatens him not to help him at all with deeds, but merely to persuade him to be courteous in all that he does, is no different from deceiving with gentle flattery a friend who trusts you and then trying to boast of it. It is like a wicked priest who by pretending to do many good deeds and by urging upon others the works of eternal life condemns himself by his own judgment, while he shows others how to obtain heavenly reward. Your statement that God is offended by love cannot keep you from it; it seems to be generally agreed that to serve God is a very great and an extraordinarily good thing, but those who desire to serve Him perfectly ought to devote themselves wholly to His service, and according to the opinion of Paul they should engage in no worldly business.[52] Therefore if you choose to serve God alone, you must give up all worldly things and contemplate only the mysteries of the Heavenly Country, for God has not wished that anybody should keep his right foot on earth and his left foot in heaven, since no one can properly devote himself to the service of two masters. Now since it is clear that you have one foot on earth from the fact that you receive with a joyful countenance those who come to you and that you exchange courteous words with them and persuade them to do the works of love, I believe you would do better to enjoy love thoroughly than to lie to God under cloak of some pretense. I believe, however, that God cannot be seriously offended by love, for what is done under the compulsion of nature can be made clean by an easy expiation. Besides, it does not seem at all proper to class as a sin the thing from which the highest good in this life takes its origin and without which no man in the world could be considered worthy of praise. Again, one's neighbor feels no injury from love—that is, he should feel none—because whatever one person asks of another—that is, whatever he should ask—he is bound to suffer freely when another asks it of him. Many, however, include among their wrongs things which seem to contain no wrong. And let it not seem to you absurd that I have explained it to you in this way: 'he asks—that is, he should ask'—since we are taught to explain in the same way a certain word in the Gospel law upon which dependeth the whole law and the prophets.[53] For we say, 'What you do not wish others to do to you—that is, what you should not wish—do not do to others.'[54] You said, too, that everybody ought to avoid love because from it come torments and grave perils. But the greater the danger connected with the pursuit of a thing which we cannot obtain without great effort, the more eagerly are we bound to seek it, for after a great misfortune safety is the more pleasant. You cannot, there-

---

[52] I Cor. 7:32-35.   [53] Matt. 22:40.   [54] Compare Matt. 7:12.

fore, defend yourself with the argument that love is not for all a desirable good toward which we are bound to strive with all our might. I do not believe, either, that you do not know whom you ought to love, for it seems that you should love the man who has placed in you all the force of his devotion and strives to do all good things for your sake. But if the ill-will of jealousy had not spread false rumors about me, you could find no one more worthy of your love than I am, because you will find that for your sake I am humble and devoted to all, that I give generously of my goods to everybody, and that whatever good deeds anybody else under heaven can think of I strive with all my might to do. Therefore let Your Prudence learn to favor anyone who deserves it, because not only the glib talker who is ready to claim his rights but even the faithful dumb man is found to be worthy to receive the reward of his service."

The woman says: "Indeed I have no desire for the empty glory of the world, nor am I trying to enrich my friends with words that have nothing substantial back of them; but I am trying to induce you to seek the rewards of a better life—not because I am one who wishes to condemn the service of Love, but because I desire to show you that the things above are preferable to the things on earth. But leaving for the present the discussion of divine matters, let us turn our pen [55] to the problem of love. I should be very glad if your tongue would stop talking and leave only your deeds to praise you, because Solomon tells us that all praise in one's own mouth vanishes away.[56] Besides, what has this so great and effusive generosity of yours been waiting for? How long has it waited to give away those made-over, worn-out clothes that I see? [57] Are all soldiers revelling in wealth? Can't you find anybody in need?"

[55] Andreas evidently forgets that he is supposed to be recording a conversation.

[56] Prov. 27: 2.

[57] W. Meyer considers that the poem "In nova fert animus" is by Hugo of Orleans himself, and is not a song "upon the tailors," but a satire against those niggards who instead of giving away their old clothes had them made over. "Die Oxforder Gedichte des Primas." *Nachrichten von der königlichen Gesellschaft der Wissenschaften zu Göttingen*, Phil.-hist. Klasse aus dem Jahre 1907, pp. 75–87.

The man says: "You want to make out that the author of that proverb you quote was crazy by trying to interpret his remark wrongly. It isn't proper that any man of character should praise his own deeds in the presence of other men or among the vulgar crowd, but if anyone should wish to refer secretly to praiseworthy deeds he has done, when in the presence of the lady for whose sake he confesses to have done them, there seems to be no argument against that, and you will find that there is a reason why this is permitted. For in the business of love all men are rivals and are very jealous of each other, and you will rarely find one who is so good a friend that when he is with women he will talk about the good character of some other man or will gladly call to mind the praiseworthy things that the other man has done. And it is this common vice, which infects all men, which has given occasion for the edict that this exception may be made in the proverb you mention. For if the rights of one litigant are unknown to the judge, naturally he gives the decision to the other party. Furthermore, I have put on these worn out clothes that you see to find out clearly whether you honor a man of good character because of his clothes, or the clothes because of the good character of the man. From your opinion it seems clear to me that with you the care of the clothes is more pleasing than the adornment of good character. This, as you know, detracts from your own good character, for ill-bred women put all their reliance on showy clothing, but noble and prudent women reject showy clothes unaccompanied by good breeding and think that only the cultivation of good character deserves respect in a man. Besides, I consider it sufficient for me that I have given generously of my property to others, for if any man neglects completely the distresses of other men and tries to spend as much as possible on the adornment of his own person, this can never add anything to his praise. If we were to say that a man deserves praise for the many good things that he lavishes on himself, we know we would have to damn the memory of many whose fame burns bright in the world and with good reason is commended by all. But the fame of those who completely neglect their own advantages in order that they may be able properly to care for the needs of others and to relieve their poverty deserves especial praise from everybody. So, leaving this poverty of words to the country women, as the saying is, you should seek more lofty subjects for discussion, so that your nobility of birth will be apparent and your good sense will be recognized not only from what you wear and the way you walk but even from what you say. I do not want to answer you with a proverb or a remark that doesn't mean anything, because these often disturb with shame the mind of the person who hears them, and it is clear that they make no improvement in his character; however, I do not cease to demand urgently that gift of love I have already spoken about."

The woman says: "I know it has long been a common saying that mocking proverbs which have the appearance of truth make the hearer more angry than stories which are made up and cited incidentally, and so I am sorry I suggested such things, since I see they have angered you. I shall therefore give up this matching of proverbs and try to answer your request in another way. Now I say that there is nothing in this life more praiseworthy than to love wisely, and no man can do to the full those things that make a man worthy of praise unless he does them under the compulsion of love. Therefore you do rightly if you seek for yourself a suitable love through whom your determination to do well may always be increased. But you can never get any benefit from loving me, because some of my hidden griefs absolutely prevent my loving. And even if I were absolutely free to love, still there would be one thing that would force me to deny you my love— that is, that another man forestalled you in serving me and in asking for my love, and so I have good reason to give it to him rather than to you."

The man says: "I am not quite clear as to those hidden griefs which you say you have which keep you from loving, for the solaces of love are medicines which purge away all griefs and restore all joys except in cases where one is grieving for a dead lover; in such a case Love's precept prescribes a two-year period of mourning to the survivor. But since, as I understand, you have never felt the arrow of any love, I do not believe that you are cherishing grief for a dead lover. As for your statement that another man forestalled me in serving you and in asking for your love, that seems to be no answer to my arguments, because it is wholly within your power to prefer the man whose merits make him deserve it most, even if the other had received from you the hope of your love, for in love we do not think that the preference should go to the man who first offered his services and asked for love, but to the one whose merits make him the more worthy. Besides, it is not correct to say that he forestalled me in love, when he merely asked for it first. In love we can say that one man forestalls another only if he is the first to deserve the reward. For if the request of a worthy man were to exclude a later request from a more worthy one, it would be a pernicious thing and the cause of much injustice. The thing to consider is, not when the request is made, but by whom, unless, of course, love has already been granted and consummated. And this is so because, as has already been said so well,[58] any lady may without blame deny a repetition of her favors to a man even after she has given him hope and granted him a kiss and the enjoyment of her embrace, if she has gone no further. Therefore the fact that my request came after his cannot stand in my way if my greater merits support my request."

The woman says: "Where did you get this idea that I have never felt the arrow of Love? Do you think me so low and destitute of all worth of character that my soul is not worthy to partake of the solaces of love? Besides this, what you have said seems contrary to all law and reason, for it is enough for any man if he is found worthy of being loved, even though another more worthy than he may come along later. One should not be prejudiced against the goodness of one man just because another is better. Therefore if any good man who is worthy of being loved asked for love before you did, it seems that I should

[58] See page 43.

grant his request rather than yours, even though you may be still more worthy. For if you try to defend any other course of action, you are trying unjustly to deprive him of his deserts."

The man says: "My lady, God forbid that I should ever think that you are not most worthy of the court of Love, but I spoke as I did because it seemed to me that hardly any man could be found who was worthy of your love. But if any worthy man should be found, he would hardly be so bold as not to hesitate to put forward his claims in your presence or ask for the gifts of love. As for your remark that we should not be prejudiced against the goodness of one man just because another is better, you cannot defend that by any argument, for an early petition from a good man cannot properly exclude a later one from a better. For although any one of the rival goddesses at the banquet was worthy enough to have the apple, that most just of judges, Alexander the son of Priam, did not listen to the petition of two of them, although they were worthy, and he wanted the most worthy one, that is Venus, to rejoice in the possession of the apple even though she was the last to ask.[59] Therefore you should seek out the truth and find which is the most worthy and keep for him what is rightfully his."

The woman says: "If a feigned abundance of passion did not torment you, you would never reject the solaces of your most beautiful wife and seek for love away from home."

The man says: "I admit that I have a wife who is beautiful enough, and I do indeed feel such affection for her as a husband can. But since I know that there can be no love between husband and wife (the decision of the Countess of Champagne supports this statement),[60] and that there can be nothing good done in this life unless it grows out of love, I am naturally compelled to seek for love outside the bonds of wedlock." The rest of this answer you will find excellently set forth

[59] Ovid *Heroides* XVI. 74 ff.   [60] Pages 106 ff.

in the dialogue between the man of the higher nobility and the woman of the noble class.[61]

The woman says: "Although love may be a very useful thing and one to be sought after by young people and those whom the glory of the world delights, to me, as one who is already advanced in age, it seems useless and a thing to be rejected by all means; yes, even if everything else persuaded me to love, my widowhood and my sadness over the best of husbands whom I have lost would prevent my finding any solace in life."

The man says: "If your heart doesn't prove to be worn out with old age, there seems to be a youthful enough beauty in the appearance of your person, from which it is clear that a youthful beauty is strong in your heart, for the outward appearance shows clearly what is the disposition of the mind within. Nor can your grief for the husband you have lost justly injure me, because I shall persuade you to that which will bring back to you continual joy and will keep this for you unimpaired. For love is a thing which breaks the bonds of griefs, and it is the only thing that can replace them with happy joys and furnish the sweet solaces of delight. Therefore love is a thing for all to seek after and for everyone in the world to cherish, because it can drive away everybody's sadness and bring anyone back to a state of joy. So according to the rule of the law you may after the years of grief for your husband have elapsed lay aside all sadness and join the soldiery of lovers. For to grieve for a husband beyond the period fixed by the laws is to despise them and to oppose a rebellious soul to the divine will and to be impiously disposed toward what it has done. Besides, grieving beyond the legal period doesn't seem to help your dead husband any, and it does do you a great deal of harm."

The woman says: "You seem very bold in opposing the intent of the law, since you say it is foolish to attempt to obey its mandates beyond

[61] Pages 91 ff.

the period which, with wonderful regard for the weakness of men, it has set; yet according to the Gospel the host who received the wounded Samaritan was given a certain sum of money and was told, 'If thou shalt spend aught over and above, I will repay thee.' [62] Therefore if the law, wishing, perhaps, to allow for my weakness, has set for me a moderate time to grieve, and if I add to this period something over and above to comply more fully with the law, I deserve to receive payment in overflowing measure and to enjoy a greater reward."

The man says: "Indeed the law did fix a humane period of mourning for women to observe, not out of consideration for their weakness, but out of regard for the good of the human race, so that there might be no confusion of descent or mixing of the families of different men. For where there would be no confusion of descent the apostle clearly permits a woman to marry again immediately after the death of her husband.[63] Much more, then, is it permissible for you to love after the legal period has elapsed."

The woman says: "Love may seem pleasing enough to everybody else, but it seems quite contrary to maidenly modesty, for, as you know well, a maiden quickly loses her honor, and her reputation is ruined by a slight rumor and a little word. Indeed I have not yet fully arrived at the age when I can manage love's anchor with the proper diligence, for it is said that before one reaches full maturity love cannot remain firmly established. Therefore it does not seem at all appropriate for me to love."

The man says: "If any woman has been careful to love prudently, she should never be troubled by a vain repentance and in no respect will she suffer a loss of her reputation. For if she is careful to give her love to a prudent and discreet man, the love will be kept secret and no one will ever hear of it and her modesty will not be at all injured thereby. As for what you said about age, it might have some point in the case of men, for before the age of eighteen a man can hardly be a firm

[62] A confused memory of Luke 10: 35.   [63] I Cor. 7: 39.

lover. But under the same law the case is different with regard to women, for a woman from her twelfth year onward may love firmly and keep her faith unshaken. Why the same nature acts differently in women and in men you can plainly see; for a woman's constancy is more firmly established at the beginning of her puberty and most certainly remains unchanged, and nature has permitted the act of Venus to her earlier than to the men, because in women the cold temperament dominates, while the men have a natural heat,[64] and a cold object warms up more quickly with the addition of a little heat than a hot one does if you add a little more. This will be clear from an illustration. If you put something hot into a vessel of silver or other metal, the metal vessel will heat up more quickly and to a higher temperature than a wooden one will, no matter how hot the liquid you put in it. Besides, women are sooner wasted by age than are men, who keep their vigor, and so it is no wonder that the women are earlier established in constancy, for we can see in everything in the world which has life or spirit that the sooner nature brings it to perfection the sooner, by the same law, it is wasted by age, and obviously the reverse of this is also true."

The woman says: "I shan't discuss these physiological arguments which you present me or give you the satisfaction of a reply; I have never cared to investigate physiology, except when someone was ill, so I shall pass this over in silence. But you are trying to persuade me to love wisely, and it is not quite clear how I may follow your advice. For although a lover may be deceitful and may be plotting to disgrace the service of Love, under the impulse of passion he tries in everything he does to pretend that he is a true lover and to deceive those who trust him. Who, then, is so careful that he can be cautious when things seem so true, and can recognize the frauds hidden beneath the surface? Scarcely could the wisdom of Solomon foresee it all or the experience of Cato predict it. Even though the cleverness of some women who are rather advanced in years and have already felt the darts of Cupid

---

[64] Compare [Pseudo-]Aristotle *Problems* IV. 25, 28.

may be able to avoid such deceptions, I have neither age to help me nor experience to teach me."

The man says: "You are saying things that surprise me very much. What impurity in silver could escape notice if it were rubbed on a touchstone or tried by the purging of fire? Just as the genuineness of gold or silver is tried by the fire or the touchstone, so is any man's faith and truth shown by his striving long for love. There is not in the world a lady or a damsel of so little wisdom (if she is classed among the ladies or the damsels) who cannot easily recognize the faith and truth of a man who asks for her love if she sets about investigating his love. There are, of course, many who falsely usurp the names 'lady' or 'damsel,' thinking that they are such merely because they are of the blood of the higher nobility or are married to a man of that class, when really it is only excellence of character, or wisdom, that makes women worthy of these names. Therefore it is no wonder that careless youth very often goes wrong in attributing to nobility of descent what is really an attribute of wisdom and character. So a woman ought not assent immediately to the desire of a suitor, but should first make him a great many cautious promises and should with proper moderation postpone giving him the good things she has promised him; then, to test the purity of his faith, she should sometimes say that she has completely changed her mind about what she promised him a while before and that she is not willing to do what she promised. No lover is so cautious and so clever that if the fruition of his love is long postponed, and if occasionally when the appointed time comes he is deceived by a lot of promises, he will not either be made a worthy man thereby or openly reveal his falseness. For if she sees that he is giving up his attempts because of their disputes or is defaming her with evil rumors or is placing his faith in promises to give her money, she ought to assume that he is not a faithful lover. But if she finds him persistent during this long-continued probation, she ought not delay much longer the fulfillment of her promises, lest he feel that his labor gets him very little profit. Furthermore, to have some instruction in physiology and science cannot hurt the goodness of anybody, but a man's worth is increased by the fruit of some science, which always increases a wise man's prudence. And the authority of Love warns you clearly to choose the love of a wise man and wholly to reject that of one who is not."

The woman says: "Any man will try by every argument to induce an unwilling person to assent to that which he himself wishes and desires with all his heart to have. But we do not consider a man a true friend if when giving advice he ignores the good of his friend and looks out only for himself, nor should we give in to the desire of such a friend who seeks only his own good. Love may therefore be safe for any married woman, but it seems that maidens should fear it greatly and consider it shameful. For if a woman's husband believes her a maiden when he marries her and then learns the truth of her seduction, he will always hate and despise her, and from this will come the great evil of repudiation, and it will be a never-failing cause of divorce, and so she will be very much in disgrace and will be despised by everybody. It would therefore be very improper if your blandishments persuaded me to love."

The man says: "Your theory seems to lead to a particularly grave error when you especially condemn love in maidens; countless ones of the very best character are said to have been in love, as we find in the cases of Anfelis,[65] and Iseult,[66] and Blanchefleur,[67] and many others. Unless a maiden strove to raise her reputation by the instigation of love, she would never deserve to have a praiseworthy husband, nor could she fully comprehend anything great. She cannot because of such conduct be hateful to a good husband, for a good husband always believes that he could never have found such a worthy wife if she had not learned the theory of love and carried out what it requires. And if it is her

[65] The heroine of *Folque de Candie* by Herbert le Duc de Danmartin. Several manuscripts give the name as Fenice; she is the heroine of Chrétien's *Cligès*.

[66] Of the various versions of the story of Iseult, Andreas is most likely to have known those by Chrétien and Thomas of Britain.

[67] The heroine of *Floire and Blancheflor*; the earliest known version was written between 1160 and 1170.

fate to have a bad husband, it is better for him to hate her than to have any affection exist between them, and this will not long harm the reputation of a worthy woman; the worthlessness of the hated husband will become more and more apparent.

"I want to explain to you something else that is in my mind, something which I know many keep hidden in their hearts, but which I do not think you are ignorant of, and that is that one kind of love is pure, and one is called mixed. It is the pure love which binds together the hearts of two lovers with every feeling of delight. This kind consists in the contemplation of the mind and the affection of the heart; it goes as far as the kiss and the embrace and the modest contact with the nude lover, omitting the final solace, for that is not permitted to those who wish to love purely.[68] This is the kind that anyone who is intent upon love ought to embrace with all his might, for this love goes on increasing without end, and we know that no one ever regretted practicing it, and the more of it one has the more one wants. This love is distinguished by being of such virtue that from it arises all excellence of character, and no injury comes from it, and God sees very little offense in it. No maiden can ever be corrupted by such a love, nor can a widow or a wife receive any harm or suffer any injury to her reputation. This is the love I cherish, this I follow and ever adore and never cease urgently to demand of you. But that is called mixed love which gets its effect from every delight of the flesh and culminates in the final act of Venus. What sort of love this is you may clearly see from what I have already said, for this kind quickly fails, and lasts but a short time, and one often regrets having practiced it; by it one's neighbor is injured, the Heavenly King is offended, and from it come very grave dangers.[68a] But I do not say this as though I meant to condemn mixed love, I merely wish to show which of the two is preferable. But mixed love, too, is real love, and it is praiseworthy, and we say that it

---

[68] For the Moslem *al-hawa al-ʿudri* see the Introduction, p. 11.

[68a] "O how great is the danger in adultery, wherein one sins against God, offends one's neighbor, often commits homicide, frequently disinherits a legitimate son," etc. Alanus de Insulis *Epitome of the Art of Preaching*, 45.

is the source of all good things, although from it grave dangers threaten, too. Therefore I approve of both pure love and mixed love, but I prefer to practice pure love. You should therefore put aside all fear of deception and choose one of the two kinds of love."

The woman says: "You are saying things that no one ever heard or knew of, things that one can scarcely believe. I wonder if anyone was ever found with such continence that he could resist the promptings of passion and control the actions of his body. Everybody would think it miraculous if a man could be placed in a fire and not be burned.[69] But if any man should be found with this faith and purity of love which you mention and this physical continence that you talk about, I would praise and approve his determination and consider it worthy of every honor, yet without any intention of condemning that mixed love which most of the world enjoys. But although other men may choose either kind of love, you ought not enter into the service of either, for a clerk ought to concern himself only with the services of the Church and to avoid all the desires of the flesh.[70] He ought to be a stranger to all forms of delight and above all to keep his body unspotted for the Lord,[71] since the Lord has granted him privileges of such great dignity and rank that he may consecrate His flesh and blood with his own hands and by his words he may absolve the offenses of sinners. If you should see my mind inclining to a lapse of the flesh, you are bound by virtue of the office God has granted you to call me back from the errors I am starting to commit, and to persuade me to be chaste in every respect, and to set me such an example that you may freely castigate the sins of others. For according to the Gospel truth, a man with a

---

[69] St. Jerome, in his letter to Eustochium (XXII. 14), when attacking a similar practice in the early Church, cites Prov. 6: 27–28, which is the source of Andreas's reference.

[70] According to tradition, the institution of the *subintroducta* was introduced into the monastery of Fontevraud or Fontevrault by its founder Robert d'Abrissel. (*The Dictionary Historical and Critical of Mr. Peter Bayle*, 2d ed., revised, corrected, and enlarged by Mr Des Maizeaux, London, 1736, III, 60–67.) Fontevraud was founded about 1100 in the Diocese of Poitiers, and became closely connected with the family of King Henry II.

[71] Jas. 1: 27.

beam in his own eye ought to cast it out before he tries to take out the mote from his brother's eye,[72] and anyone would be open to the derision of mankind if he were bound in this fashion and should try to loose the bonds of his fellow prisoners. Therefore it is not safe for women to stain with fleshly contagion those whom God has chosen to be His ministers and whom He wishes to keep themselves in all things pure and chaste in His service."

The man says: "Although I have cast in my lot with the clergy, I am a man conceived in sin and like other men naturally prone to a lapse of the flesh. For although God has wished the clerks to perform their duty in His services and in making known the Divine Word and has laid upon them great honor, still He has not wished in so doing to improve their condition by taking from them the stimulus of the flesh and the incitement to sin. Therefore I do not believe that God has wished to lay upon them any greater abstinence of the flesh and to weary them with a double burden. Why, then, is a clerk more bound to keep his body chaste than any layman is? You must not believe that the delight of the flesh is forbidden to the clergy alone, since God bids every Christian be on his guard against all bodily uncleanness and wholly to avoid fleshly desires. Your argument may therefore apply equally well to the laity and to the clergy. We do not believe that the power of admonishing our neighbor and calling his mind away from his error is granted by God to the clergy alone, but we know that the Lord has laid this necessity upon every Christian. For the teaching of the Gospel Truth says, 'If thy brother shall offend against thee, go, and rebuke him between thee and him alone.' [73] Now it does not say, 'If a clerk's brother shall offend against him,' but it speaks in general terms as a general command to everyone. A clerk does well, and a layman does well, if he abstains from all worldly delight and confirms the hearts of his neighbors in all good works. Nevertheless I admit, for I cannot deny it, that a clerk, by virtue of the office laid upon him, is in a special manner bound to make known the way of truth, both in church and

[72] Matt. 7: 5; Luke 6: 42.   [73] Matt. 18: 15.

among the people, and by his admonitions to confirm them in the true catholic faith. If through negligence he does not do this, he can never escape everlasting punishment unless he mitigates the sin by the medicine of fruitful repentance. But if with his tongue he rightly discharges this office, he is freed from the burden, for any other sins he may commit are no more severely punished in him than in any layman, since he is naturally driven to them by the incentive of the flesh just like all the rest of mankind. This is what the authority of the Gospel proclaims; for the Lord, seeing His clergy, in accordance with the frailty of human nature, about to fall into various excesses, said in the Gospel, 'The scribes and the Pharisees have sitten on the chair of Moses. All things whatsoever they shall say to you, observe and do: but according to their works do ye not,' [74] just as though he said, 'You must believe what the clergy say, because they are God's deputies; but because they are subject to the temptation of the flesh like other men, you must not regard their works if they happen to go astray in anything.' Therefore it is enough for me if, when I stand by the altar, I devote myself to proclaiming the word of God to my people. So if I ask any woman to love me, she cannot refuse me on the pretext that I am a clerk; indeed I shall prove to you by inevitable necessity that in love a clerk is preferable to a layman. We find that a clerk is in every respect more cautious and more prudent than a layman, and conducts himself and his affairs with greater restraint, and is accustomed to keep everything within more proper bounds; that is because a clerk, as the Scripture tells us, has an experienced knowledge of all things.[75] Therefore in love he is to be preferred to a layman, because it has been found that nothing in the world is so necessary as to be experienced in carrying on all things connected with love. So if you find me otherwise worthy of your love, you cannot with propriety cast me aside just because you see that I am enrolled among the clergy."

The woman says: "I marvel greatly at your remark that a clerk is not punished more severely than a layman for indulging in the pleasures

---

[74] Matt. 23: 2–3.   [75] Mal. 2: 7.

of the world, since we find in Holy Writ that the greater the prerogative of any living man in rank and dignity, the greater is his fall if
he neglects his duty.[76] But even if we do not find a greater sin in the
love of a clerk than in that of a layman, there is something else that
most emphatically keeps women from loving a clerk. For although
love, by its very nature, seeks for a pleasing and beautiful bodily appearance and demands that a man should be ready to make gifts to
anybody at the proper time, that he should be courageous against those
who make war on him, should rejoice greatly in the stress of battle and
take part constantly in the toil of wars, a clerk comes before us dressed
in women's garments, unsightly because of his shaven head, he cannot aid anybody with gifts unless he wants to take some other man's
property, and we find him given up to continual indolence and devoted
only to serving his belly; for these reasons if he dares to speak a word
of love to any woman of character, she should prudently check him as
soon as he begins to speak, and he will deserve to be rejected ig-
nominiously and in disgrace, so that not only may he be overcome by
shame and compelled to refrain from such unlawful actions, but that
others, for fear of the same shame, may be afraid to make the same
request. For many people abstain from things that are forbidden and
wicked more because of the disgrace in this world than to avoid the
torments of the everlasting death."

The man says: "It is true, as you say, that the greater a man's dignity
the greater is the fall if he sins, not however in God's sight, but only in
the opinion of the evil-speaking crowd. For everybody is more worked
up over a minor offense by a single clerk whose fault they exaggerate
and whose life they reproach than they are if they find that a thousand
common men have committed the foulest of crimes. Why this is I
shall refrain from telling you at present. As for the womanish garb
assigned to the clergy, that cannot do me any harm, because this costume
was assigned to me in accordance with my order by the ancient good
sense of the fathers, so that the clergy might be distinguished from

[76] Luke 12:48.

other men by their habit and their gait. Wherefore if in such a minor matter I should overthrow the precepts of the fathers and neglect their mandates, you ought not to believe that I would obey the greater mandates of you who are, as it were, a woman of a different race; besides you might object to me with the remark, 'Go away, you apostate who are clearly a traitor to your order.' As for what you say about giving gifts, that seems to have arisen out of a great mistake, for although giving is commended to all men by the Author of truth Himself,[77] and the way of avarice is forbidden to everybody, I do not see how you have the face to try to deny to the clerks acts of generosity, unless perhaps you wish your words to be understood as referring to those clerks who, as everybody knows, have wholly renounced the world and all worldly property. But even in the case of these, if we look at the matter carefully, your remark doesn't seem to be based upon truth. Engaging in battle is, of course, forbidden us by God; that is so that our hands may always be innocent of the shedding of blood and we may not be driven from His service as unworthy because we have shed it. For a man polluted by shedding blood is not acceptable for the service of God. It was for this reason that David, that most holy of kings, might not build a temple to the Lord, since he had shed human blood; he heard the Lord himself say to him, 'Thou shalt not build me a temple: because thou art a man of blood.'[78] Now if I were not prevented by this argument, there is nothing in the world that would be more pleasing to me than to do warlike deeds and to show my boldness of heart.

"As for what you chose to say about serving the belly, that can in no way harm me, because you cannot find anyone, clerk or layman, man or woman, young or old, who does not gladly devote himself to the services of the belly. But if anyone is too much inclined that way, it is

[77] Matt. 5:42; 10:8, and elsewhere.
[78] I Paralipomenon (Chronicles) 28:3. But St. Jerome says (*Against Jovinian* I. 24), "And because he was a man of blood—the reference is not, as some think, to his wars but to the murder [of Urias]—he was not permitted to build a temple to the Lord."

clear before God and all men that this is just as harmful to a layman as to a clerk, and it deserves every reprehension. Nor must you presume, because clerks are idle so much, that they are great gluttons; if you were to assume that those who are idle are the greatest gluttons, you would by all living reason have to assume it of all women, for they all live in a state of continual bodily rest. Indeed, if you are looking for the truth, you can bring this charge against women more than against either clerks or laymen, because we read that the woman defied God's mandate and served her belly before the man did and that out of gluttony she transgressed God's precept. Indeed, the man would never have done so if he had not first been overpersuaded by the woman and duped by her urgings."

The woman says: "If you are so stirred up by what I have said, you ought to get even with me alone with your belligerent examples—not rage indiscriminately against all women because of the offense of one of them. For if it was the woman who first out of gluttony disobeyed the divine command, she did it because she was deceived by the cleverness of the demon; she never thought about restraining her appetite, since that didn't amount to anything, but like a fool she believed the words of the deceitful demon, and she wanted the knowledge of good and evil which the Lord had forbidden."

The man says: "But why was the woman tempted to eat before the man was (since a victory over the man would have been more to the demon's credit), except that he foresaw that the woman would be more inclined to yield to her gluttonous appetite than the man would?" [79]

The woman says: "This was because women are by nature more ready to believe anything than men are; they are innocent and guileless, and so they believe everything. The demon, therefore, seeing that the

[79] Thomas Aquinas, apparently following ecclesiastical tradition, tells us that the Devil chose the woman as the instrument of temptation because she was weaker than the man and more liable to be deceived (*Theological Summa* II. II, Qu. 165. art. 2). See also Jerome (*Against Jovinian* I. 27), and I Tim. 2: 14.

man was not so ready and prone to believe anything, because he himself was shrewd and tricky in all things, decided to try his temptation on the woman; since if he had begun by tempting the man and had failed to get results, the woman would have strengthened her mind by the example of the man."

The man says: "It will be a long time before we run out of material for arguing along this line, and so I ask you to drop the discussion and to give me an answer to my main proposition, for the objections you have already made do not seem to me to hold good at all against that."

The woman says: "Even if your good qualities do make you worthy of such an honor, there is another thing that stands in the way of your love. There is another man, equal to you in character and family and no different in his desire to serve me, who asks for love by his services alone and is reluctant to mention the matter with his tongue, and it is most fitting that in love he should be preferred to you. For I think that the man who puts all his hope and trust in the purity of my faith and does not trouble me with constant importunities, since he feels confident that his hope will be fulfilled just because of my liberality, deserves to get from me what he wants more than the one who has laid before me in so many words the secrets of his heart and puts all his trust in his fluency of speech, having more trust apparently in the force of his own remarks and the duplicity of his words than in the honesty of my judgment. A judge is more obligated to bring out the rights of the party who has no lawyer to help him and leaves the merits of the whole case to the mercy of the judge than of the one who has appeared at the trial supported by the influence of skilled men and with a great many people to give him strength."

The man says: "It seems to me that your opinion in this case is open to a good deal of argument, for what wise man ever said that a mute who tries with unintelligible gestures to indicate what he wants deserves to have it more than the man who can ask with words of deepest wisdom and all the ornaments of language for what his soul desires? Among the popular sayings men quote is, 'Never have a mute for a sailor on any ship.' Besides there seems to be every argument in favor of my being permitted to ask for what I want and urgently desire; even the Author of truth Himself said, 'Ask, and it shall be given you: knock and it shall be opened to you.' [80] For the custom has grown up in the world that far from getting what we want or obtaining the result we hope for, by keeping silent, we can hardly get it by the most insistent demands. Indeed, I shall show you by stronger arguments that what I ask for should be given to me rather than to this silent man you speak of, for you owe it to me not only because of my services but even more because of the great urging of my petition. For a thing which is asked for more than once very properly seems dearly bought, and you should favor my petition rather than his, because you owe it to him on one count, but to me on two; and I believe there never was a woman in the world who would of her own accord offer to give such a thing to people who did not ask for it—the normal modesty of women would prevent that."

The woman says: "The reason sailors refuse to take mutes on board a ship is that in time of urgent peril they cannot hear what their fellows tell them to do and they cannot tell the others what they think ought to be done to help the ship. But the labor of a mute should not go without its proper reward, even though he cannot express in words what he wants, and the example you cite from the Gospel cannot make any difference here. He whose own merits speak for him and who is aided by the purity of his faith is considered, so far as the judgment of the Eternal King goes, to be asking urgently and knocking incessantly at the door. If you wish to restrict the meaning of the word and take only what it actually says, you will be forced to say emphatically that all mutes are absolutely denied entrance into Paradise, since because of a natural defect in their tongues they can never ask in articulate words for what they desire in their hearts. Neither can you defend with any good argument your statement that you are the more deserv-

[80] Matt. 7:7; Luke 11:9.

ing of what you seek since it is owed to you on two counts; that is, indeed, said to be true of things that are a subject of trade among men, but God forbid that anyone should ever buy love for a price. For love is a gracious thing, arising only out of nobility of the heart and pure liberality of the mind, and so should be given to everybody without cost and with no idea of payment, although lovers may, for mutual solace, honor each other with certain gifts. But if they are found to be engaged in the service of Love solely with an eye to the payment, after that their love is considered, not true love, but feigned love. Besides, I ought not lose credit for my liberality just because of your request, which is what would happen if your demand for what you want made it due to you; for when anything is demanded as one's due, there is no place for liberality. As for your saying that a thing we beg for is thus fully paid for, that is true as regards the asker but not as regards the possessor. For if we were to consider that a thing was owed to a man just because he asked for it, many people would become very wealthy who otherwise will be perpetually poor and oppressed by very great poverty." (Here the author wished to refer aptly to a proverb, for when any man spends a great deal of money or wears himself out with a great deal of labor, people commonly say of him, "That man bought that at far too high a price, yet nobody owed it to him at all.") "Nor can your remark that it is contrary to a woman's modesty for her to give her love when it is not asked for, stand in the way of what I said, for there is no rule to forbid women of their own accord giving their love to any worthy man. For a woman can, if any man inspires her with love, gracefully and courteously ask him to love her, if she knows that for some reason he does not say anything about it. This opinion is very much strengthened by the example of the daughter of King Charles the Great, who asked Hugo of Alverne for his love in the most specific terms; but he, since he was in love with another daughter of the same king, refused her his love, because he did not wish knowingly to commit the crime of incest.[81]

[81] The romance of Hugo d'Alverne has been preserved only in later Italian versions.

Therefore there is no reason why I am forbidden to love the silent man."

The man says: "I would be very glad if your opinion on this matter were accepted by all women, because then the labor of all men who wanted to love would be made light enough and their condition would be improved. But I cannot agree with you that a man deserves more honor if he merely keeps silent than he does when he expresses himself wisely and courteously. Nor does your liberality thereby lose its effect, because when I said what I did about the laws of trade and the debts of love I did not say it with the idea that your love was, strictly speaking, due to me or that it ought to be degraded by the giving of money, but in the firm belief that Your Grace ought to be more gracious to me, who am asking urgently for it, than to a taciturn man who keeps silent and does not expect anything."

The woman says: "Your urging seems to me too insistent, because you are trying to obtain the gift of love in such a hurry. For even if your good qualities made you most worthy of every honor, you ought not ask to have love granted you so suddenly. No woman of any character ought to be so quick to assent to her lover's desire, for the quick and hasty granting of love arouses contempt in the lover and makes the love he has long desired seem cheap; while even simulated love is purified and all the rust is removed from it if the attainment is put off for a long time. Therefore a woman ought first to find out the man's character by many tests and have clear evidence of his good faith."

The man says: "In the case of a sick man who seems to be on the verge of death we ought not follow the usual diet or give him his regular medicine; a wise physician will usually, out of pity, give him whatever he has an appetite for, although normally this is bad for his disease. Therefore the pains and the continual griefs which threaten a bitter death to me who am languishing for love of you forcibly compel me to ask insistently and contrary to rule for something that will keep me from this death. Your argument that it is improper for women to give their love to anybody all of a sudden cannot help you; you ought to leave that answer to the country women who are always saying, 'A tree doesn't fall completely at the first blow.' [81a] A wise and discreet woman is usually moderate about delaying the grant of her lover's request, because if he is carelessly kept in suspense when he is badly smitten with love for a woman, he cannot keep from haunting the place where she is and staring at her with his longing eyes. So it often happens that because of such meetings the relationship of the lovers is shamefully maligned by the vulgar crowd; sometimes a love scarcely begun is talked about as though it were consummated, and so good men's intentions are interfered with. Therefore when a woman is asked for her love she ought to put her suitor off for only a short time if she is inclined to love him."

The woman says: "For the sake of those great good things which you are asking for, you ought patiently to endure the great torments and serious difficulties which you say are threatening you, for we cannot fully appreciate good things unless we have previously experienced bad ones. As for your remark that a woman should be moderate about her delay in granting a man's request, that is true where she has fully made up her mind to love the man. But when she has fully determined not to love a suitor, she should pleasantly and prudently and politely tell him he is rejected, not upset his soul by any rude remark or keep him in suspense by any promise. Therefore, since I am still unshaken in my determination not to love you, you must not take it amiss if I refuse to cheat you with deceitful postponements. But in order not to offend you by saying this, I will tell you why I do not love you: it is that I am in love with another man, and I am bound to him by unbreakable ties."

The man says: "Any tortures would be very sweet to me if I could find in them any indication of future good. As for your statement that you are in love with another man, I think there is no doubt that you are looking for a way of escape and want to cut off my opportunity of talk-

---

[81a] See A. Tobler, *Li proverbe au vilain* (Leipzig, 1895), stanza 5, and p. 118*n*.

ing with you, because Love's mandate says that no one should knowingly subvert a love which has been properly established by anyone else. But since I cannot infer from any indications that this is such a case, there is no reason why I should not be ignorant of it, and so it seems that I am not violating Love's mandate. But even if I did know surely that you were engaged to another man, and I thought he was not a fit match for you, if I could talk you out of such a match I would not feel that by doing so I was violating Love's precepts, but rather that I was faithfully obeying his mandates. For that precept of his that we are talking about now speaks of people who are *properly* joined, and this adverb *properly* shows that it was put in very deliberately. For a woman is not properly joined in love when the character of the man is not as good as that of the woman or when the pure affection of the heart is not equal on both sides. Moreover, even if I did know well that you were properly joined in love, although it would not then be correct for me to ask for your love, since Love's mandate forbids me to do that, I do think it would be proper for me to beg you to allow me to be well disposed toward you and for you to praise my praiseworthy deeds by accepting them and to set me right with a secret reproof if through thoughtlessness I go wrong in anything. Therefore if you are in love with anyone, which I can by no means believe, Your Prudence should be careful to find out whether such a love is a proper one for you."

The woman says: "I cannot convince you of the truth of what I say except by giving you my word for it, because according to the teaching of Love no one may expose the secrets of his love to many people. Therefore I consider it most discourteous for you to say that you cannot accept my word or that of any woman on this point. But to give you permission to be well disposed toward me is to give you nothing, for this depends wholly upon yourself; I do, however, gladly promise to praise anything you do that deserves praise. I do not take upon myself the task of correcting you, for that service belongs only to lovers. Now, whether people are joined together by a proper love is not easy to tell, nor does it seem very proper to insist on an investigation of this kind in cases where both parties are equally in love, unless their inequality is too obvious and the admonition of the woman cannot make any improvement on the situation. May God grant you, therefore, that which is pleasing to your desire, but by which no worthy man may feel that he is injured.

"However, from the replies that you made to me, I know that you have had a great deal of experience in the art of love, so I am asking your opinion upon a certain matter connected with it. Now, since a certain woman of the most excellent character wished to reject one of her two suitors by letting him make his own choice, and to accept the other, she divided the solaces of love in her in this fashion. She said, 'Let one of you choose the upper half of me, and let the other suitor have the lower half.' Without a moment's delay each of them chose his part, and each insisted that he had chosen the better part, and argued that he was more worthy of her love than the other man was because he had chosen the worthier part. Since the woman I have mentioned did not wish to make a hasty decision she asked me, with the consent of the contenders, to give my decision as to which of them should be considered better in what he asked for. I therefore ask you which seems to you to have made the more praiseworthy choice."

The man says: "Since I am asking you for your love and you give me your pretext for not loving, you ought not to consider it discourteous of me if I try in every way to get rid of this excuse that is doing me the harm or to say something that will nullify it. Besides, you know that it will not take anything away from the rights of any lover if Your Prudence chooses to restrain my thoughtless acts. You should therefore be careful to do these things that you ought to do, because I shall never be separated from my determination to love you.

"You ask me, also, to give you my opinion on a matter on which no man of experience should hesitate, for who doubts that the man who chooses the solaces of the upper part should be preferred to the one who seeks the lower? For so far as the solaces of the lower part go, we are in no wise differentiated from brute beasts; but in this respect nature joins us to them. But the solaces of the upper part are, so to speak, attributes peculiar to the nature of man and are by this same nature denied to all the other animals. Therefore the unworthy man who chose the lower part should be driven out from love just as though he were a dog,[82] and he who chose the upper part should be accepted as one who honors nature. Besides this, no man has ever been found who was tired of the solaces of the upper part, or satiated by practicing them, but the delight of the lower part quickly palls upon those who practice it, and it makes them repent of what they have done."

The woman says: "Your opinion in this case seems to be greatly at fault and very far from the truth. Whatever solaces men use to drive away their cares always take their beginning from that which lies hid in the lower part, and thence is derived the origin of all of them. For if there were a woman whose beauty was famous throughout the world, but who was found to be wholly useless for the work of Venus, no one would want her solaces, and she would be rejected by everyone as unclean. For the delight of the upper part would be absolutely nothing unless it were indulged in with an eye to the lower and were kept alive by contemplation of it. If you want to deny the truth of this, you will be forced to admit that two men can give each other the solaces of love, a thing which would be disgraceful enough to speak of and criminal to practice. Then again, if a man is found to be frigid or otherwise incapable of carrying out the works of Venus, he never wants to enjoy any of the delights of the flesh, because the efficient cause of love, which without a doubt reigns in the lower part, is found to be lacking in him. For if the efficient cause is removed, its effect must necessarily cease. It is no objection that, as you say, we share this nature with the beasts, because in all things that must be considered the principal and the

---

[82] "But these two pleasures of taste and touch, namely, gluttony and venery, are the only ones common to man with the lower animals, and therefore whoever is enslaved to these beastly pleasures is regarded as in the number of brutes and beasts." Aulus Gellius *Attic Nights* XIX. ii. 3. Macrobius *Saturnalia* II. viii. 12 has practically the same. Both are paraphrasing Aristotle's *Ethics*.

natural thing which in its use agrees with the nature of other things of its own kind and is found to be in union with them. Nor can you help your argument by the opinion you give that men are never satiated by the solace of the upper part, but quickly tire of that of the lower. We think that everyone should reject that food which never satisfies the hunger when it is eaten, but stuffs the body without nourishing it and fills the bowels with discomfort; and on the contrary we ought to choose that food which when eaten fills us up and satiates by invigorating and when digested allows us to hunger again. Furthermore, no one ought to have any doubt that the lower parts of anything should be considered more worthy than the upper, for even in secular buildings we see that the foundations are called the most worthy part of them. We know that the same is true of those things which draw their nourishment from the earth, because men judge them according to their lower parts. Indeed, I will go further and say that whatever lovers do has as its only object the obtaining of the solaces of the lower part, for there is fulfilled the whole effect of love, at which all lovers chiefly aim and without which they think they have nothing more than certain preludes to love. Therefore the man who chose the lower part made the more praiseworthy choice, since he preferred to enjoy the fruition of the more worthy part instead of asking, like the one who chose the upper part, for its preludes."

The man says: "Anybody who after thinking the matter over would say what you do is surely suffering from a deranged mind. For although any lover may be chiefly inclined toward the solaces of the lower part, and the final cause of love may be there, still it would seem a very shameful and improper use of the body and a great disgrace for women to practice the lower solaces without the upper. Indeed, it seems impossible to enjoy the delight of the lower part without that of the upper, unless we are to have too indecent and shameful a use of the body. For the solaces of the upper part are most proper and refined and can be indulged in without any violation of modesty on the part of either participant, even if the lower delight is omitted. Indeed, the rational order in love requires that one should first, after much urging, obtain the wanton solaces of the upper part, and after that go on step by step to the lower ones. Only those women who wish to make a profit from their bodies and who are prostituted to the public traffic of Venus seek the solaces of the lower part alone and despise all those of the upper. Therefore everybody should follow the order I have indicated as the natural one, lest we be caught by the old saying, 'Don't try to put on the horse's bridle from the tail end.' The comparison you make with food is not a good one, because food is eaten in order that the body may be satisfied, but these solaces are really practiced in order that the delight of the flesh may ever increase—and so, too, may the will to preserve love. You tried to say that lower things are regularly to be preferred to higher ones, but no wise man can have any doubt that higher things are preferable to lower ones, for heaven is preferable to earth, paradise to hell, and angels to men. Also, the upper part of a man—that is, the head—is considered the more worthy, because it is with regard to his face that a man is said to be formed in the image of his Creator, and a man is said to be buried where his head is interred. Besides, when a man's head is removed there is no telling whose the body is, but anyone who looks at the amputated head will easily know what the body was like. As for your other illustrations, secular buildings are praised for the beauty of their upper parts, not of their foundations, and trees earn their praise from men by their production of fruit or by the regular arrangement of their branches. Contrary to your opinion, therefore, the man who chose the upper part should be the preferred lover."

The woman says: "Although your opinion may seem to be opposed by many arguments, still, because I see that all justice is on its side and that it is defended with the more rational firmness, I think I ought to assent and follow it as the one that has the truth back of it. Furthermore, I am not sorry to test the fulness of your knowledge on another matter. The noble lover of a certain woman set out with the royal expedition, and while he was gone false rumors were spread everywhere that he had died; after the woman had heard them and had carefully inquired into the matter, she observed the customary and reasonable period of mourning which she thought was due to dead lovers; then she took another lover. But after a short space of time had elapsed, the first lover came back and asked to be given the usual embraces; but the second lover forbade her to give them to him, for he said that the second love had been perfected and reciprocated. Now neither of the lovers ought to be deprived of love without some fault on his own part. But, also, if in the presence of the first lover the woman should be driven by love to ask the second to embrace her, such a love might prove injurious to the other man, but the woman could make the excuse that she had done this under the compulsion of love. No one can love anywhere except where the spirit of love leads him and his will compels him, and so there is good reason why this second lover, too, should remain in the position in which he is firmly established."

The man says: "The unraveling of the present question depends more upon the choice or the desire of the woman than upon the understanding of either a regular precept or a special mandate of Love. I think the lady we are talking about would do well if she restored herself completely to the first lover, provided only that she was induced to do so by a tie of affection for him.[83] But if the spirit in her impels her not at all toward him, or only a little, still I say that she ought by force to compel her will to seek after what formerly she embraced with great eagerness and approved with the desire of her heart, for it is the height of wisdom for anyone to withdraw her mind from that to which she has consented through error. Nor could the second lover properly consider this an injury to him, because we do not consider that a man has lost anything if through error he gets a thing that belongs to someone else and then, after the error is discovered, gives it up. But if she should see that her will does not respond to any coercion and should

[83] According to Hugo of St. Victor (*The Sacrament of Marriage*) a woman who marries under such circumstances must return to the first husband if he wants her. If she desires to keep the second husband, she is to be excommunicated.

know that her feeling for the first lover is dead and cannot be revived, she may keep the second lover. For to say that she should, absolutely, return to the first one, unless she does it under the persuasion of love's remorse, would be a shameful thing to say and would defeat the precept of Love. Nor can that rule you quoted—that no one should be deprived of his love without some fault on his part—stand in the way, because the first lover, who finds himself deprived of his love without any fault of his, cites it in his own defense. I have learned from people experienced in the law of Love that the rule we have just mentioned must be understood when it says 'without any fault of his' as meaning also 'or without any other good reason.' Therefore it cannot rightly follow, as you said it did, that a woman may spurn the love of one man and accept that of another if she is driven to do so by love's remorse; but if any man attempts to undermine her good faith, she must try to turn him away politely, and if he is too insistent she must finally tell him that she is already in love with someone else, that she ought not incline her heart to his words or remember what he tells her, or keep his image in her mind, or even think about him very often lest because women are weak she might open the way for some spark of love to enter and might direct her mind toward him. For if a woman does not begin to fall in love by thinking about a man continually and immoderately or by imagining the acts of delight, she will never care to seek a new love with any man."

The woman says: "I am very well pleased with your answers on both questions, because they seem to be supported by all the wisdom of erudition. Now, to keep anybody from having any reason to suspect evil of us because we have been talking so long, it seems to me proper that our discussion should end here."

The man says: "What you say seems to me very proper, but since I am yielding to you in this, I ask you to be so good as to answer me one question first: that is, whether a lover who comes to a second woman, but with no intention of loving her or of forgetting his affection for the first one, ought to be punished by losing the love he has. It seems to me that no matter what one of the lovers does, if his feeling of love is not thereby lessened his fellow-lover ought to endure it patiently and by her rebukes teach him better."

The woman says: "I shall not be too eager with my answer to you on this point, but I wonder how your good sense can have any doubt about it, since a rule of Love clearly teaches us that a lover is bound to keep himself chaste for his beloved. I have therefore reason to infer, from a logical interpretation of this, that in the present case the lover should be punished by the loss of his love; I think it is sufficient that this conduct is forbidden by Love's mandate. However I believe that his beloved may, if she wishes, pardon the excesses of the offender."

The man says: "Your interpretation seems to me very severe, but I am afraid to oppose so great an authority. But there is still another doubt that disturbs my soul—that is, whether a lover should be punished by the loss of his love if he goes to another woman with no feeling of love for her and he fails to accomplish his desire. For it seems that he ought not be so severely punished for so slight an offense, when the other lover has sustained no injury."

The woman says: "This too deserves to be condemned by the same opinion, unless spontaneous repentance for his offense and every proof of the good faith of the offender should happen to soften the heart of his beloved. It does not seem to be in accordance with Love's precept to keep oneself chaste for a lover whose shameless attempt betrays a shameless mind."

CHAPTER VII. THE LOVE OF THE CLERGY

Now, since in the preceding sections we have dealt with three classes of men: namely, commoners, simple nobility, and the higher nobility, and we recall mentioning at the beginning of the discussion the noblest class of all—that is, the clergy—let us speak briefly concerning their love affairs and see where the men of this fourth class get their nobility. Now the clerk is considered to be of the most noble class by virtue of his sacred calling, a nobility which we agree comes from God's bosom and is granted to him by the Divine Will, as God tells us Himself when he says, "He that toucheth you toucheth me," and, "He that toucheth you, toucheth the apple of my eye." [84] But so far as this nobility goes, a clerk cannot look for love, for on the strength of it he ought not devote himself to the works of love but is bound to renounce absolutely all the delights of the flesh and to keep himself free from all bodily filth, unspotted for the Lord whose service, according to our belief, he has taken upon him. A clerk's nobility, therefore, is not derived from his ancestors, nor can the secular power deprive him of it, but by God's grace alone, as we know, is it granted, and by His gift is it given, and by God alone may the privileges of this kind of nobility be annulled if His commands are violated. So it is very clear that a clerk, so far as concerns the distinction of this clerical nobility, cannot love, and thus it would be improper for me to treat of his love according to the dignity of this rank and the nobility of the order. A clerk ought therefore to be a stranger to every act of love and to put aside all uncleanness of body, or he will deserve to be deprived of this special nobility granted him by God. But since hardly anyone ever lives without carnal sin, and since the life of the clergy is, because of the continual idleness and the great abundance of food, naturally more liable to temptations of the body than that of any other men, if any clerk should wish to enter into the lists of Love let him speak and apply himself to Love's service in accordance with the rank or standing of his parents, as we have already fully explained in regard to the different ranks of men.

CHAPTER VIII. THE LOVE OF NUNS

You may be interested enough to ask what we have to say regarding the love of nuns. What we say is that their solaces must be absolutely

[84] Zach. 2: 8.

avoided just as though they were a pestilence of the soul, because from them comes the great wrath of our Heavenly Father and the civil authorities are greatly stirred up and threaten the most severe punishments, and by all of this we become infamous among men and our good reputation is destroyed. Even Love's commandment warns us not to choose for our love any woman whom we may not properly seek to marry. And if anybody should think so little of himself and of both laws as to seek for the love of a nun, he would deserve to be despised by everybody and he ought to be avoided as an abominable beast. There is no reason to have any doubt about the faith of a man who for the sake of one act of momentary delight would not fear to subject himself to the death penalty and would have no shame about becoming a scandal to God and men. We should therefore condemn absolutely the love of nuns and reject their solaces just as though they carried the plague. We do not say this with the idea that one cannot love a nun, but because by such love body and soul are condemned to death. Therefore we do not want you to know any words that may be used to solicit them. For one time when we had a chance to speak to a certain nun we spoke so well on the art, not being ignorant of the art of soliciting nuns, that we forced her to assent to our desire; we were smitten with what we may call mental blindness, and wholly forgetting what was seemly (since "no lover ever sees what is seemly" [85] and also "Love does not see anything well, he sees everything with his blind eye") we straightway began to be violently attracted by her beauty and captured by her pleasant conversation. But in the meantime we realized the madness that was carrying us away, and with a great effort roused ourselves up from the deadly sleep. And although we consider ourselves very expert in the art of love and well instructed in its cure, we were barely able to avoid her pestilential snares and escape without contamination of the flesh. Be careful therefore, Walter, about seeking lonely places with nuns or looking for opportunities to talk with them, for if one of them should think that the place was suitable for wanton dalliance, she would have no hesitation in granting you what you desire

[85] Ovid *Heroides* IV. 154.

and preparing for you burning solaces, and you could hardly escape that worst of crimes, engaging in the work of Venus. For if the charm of such women forced us, who are experienced in every trick and esteemed for our knowledge of the art of love, to waver, how can your inexperienced youth prevent it? Therefore you should avoid a love of this kind, my friend.

CHAPTER IX. LOVE GOT WITH MONEY

Now let us see whether real love can be got with money or any other gift. Real love comes only from the affection of the heart and is granted out of pure grace and genuine liberality, and this most precious gift of love cannot be paid for at any set price or be cheapened by a matter of money. If any woman is so possessed with a feeling of avarice as to give herself to a lover for the sake of pay, let no one consider her a lover, but rather a counterfeiter of love, who ought to join those shameful women in the brothel. Indeed the wantonness of such women is more polluted than the passion of harlots who ply their trade openly, for they do what one expects them to, and they deceive no one since their intentions are perfectly obvious. But those others who pretend to be fine ladies of the very best breeding force men to languish for love of them, and under the false veil of affection they gleefully rob of all their wealth those who have been smitten by Cupid's arrow. Men are deceived by their fallacious looks, outwitted by their crafty beckonings, and impelled by their clever and deceitful demands; they are kept busy giving them as many good things as they can, and they get more pleasure out of what they give away than from what they keep for their own use. These women have all sorts of ways of asking for things, and so long as they see that a man can respond to their greedy desire for gifts, they say that he is their adored lover, and they never cease to drain away his property or ruin him by their constant demands. But when his substance is gone and his patrimony is exhausted they despise and hate him and cast him aside like an unproductive bee, and then they begin to appear in their real colors. Any man who would seek for the love of women like these ought to be classed with shameless dogs and deserves no help from anybody. It ought therefore to be clear to everyone that the love which seeks for rewards should not be called love by anybody, but rather shameful harlotry and greedy wantonness, which no man's property can satisfy, nor can anybody's generosity mitigate it in the least by giving these women money. Anyone who has a firm manly character ought to exert himself to keep away from the allurements of women like these and to avoid their dangerous frauds. For a woman who is really in love always rejects and hates gifts from her lover, and devotes her efforts to increasing his wealth so that he may always have something he can give away and thereby increase his good name; she does not expect anything from him except the sweet solaces of the flesh and that her fame may increase among all men because he praises her. For a woman thinks that anything that her lover gives to others for her sake and for the sake of acquiring praise benefits her. Even though a woman is in need of a great many things, if she is really in love she thinks it a very serious thing to lessen her lover's property; but the lover, for his part, ought never to permit her to suffer for lack of anything if he can be of any assistance. It is a great disgrace for a lover to allow his beloved to be in need of anything when he himself has plenty. It is never held to the discredit of a woman if in a time of urgent need she accepts gifts from her lover and takes full advantage of his generosity. But when a woman has plenty of money it is enough that for her sake her lover gives gifts to others so far as is seemly.

A woman who you know desires money in return for her love should be looked upon as a deadly enemy, and you should be careful to avoid her like a venomous animal that strikes with its tail and fawns with its mouth. If you are so driven by wantonness of the body that you want to seek paid women, it would be better for you to do business with the women who openly loiter in the brothels and sell their bodies for a small price than to be robbed of your property, under the fiction of love, by some woman who pretends to be a lady, but acts like a strumpet. In such a business he is said to drive the best bargain who gets what he wants at the lowest price, and you get a thing more cheaply when it is offered for sale than when the buyer asks the other to sell. Alas, we grieve because we see the honorable name of ladies profaned by meretricious actions! Therefore let all worthy ladies take up arms when they see their rights usurped by unworthy women, and let them be zealous to avenge such infamous conduct, lest such a ruinous example spread further through the world.

Therefore do not let the distinguished but false outward show of a woman deceive you, or the ancestry of a degenerate woman, whose first enticements are sweeter than any honey, but whose last prove more bitter than gall or wormwood.[86] Whenever you notice a woman reminding you how generous someone else was in showering gifts upon his beloved, or hear her praise someone else's jewelry, or complain that some of her things have been pawned, or, under some pretext or other, ask for a piece of jewelry,[87] you must take good care to guard yourself against her wiles, for she doesn't want to be loved, but to draw money out of you. If nothing else could convince you of the truth of this, the rule of Love which says that love and avarice cannot dwell in the same abode would prove it. For if love does not come from the pure pleasure of giving and is not given without payment, it is not love, but a lying and profane imitation of it.

But although such an agreeable love can rarely be found, because the craving for money debases many women, you should strive with all your might to find a loved one whose faithfulness to you will not be changed if great poverty or misfortune should come upon you. For if you fall in love with a woman who is deceitful and desirous of being made rich, you can never gain her love, but she will deceive you by her foxy tricks; because when for the sake of what she can get out of you she makes you false signs of love, she will be giving you only a breath of empty air, while she leads you on to give her presents. And

---

[86] Prov. 5 : 3–4.   [87] Compare with Ovid's *Art of Love* I. 417 ff.

then your dearest possession will seem very little to give in return for one of those expensive, deceitful nods, and so, taken in by a clever woman, you will be forced to sail to the coast of poverty and will be in all respects an object of contempt. All men throughout the world agree that there is nothing so contemptible as for a man to waste his substance on the work of the flesh and the solace of Venus, and what sort of love it is that is granted for a price can be very clear to you from this book. Therefore, my friend, you should always follow this maxim: whenever you have reason to believe that a woman is interested in piling up the coin, be careful to avoid her in the very beginning and not to involve yourself at all in her snares. For if you try to fall in with what she says in order to find out what her real intention is, you will find yourself foiled by your own plan, because no amount of searching will reveal how she feels and what she means to do until the leech is full of blood and leaves you only half alive with all the blood of your wealth drained off.[88] A wise man's best efforts can hardly find out what is beneath the guile of a deceitful lady-love, for she knows how to color her frauds by so many arts and with so much cleverness that the faithful lover is rarely clever enough to see through them. The ability of a greedy woman is greater than that of the Ancient Enemy was when by his shrewdness he cleverly perverted the mind of our first parent. Therefore you should use all your cleverness to see that you are not tripped up by the snares of such a woman, because a woman of that kind does not want to love, but to revel in your wealth. If we wanted to devote ourselves to the reform of such women and to call to mind their lives and their deeds, our span of life would be spent before there was any lack in the abundance of material to write about. We do not say these things with the desire of running down honorable women, but because we want to expose the lives of those who do not blush to bring disgrace upon the military service of a host of honorable women by the way they act, and to profane this service under the pretense of love. God forbid that we should ever

[88] Horace *Art of Poetry*, l. 476.

wish, or be able, to cast a slur upon the deeds of honorable women, or to run them down in the least in this little book of ours, because it is through them that all the world is induced to do good deeds, the rich increase in wealth, abundant provision is made for the needs of the poor, and the avaricious are brought back again to the path of rectitude and learn the way of generosity. Indeed, since women are able to confer praise, they give the occasion for doing all the good things that are done in the world. Now, Walter, if by continual reading you learn those things which we are telling you with such splendid brevity, it is not likely that you will be overreached by the tricks of a deceitful woman.

CHAPTER X. THE EASY ATTAINMENT OF ONE'S OBJECT

Let us see next whether if one attains one's object easily it may lead to love. First we must see what we mean by attaining it easily. We may say it is easily attained when a woman, under the impulse of carnal passion, readily gives herself to a man who asks her and will easily do the same to another who asks, feeling no trace of love when the deed is done, but accepting no pay for it. Do not fall into the toils of such a woman, because you cannot win her love no matter how hard you try. This kind of woman has so much of the spirit of Venus in her that she cannot confine herself to the love of any one man, but she desires to sate her lust with many. Therefore it is idle for you to seek her love unless you know that you are so potent at Venus's trade that you can satisfy her; that would be harder for you to do than to dry up the oceans, so we think that there is good reason for you to have nothing to do with her love. Although you may enjoy her embraces as fully as you wish, her solaces will cause you intolerable pain and will give rise to many woes for you. You can never know, until you have been through it, how bitter will be your grief when, as lovers will, you want to believe that you are the only one to enjoy her solaces, but you know that she has gratified the passion of another man and made you share her with him. From what we have said it should be perfectly clear to you that where you find it easy to attain your desire you may be sure there is no love; for when a woman is so passionate that she cannot confine herself to one man, but desires to gratify the passion of many, there love can find no place at all. For true love joins the hearts of two persons with so great a feeling of delight that they cannot desire to embrace anybody else; on the contrary they take care to avoid the solaces of everybody else as though they were horrible things, and they keep themselves for each other. This readiness to grant requests is, we say, the same thing in women as overvoluptuousness in men—a thing which all agree should be a total stranger in the court of Love. For he who is so tormented by carnal passion that he cannot embrace anyone in heart-felt love, but basely lusts after every woman he sees, is not called a lover but a counterfeiter of love and a pretender, and he is lower than a shameless dog. Indeed the man who is so wanton that he cannot confine himself to the love of one woman deserves to be considered an impetuous ass. It will therefore be clear to you that you are bound to avoid an overabundance of passion and that you ought not to seek the love of a woman who you know will grant easily what you seek.

CHAPTER XI. THE LOVE OF PEASANTS

But lest you should consider that what we have already said about the love of the middle class applies also to farmers, we will add a little about their love. We say that it rarely happens that we find farmers serving in Love's court, but naturally, like a horse or a mule,[89] they give themselves up to the work of Venus, as nature's urging teaches them to do. For a farmer hard labor and the uninterrupted solaces of plough and mattock are sufficient. And even if it should happen at times, though rarely, that contrary to their nature they are stirred up by Cupid's arrows, it is not expedient that they should be instructed

[89] Tob. 6: 17.

in the theory of love, lest while they are devoting themselves to conduct which is not natural to them the kindly farms which are usually
made fruitful by their efforts may through lack of cultivation prove
useless to us. And if you should, by some chance, fall in love with some
of their women, be careful to puff them up with lots of praise and then,
when you find a convenient place, do not hesitate to take what you seek
and to embrace them by force. For you can hardly soften their outward
inflexibility so far that they will grant you their embraces quietly or
permit you to have the solaces you desire unless first you use a little
compulsion as a convenient cure for their shyness. We do not say these
things, however, because we want to persuade you to love such women,
but only so that, if through lack of caution you should be driven to
love them, you may know, in brief compass, what to do.

CHAPTER XII. THE LOVE OF PROSTITUTES

Now in case anybody should ask how we feel about the love of
prostitutes we say that they are all to be shunned absolutely, because it
is most shameful to have dealings with them, and with them one almost
always falls into the sin of lewdness. Besides, a prostitute seldom gives
herself to anyone until she has been given a present that pleases her.
Even if it should happen once in a while that a woman of this kind
does fall in love, all agree that her love is harmful to men, because
all wise men frown upon having familiar intercourse with prostitutes,
and to do so spoils anybody's good name. Therefore we have no desire to explain to you the way to gain their love, because whatever the
feeling that makes them give themselves to a suitor they always do
so without much urging, so you don't need to ask for instructions on
this point.

BOOK TWO

How Love May Be Retained

CHAPTER I. HOW LOVE, WHEN IT HAS BEEN ACQUIRED, MAY BE KEPT

Now since we have already said enough about acquiring love, it is not unfitting that we should next see and describe how this love may be retained after it has once been acquired. The man who wants to keep his love affair for a long time untroubled should above all things be careful not to let it be known to any outsider, but should keep it hidden from everybody; because when a number of people begin to get wind of such an affair, it ceases to develop naturally and even loses what progress it has already made. Furthermore a lover ought to appear to his beloved wise in every respect and restrained in his conduct, and he should do nothing disagreeable that might annoy her. Moreover every man is bound, in time of need, to come to the aid of his beloved, both by sympathizing with her in all her troubles and by acceding to all her reasonable desires. Even if he knows sometimes that what she wants is not so reasonable, he should be prepared to agree to it after he has asked her to reconsider. And if inadvertently he should do something improper that offends her, let him straightway confess with downcast face that he has done wrong, and let him give the excuse that he lost his temper or make some other suitable explanation that will fit the case. And every man ought to be sparing of praise of his beloved when he is among other men; he should not talk about her often or at great length, and he should not spend a great deal of time in places where she is. When he is with other men, if he meets her in a group of women, he should not try to communicate with her by signs, but should treat her almost like a stranger, lest some person spying on their love might have opportunity to spread malicious gossip. Lovers should not even nod to each other unless they are sure that nobody is watching them. Every man should also wear things that his beloved likes and pay a reasonable amount of attention to his appearance—not too much because excessive care for one's looks is distasteful to everybody and leads people to despise the good looks that one has. If the lover is lavish in giving, that helps him retain a love he has acquired, for all lovers ought to despise all worldly riches and should give alms to those who have need of them. Nothing is considered more praiseworthy in a lover than to be known to be generous, and no matter how worthy a man may be otherwise, avarice degrades him, while many faults are excused if one has the virtue of liberality. Also, if the lover is one who is fitted to be a warrior, he should see to it that his courage is apparent to everybody, for it detracts very much from the good character of a man if he is timid in a fight. A lover should always offer his services and obedience freely to every lady, and he ought to root out all his pride and be very humble. He ought to give a good deal of attention to acting toward all in such fashion that no one may be sorry to call to mind his good deeds or have reason to censure anything he has done. Then, too, he must keep in mind the general rule that lovers must not neglect anything that good manners demand or good breeding suggests, but they should be very careful to do everything of this sort. Love may also be retained by indulging in the sweet and delightful solaces of the flesh, but only in such manner and in such number that they may never seem wearisome to the loved one. Let the lover strive to practice gracefully and manfully any act or mannerism which he has noticed is pleasing to his beloved. A clerk should not, of course, affect the manners or the dress of the laity, for no one is likely to please his beloved, if she is a wise woman, by wearing strange clothing or by practicing manners that do not suit his status. Furthermore a lover should make every attempt to be constantly in the company of good men and to avoid completely the society of the wicked. For association with the vulgar makes a lover who joins them a thing of contempt to his beloved.

What we have said about retaining love you should understand as referring to a lover of either sex. There are doubtless many other things which may be useful in retaining love that a wide-awake diligent lover may discover for himself.

CHAPTER II. HOW A LOVE, ONCE CONSUMMATED, MAY BE INCREASED

We shall attempt to show you in a few words how love may be increased after it has been consummated. Now in the first place it is said to increase if the lovers see each other rarely and with difficulty; for the greater the difficulty of exchanging solaces, the more do the desire for them and the feeling of love increase. Love increases, too, if one of the lovers shows that he is angry at the other; for the lover falls at once into a great fear that this feeling which has arisen in his beloved may last forever. Love increases, likewise, if one of the lovers feels real jealousy, which is called, in fact, the nurse of love. Even if he does not suffer from real jealousy, but from a shameful suspicion, still by virtue of this his love always increases and grows more powerful. What constitutes real jealousy and what shameful suspicion you can easily see in the discussion between the man of the higher nobility and the noblewoman.[1] Love increases, too, if it happens to last after it has been made public; ordinarily it does not last, but begins to fail just as soon as it is revealed. Again, if one of the lovers dreams about the other, that gives rise to love, or if love already exists it increases it. So, too, if you know that someone is trying to win your beloved away from you, that will no doubt increase your love and you will begin to feel more affection for her. I will go further and say that even though you know perfectly well that some other man is enjoying the embraces of your beloved, this will make you begin to value her solaces all the more,

---

[1] Pages 103 ff.

unless your greatness of soul and nobility of mind keep you from such wickedness. When you have gone to some other place or are about to go away—that increases your love, and so do the scoldings and beatings that lovers suffer from their parents, for not only does a scolding lecture cause love to increase after it is perfected, but it even gives a perfect reason for beginning a love affair that has not yet started. Frequent dwelling with delight on the thought of the beloved is of value in increasing love; so is the sight of her eyes when you are by yourselves and fearful, and her eager acceptance of a demand for the acts of love. Love is greatly intensified by a carriage and a way of walking that please the beloved, by a readiness to say pretty things, by a pleasant manner of speaking, and by hearing men sing the praises of the loved one. There are doubtless still other things by which love is increased which you can find out for yourself if you will study the matter attentively and if you have paid careful attention to those things that we have set down. For all the other things that are effective in such an affair seem to be dependent upon those which we have mentioned and to grow out of them.

CHAPTER III. IN WHAT WAYS LOVE MAY BE DECREASED

Now let us see in what ways love may be decreased. Too many opportunities for exchanging solaces, too many opportunities of seeing the loved one, too much chance to talk to each other all decrease love, and so does an uncultured appearance or manner of walking on the part of the lover or the sudden loss of his property. For a lover who suffers from great poverty is so tormented by the thought of household affairs and his urgent necessities that he can give no heed to the impulses of love and cannot allow it to increase as it should; as a result everybody tries to find fault with his character and his life, and he is despised and hated by all, and no one will look upon him as a friend because

> While you are fortunate you will number many friends,
> When the skies grow dark you will be alone.[2]

Because of all these things a man's face and figure begin to change, and restful sleep deserts him, and so he can hardly escape becoming contemptible in the eyes of his beloved. It also decreases love if one discovers any infamy in the lover or hears of any avarice, bad character, or any kind of unworthiness; so it does for him to have an affair with another woman, even if he is not in love with her. Love decreases, too, if the woman finds that her lover is foolish and indiscreet, or if he seems to go beyond reasonable bounds in his demands for love, or if she sees that he has no regard for her modesty and will not forgive her bashfulness. For a faithful lover ought to prefer love's greatest pains to making demands which deprive his beloved of her modesty or taking pleasure in making fun of her blushes; he is not called a lover, but a betrayer, who would consider only his own passions and who would be unmindful of the good of his beloved. Love decreases, too, if the woman considers that her lover is cowardly in battle, or sees that he is unrestrained in his speech or spoiled by the vice of arrogance. For nothing appears more seemly in the character of any lover at all than that he should be clad in the garment of humility and wholly lack the nakedness of pride. The utterance of silly and foolish words frequently decreases love. Many men, when with a woman, think that they will please her if they utter the first silly words that come into their heads, which is really a great mistake. The man who thinks he can please a wise woman by doing something foolish shows a great lack of sense.

Other things which weaken love are blasphemy against God or His saints, mockery of the ceremonies of the Church, and a deliberate withholding of charity from the poor. We find that love decreases very sharply if one is unfaithful to his friend, or if he brazenly says one thing while he deceitfully conceals a different idea in his heart. Love decreases, too, if the lover piles up more wealth than is proper, or if

---

[2] Quoted, not quite accurately, from Ovid *Tristia* I. ix. 5–6.

he is too ready to go to law over trifles. We could tell you many more things about the weakening of love, but we leave you to find these out for yourself, for we see that you are so devoted to the practice of love as to neglect all other business and so determined to love that nothing in the art of love can escape you, since there is not a thing in it that you leave undiscussed. But we do not want you to overlook the fact that when love has definitely begun to decline, it quickly comes to an end unless something comes to save it.

CHAPTER IV. HOW LOVE MAY COME TO AN END

Now having treated briefly of the lessening of love we shall try next to add for you an explanation of how it may come to an end. First of all we see that love comes to an end if one of the lovers breaks faith or tries to break faith with the other, or if he is found to go astray from the Catholic religion. It comes to an end also after it has been openly revealed and made known to men. So, too, if one of the lovers has plenty of money and does not come to the aid of the other who is in great need and lacks a great many things, then love usually becomes very cheap and comes to an ignominious end. An old love also ends when a new one begins, because no one can love two people at the same time. Furthermore, inequality of love and a fraudulent and deceitful duplicity of heart always drive out love, for a deceitful lover, no matter how worthy he is otherwise, ought to be rejected by any woman; it does not matter how well known his good qualities are and how great his wisdom, if he comes to love with a mind full of deceit, he deserves to be driven out of Love's court. Love seeks for two persons who are bound together by a mutual trust and an identity of desires, and other people lack all merit in love and are considered as strangers to his court. Again, if the parties concerned marry, love is violently put to flight, as is clearly shown by the teaching of certain lovers. Again, if by some chance one of the lovers becomes incapable of carrying out love's duties, love can no longer last between them and deserts them completely. Likewise if one of the lovers becomes insane or develops a sudden timidity, love flees and becomes hateful. Having indicated these things to you briefly and in general terms, my friend, we leave it to you to figure out the other ways that love may be ended, for we do not want to indulge you in your indolence or to save you all exertion.

You may, however, ask whether a love once ended can ever come to life again. If this failure of love comes from ignorance of some particular thing, there is no doubt but that it may be revived; however, where it grows out of some misdeed of the lover or of some defect in his nature, we cannot remember any case where it has revived, although we do not say that it cannot, except perhaps in cases where this failure is due to some defect in the lover's nature. And if love should at some time happen to come to life again, we do not think that the lovers would have perfect confidence in each other.

CHAPTER V. INDICATIONS THAT ONE'S LOVE IS RETURNED

Now that we have thus disposed of these questions and have, in a short space, finished them up, let us add to them a discussion of how to find out whether one's love is returned—something that we think will be useful and helpful to all lovers. Nothing is more necessary to lovers than to know beyond a doubt how the people they love feel towards them, for if they should go wrong on this point, they would get little honor from such a love affair and they might suffer a great loss. There are many ways in which a lover can find out the faith of his beloved and test her feelings. If you see that your loved one is missing all sorts of opportunities to meet you or is putting false obstacles in your path, you cannot hope long to enjoy her love. So, too, if you find her, for no reason at all, growing half-hearted about giving you the usual solaces, you may see that her faith is wavering. If you find that she keeps out of your sight more than she was accustomed to do, her feelings are not very stable; and if she tries to hide from your faithful messenger, there is no doubt that she has turned you adrift in the mighty waves and that her love for you is only feigned. Again, if you find that she is refraining from sending you the usual messages or that her particularly faithful messenger is getting lax about bringing them to you as he used to do or is becoming a stranger to you, you may believe that your love has turned against you. If at the very moment of delight when she is offering you her sweet solaces the act is more wearisome to her than usual, or if you see that your solaces bore her, you need not doubt that she has no love for you. So, too, if she finds more fault with you than usual or demands things that she has not been in the habit of demanding, or if you find her less ready than usual to grant or to seek solaces, you may know that your love will not last much longer. Again, if when she is with you or someone else she frequently talks about what you did and what the other man did, without making any distinction between you, or if on some clever pretext she asks what sort of man he is or what sort of character he has, you may know that she is thinking about the love of the other man. Moreover, if you find that she is paying more attention to the care of her person than she had been doing, either her love for you is growing or she is interested in the love of someone else. On the other hand, a woman who turns pale in the presence of her lover is without a doubt really in love. He who wants to make a real test of the faith and affection of his beloved should, with the greatest care and subtlety, pretend to her that he desires the embraces of some other woman, and he should be seen near this woman more often than he has been. If he finds that this upsets his beloved he can be sure that she is very much in love with him and most constant in her affection. For when one of the lovers is seen to be enjoying the embraces of a new love, or for some reason or other the woman suspects that he is thinking of doing so, she begins at once to be greatly disturbed in heart and soul and to be deeply smitten with an unbearable jealousy; at once her face begins to make manifest this inner suffering of her soul. It is well if lovers pretend from time to time to be angry at each other, for if one lets the other see that he is angry and that something has made him indignant with his loved one, he can find out clearly how faithful she is. For a true lover is always in fear and trembling lest the anger of his beloved last forever, and so, even if one lover does show at times that he is angry at the other without cause, this disturbance will last but a little while if they find that their feeling for each other is really love. You must not think that by quarrels of this kind the bonds of affection and love are weakened; it is only clearing away the rust. Another thing is that if one of the lovers is too much concerned with asking the other for gifts, unless he is driven to this by urgent necessity, he may pretend that he is in love, but he is a long way from having the affection of a lover; what he wants is, not to love, but to enjoy the wealth of somebody else.

There are, I suppose, a great many other things that may be of value as indications that one's love is returned, which an attentive reader can easily discover from what I have said.

CHAPTER VI. IF ONE OF THE LOVERS IS UNFAITHFUL TO THE OTHER

If one of the lovers should be unfaithful to the other, and the offender is the man, and he has an eye to a new love affair, he renders himself wholly unworthy of his former love, and she ought to deprive him completely of her embraces, because the feeling of love he formerly had is now completely gone. With good reason it has been shown to be wholly impossible for a man to think continually and excessively about a woman so as to give rise to a new love without completely driving out the old, for we are taught by the natural and universal tradition of love that no one can be bound by a twofold love. Therefore, if such a lover as this should seek for the usual embraces and ask to be rewarded with his former joys, the first woman should forbid him the house and treat him like a perfect stranger, because in such a case as this no amount of submission will help him unless the woman wishes to show him favor.

But let us see whether the woman, if she does accept such a lover, does a praiseworthy act. I want to make it very clear to the women that it is a great blot on a woman's character if she has anything more to do with a lover who has engaged in a new love; a man deserves no mercy if he forgets honors of this kind which he has received and is so lacking in gratitude that he is not ashamed to think of embracing some other woman. For what greater favor can be shown to any man in the world than for him to have the love of the woman he desires? But if, as so often happens, the woman cannot get out of her mind her love for this deceiver, and if he persists with his new love, she may be very sure that she will suffer great torments every day before her desire comes to pass. For when a lover has taken up with a new love, he can rarely be won back easily to the old one; because a love that has died out can seldom be brought to life again. To a woman in such a position I cannot refuse this advice: if such a woman wants to keep hold of a wavering lover, she must be careful not to let him know her intentions and she must hide her real feelings and by careful dissimulation make it seem to him that she is not distressed by the upsetting of their love affair, and she must pretend to endure with patience and equanimity what her lover is doing. If she knows that he is walking through her neighborhood, she must not go where he can see her, as she has been in the habit of doing, but she must keep completely out of his sight. If the woman sees that she is getting no results by this method, she must very cautiously pretend that she is thinking about the embrace of some other man, so that the lover, when he thinks that those delightful solaces which formerly he was so eager to accept are now being given to someone else, may become jealous and fall to longing for them as he used to do. If the lost love cannot be recovered by these devices, the wisest plan would be for the woman to see if she couldn't forget him entirely and put quite out of her mind all remembrance of his love. Then if she has discreetly tried these remedies which I have mentioned and she doesn't notice that the wounds show any improvement, she will do wisely and well if she stops worrying over the love of such a man, because in a storm of this kind you can never cast anchor on the shore you are seeking. Women should therefore take great care not to bind themselves to lovers of this kind, because from such a love they will get no true joy, but will be exposed to innumerable troubles and infinite griefs. Therefore, when a woman is asked for her love, before she grants it she should make every effort to find out the character and the good faith of the man who is asking, so that there will be nothing she does not know about him; because after she has heedlessly gone into the affair it is too late to seek the advice of a wise man or to torment herself with a tardy repentance. A woman must therefore be careful not to be tripped up by the snares of a deceitful lover, because so many of them do not desire to be loved, but merely to gratify their passions or to boast in company of their conquests over women. These men, before they get from a woman the fruit of their efforts, seem to say everything charmingly and in good faith and without guile; but after they attain their object they turn their backs upon the loved one, the duplicity which was hidden in their hearts begins to appear, and the poor, simple, overcredulous woman finds herself mortally deceived by the trickery of the pretended lover.

But what if the man should be unfaithful to his beloved—not with the idea of finding a new love, but because he has been driven to it by an irresistible passion for another woman? What, for instance, if chance should present to him an unknown woman in a convenient place or what if at a time when Venus is urging him on to that which I am talking about he should meet with a little strumpet or somebody's servant girl? Should he, just because he played with her in the grass, lose the love of his beloved? We can say without fear of contradiction that just for this a lover is not considered unworthy of the love of his beloved unless he indulges in so many excesses with a number of women that we may conclude that he is overpassionate. But if whenever he becomes acquainted with a woman he pesters her to gain his end, or if he attains his object as a result of his efforts, then rightly he does deserve to be deprived of his former love, because there is a strong presumption that he has acted in this way with an eye toward a new one, especially where he has strayed with a woman of the nobility or otherwise of an honorable estate.

But perhaps you will ask what a woman is to do if her adored lover asks for permission to leave her in favor of some other woman. We are bound to say emphatically that a woman ought by no means to give her lover permission to enjoy the embraces of another woman; instead she should in very plain words forbid him the other woman's embraces. But if she has granted him such permission and he has taken advantage of this, it is just as useless for him to go back to his former love as if he had left her without receiving permission. For although by granting such a request the woman has clearly committed a sin against love, still her error cannot excuse the bad faith of the lover or cover up his offense. On the other hand, if the lover tried to take advantage of the permission she gave him but his attempt was unsuccessful, the woman cannot on this account deny him the regular solaces, since she, too, is at fault and one misdeed may balance the other.

But now let us discuss the old mistake and see what should be done if it is the woman who is unfaithful to her lover. The old opinion, held by some, is that when the woman is at fault the same rule should be followed as in the case of the man just mentioned. But this rule, although old, should not be respected on that account, since it would lead us into great error. God forbid that we should ever declare that a woman who is not ashamed to wanton with two men should go unpunished. Although in the case of men such a thing is tolerated because it is so common and because the sex has a privilege by which all things in this world which are by their nature immodest are more readily allowed to men, in the case of a woman they are, because of the decency of the modest sex, considered so disgraceful that after a woman has indulged the passions of several men everybody looks upon her as an unclean strumpet unfit to associate with other ladies. Therefore if a woman goes back to her former lover after enjoying the embraces of someone else, it is a disgrace to him, for he can see perfectly well that she no longer has any love for him. Why, therefore, should he place his affection on her?

But perhaps you will say, "The lover so pines for love of this woman that he cannot by any means forget her or get her out of his mind; therefore, master, give him some means of saving himself." But may Andreas never enjoy the thing he desires most in this world, that without which he cannot even be happy in this mortal life, if he will ever give his aid to such a wretched man. It would seem more profitable to mankind for us to leave such a man to his own devices, letting his wounds go untouched like those of a dead man, than to teach him cures for love. For when a man is known to have degenerated so far from manly firmness as to love such women, he ought to be considered wholly unworthy of any help and worse than a dead man. I would prefer to have such a man, who has found a fit match in such a woman, continue to enjoy such a love.

But what if a woman should give kisses to such a man or let him hold her in his arms, but goes no further? We would like to give her the scolding she deserves and tell her that a woman who gives any man other than her lover a kiss or an embrace is acting shamefully, since these are always considered signs of love and are given to men as an indication that love is to follow.

But whether the woman or the lover may properly seek a new love we shall not trouble to explain to you here, because, rightly or wrongly, people do it, and after one has been smitten with a new love he is just as forcibly compelled to give way to his own impulses as though he were under the domination of some other person. But I know that once when I sought advice I got the answer that a true lover can never desire a new love unless he knows that for some definite and sufficient reason the old love is dead; we know from our own experience that this rule is very true.[3] We have fallen in love with a woman of the most admirable character, although we never have had, or hope to have, any

---

[3] The change in number follows the Latin.

fruit of this love. For we are compelled to pine away for love of a woman of such lofty station that we dare not say one word about it, nor dare we throw ourself upon her mercy, and so at length we are forced to find our body shipwrecked. But although rashly and without foresight we have fallen into such great waves in this tempest, still we cannot think about a new love or look for any other way to free ourself.

But since you are making a special study of the subject of love, you may well ask whether a man can have a pure love for one woman and a mixed or common love with another.[4] We will show you, by an unanswerable argument, that no one can feel affection for two women in this fashion. For although pure love and mixed love may seem to be very different things, if you will look at the matter properly you will see that pure love, so far as its substance goes, is the same as mixed love and comes from the same feeling of the heart. The substance of the love is the same in each case, and only the manner and form of loving are different, as this illustration will make clear to you. Sometimes we see a man with a desire to drink his wine unmixed, and at another time his appetite prompts him to drink only water or wine and water mixed; although his appetite manifests itself differently, the substance of it is the same and unchanged. So likewise when two people have long been united by pure love and afterwards desire to practice mixed love, the substance of the love remains the same in them, although the manner and form and the way of practicing it are different.

You may perhaps inquire, Walter, whether one should reject a woman who has been carried away by force and violated by another man. In such a case we say that it is not right for anybody to blame a woman for what she did under compulsion unless she has consented to the act by repeating it afterward. You will ask, too, whether a woman sins against the precepts of Love when she persuades some other lady to accept a new love although she knows that she already has a suitable lover. Reason forces us to say that no one may solicit, either for himself

4 See p. 122.

or for somebody else, any woman whom he knows to be already properly matched.

And now you may ask whether a woman who has made a mistake and has offered her love to a man not worthy of her may deprive him of this love and freely seek the solaces of another lover. If any woman has made a mistake of this kind and has obligated herself to an unworthy lover, she ought to devote all her efforts to improving his character and drawing him away from his evil practices. But if she sees that all her efforts will not make any improvement in him, she may freely and without fear of blame send him away and never give him another embrace. The same thing should, we think, be said of a man who makes a mistake and carelessly joins himself to a woman of bad character.

You may possibly ask me whether if one of the lovers should not care to indulge in love's solaces any longer and holds aloof from the other he may be said to be unfaithful to her. We dare not presume to say that no one may refrain from the delights of the world, lest such a doctrine should seem to be contrary to the commands of God Himself, nor would it be safe to hold that a man ought not rather to devote himself to God than to worldly pleasures. But we do say that if he should afterwards decide to love again, according to the opinion of the ladies he must return to the arms of his first love if she cares to ask him to. But perhaps you will say: "Then this is contrary to that rule of Love which says that one's love must not be revealed." To this objection we answer that love may be revealed to three people besides the lovers themselves, for the lover is allowed to find a suitable confidant from whom he may get secret comfort in his love affair and who will offer him sympathy if things turn out badly; the woman may choose a similar confidante. Besides these they may have one faithful intermediary, chosen by common consent, through whom the affair may always be managed in secret and in the proper fashion. These two confidants are bound, when both of the lovers wish it and the occasion demands, to go before the ladies and tell them what has happened, but without giving any information as to the identity of the lovers concerned in the case.

You may well ask, too, whether when love has been encouraged by the granting of hope or even has advanced to the second or third stage and then the woman has refused to grant the love she has promised, she may be said to be unfaithful to her lover. We believe we must firmly hold that when a woman has granted any man the hope of her love or has given him any of the other preliminary gifts, and she finds him not unworthy of this love, it is very wrong for her to try to deprive him of the love he has so long hoped for. It is not proper for any honest woman to put off without good cause the fulfillment of any of her promises; if she is fully determined not to listen to a suitor, she must not grant him hope or any of the other preliminary gifts of love, because it is considered very deceitful for her not to do what she has promised him. It is thought very shameful in a woman not to be careful to keep her promises; that is usually looked upon like the deceit of harlots, who in all their deeds and words are full of falsehood and all of whose thoughts are full of guile.

There is one thing about a harlot that we want you particularly to notice: if by some miracle she should happen some time to fall in love, she can never be unfaithful to her lover. We know, from some of her remarks, that the Countess of Champagne knew this, and we think that she mentioned it because she wanted to call attention to the baseness of a man who would chase after harlots, and to punish his expertness. The man who has indulged in so filthy a love does not deserve to be aided by any of the privileges of love when things turn out badly; he is bound to suffer in patience, since he joined himself to her with his eyes open. What we have said here about harlots applies not only to those who inhabit the stews but also to all women who give themselves to a lover in the expectation of payment of any kind.

You ask too, Walter, whether if two lovers are enjoying by mutual agreement a pure love and later one of them desires a mixed or common one [5] the other may hold back. Now, we want you to be fully instructed on this point—that although all men ought to choose a pure love rather than a mixed or common one, still one of the lovers may not oppose the desire of the other unless at the beginning of the attachment they made an agreement that they would never engage in mixed love except by the free will and the full consent of both parties. But even if the lovers have made an agreement that neither may ask for anything more unless both are agreed to it, still it is not right for a woman to refuse to give in to her lover's desire on this point if she sees that he persists in it. For all lovers are bound, when practicing love's solaces, to be mutually obedient to each other's desires.

CHAPTER VII. VARIOUS DECISIONS IN LOVE CASES

Now then, let us come to various decisions in cases of love:

1. A man who was greatly enamoured of a certain woman devoted his whole heart to the love of her. But when she saw that he was in love with her, she absolutely forbade him to love. When she discovered that he was just as much in love with her as ever, she said to him one day, "I know it is true that you have striven a very long time for my love, but you can never get it unless you are willing to make me a firm promise that you will always obey all my commands and that if you oppose them in any way you will be willing to lose my love completely." The man answered her, "My lady, God forbid that I should ever be so much in error as to oppose your commands in anything; so, since what you ask is very pleasing, I gladly assent to it." After he had promised this she immediately ordered him to make no more effort to gain her love and not to dare to speak a good word of her to others. This was a heavy blow to the lover, yet he bore it patiently. But one day when this lover and some other knights were with some ladies he heard his companions speaking very shamefully about his lady and

[5] See p. 122.

saying things about her reputation that were neither right nor proper. He endured it for a while with an ill grace, but when he saw that they kept on disparaging the lady he burst out violently against them and began to accuse them of slander and to defend his lady's reputation. When all this came to her ears she said that he ought to lose her love completely because by praising her he had violated her commands.

This point the Countess of Champagne [6] explained as follows in her decision. She said that the lady was too severe in her command, because she was not ashamed to silence him by an unfair sentence after he had wholly submitted himself to her will and after she had given him the hope of her love by binding him to her with a promise which no honorable woman can break without a reason. Nor did the aforesaid lover sin at all when he tried to deliver a well-deserved rebuke to those who were slandering his lady. For although he did make such a promise in order the more easily to obtain her love, it seems unfair of the woman to lay upon him the command that he should trouble himself no more with love for her.

II. Again. Another man, although he was enjoying the embraces of a most excellent love, asked her for permission to obtain the embraces of a different woman. Having received this he went away and refrained longer than usual from the solaces of the first lady. But after a month had elapsed he came back to the first one and said that he had never received any solaces from the other lady, nor had he wished to receive them, but he had merely wanted to test the constancy of his loved one. This woman refused him her love on the ground that he was unworthy, saying that for him to ask and receive such permission was reason enough for her to deprive him of her love. But the opinion of Queen Eleanor,[7] who was consulted on the matter, seems to be just the opposite of this woman's. She said, "We know that it comes from the nature of love that those who are in love often falsely pretend that they desire new embraces, that they may the better test the faith and constancy of their co-lover. Therefore a woman sins against the nature

---

[6] See Introduction, p. 13.   [7] See Introduction, p. 15.

of love itself if she keeps back her embraces from her lover on this account or forbids him her love, unless she has clear evidence that he has been unfaithful to her."

III. There were two men who were equal in birth and life and morals and everything else except that one happened to have more property than the other, so that many wondered which was preferable as a lover. From this case came the dictum of the Countess of Champagne, who said, "It would not be right for one to prefer a vulgar rich man to a noble and handsome poor one. Indeed a handsome poor man may well be preferred to a rich nobleman [8] if both are seeking the love of a rich woman, since it is more worthy for a woman who is blessed with an abundance of property to accept a needy lover than one who has great wealth. Nothing should be more grievous to all good men than to see worth overshadowed by poverty or suffering from the lack of anything. It is right, therefore, for men to praise a wealthy woman who disregards money and seeks a needy lover whom she can help with her wealth, for nothing seems so praiseworthy in a lover of either sex as to relieve the necessities of the loved one so far as may be. But if the woman herself is in need, she is more ready to accept the rich lover; for if both lovers are oppressed by poverty there is little doubt that their love will be of short duration. Poverty brings a great feeling of shame to all honorable men and gives them many an anxious thought and is even a great disturber of quiet sleep; so as a result it commonly puts love to flight.

IV. Another question like this came up: two men who were in all things absolutely equal began to pay court at the same time and in the same manner and demanded urgently that they be loved. Therefore it was asked which man's love could be chosen in such a case. We are taught by the admonition of the same countess that in such a case the man who asks first should be given the preference; but if their proposals seem to be simultaneous, it is not unfair to leave it to the woman

---

[8] "We prefer a virtuous poor man to an unmannerly rich one." Seneca *Benefits* IV. iii.

to choose the one of the two toward whom she finds her heart inclining.

V. A certain knight loved his lady beyond all measure and enjoyed her full embrace, but she did not love him with equal ardor. He sought to leave her, but she, desiring to retain him in his former status, opposed his wish. In this affair the Countess gave this response: "It is considered very unseemly for a woman to seek to be loved and yet to refuse to love. It is silly for anybody disrespectfully to ask of others what she herself wholly refuses to give to others."

VI. Then a question like this came up: A worthless young man and an older knight of excellent character sought the love of the same woman. The young man argued that she ought to prefer him to the older man because if he got the love he was after he might by means of it acquire an excellent character, and it would be no small credit to the woman if through her a worthless man was made into a man of good character.

To this Queen Eleanor replied as follows: "Although the young man may show that by receiving love he might rise to be a worthy man, a woman does not do very wisely if she chooses to love an unworthy man, especially when a good and eminently worthy one seeks her love. It might happen that because of the faults of the unworthy man his character would not be improved even if he did receive the good things he was hoping for, since the seeds which we sow do not always produce a crop."

VII. This other love affair was submitted to the decision of the same queen. A certain man who had in ignorance joined in love with a woman who was related to him, sought to leave her when he discovered his fault. But the woman was bound by the chain of love and tried to keep him in love's observances, saying that the crime was fully excused by the fact that when they began to enjoy the love it was without any sin.

In this affair the Queen answered as follows: "A woman who under the excuse of a mistake of any kind seeks to preserve an incestuous love is clearly going contrary to what is right and proper. We are always bound to oppose any of those incestuous and damnable actions which we know even human laws punish by very heavy penalties."

VIII. A certain lady had a proper enough lover, but was afterward, through no fault of her own, married to an honorable man, and she avoided her love and denied him his usual solaces. But Lady Ermengarde of Narbonne [9] demonstrated the lady's bad character in these words: "The later contracting of a marital union does not properly exclude an early love except in cases where the woman gives up love entirely and is determined by no means to love any more."

IX. A certain man asked the same lady to make clear where there was the greater affection—between lovers or between married people. The lady gave him a logical answer. She said: "We consider that marital affection and the true love of lovers are wholly different and arise from entirely different sources, and so the ambiguous nature of the word prevents the comparison of the things and we have to place them in different classes. Comparisons of more or less are not valid when things are grouped together under an ambiguous heading and the comparison is made in regard to that ambiguous term. It is no true comparison to say that a name is simpler than a body or that the outline of a speech is better arranged than the delivery.

X. The same man asked the same lady this question. A certain woman had been married, but was now separated from her husband by a divorce, and her former husband sought eagerly for her love. In this case the lady replied: "If any two people have been married and afterwards separate in any way, we consider love between them wholly wicked."

XI. A good and prudent man sought the love of a woman; then later a still more worthy man came and urgently sought her love. Which lover, then, should she choose? Ermengarde of Narbonne settled the case in this way: "It is left to the woman to choose whether she will listen to the good man or to the better one."

XII. Another case in love runs like this: A man who had a suitable enough lover most urgently besought another lady for her love just as though he didn't have the love of any other woman; and from her he obtained all his heart's desire, all he so ardently sought. After his

[9] She became Viscountess of Narbonne about 1142 and died about 1187.

efforts had been rewarded he sought again the embraces of the first lady and turned his back on the second. What punishment, then, should be given to this wicked man? In this affair the opinion of the Countess of Flanders [10] attracted notice.

"The man who plotted so fraudulently ought to be deprived of the love of both women and should never in the future enjoy the love of any honorable lady, since we think he is swayed by strong voluptuousness and this is a direct enemy of love as you are shown more fully in the teaching of the Chaplain. But the woman should not consider it any reflection on her reputation, since any woman who wants to have the praise of the world must indulge in love, and it is not easy for anybody to examine a man's innermost faith and the secrets of his heart, and so we often find wisdom deceived under the cloak of many words. However, if the man does not return to his first love, but desires to stay in love with the second, the first has no cause for complaint against the other if she tries to cultivate his new-born love and allows another woman rather than herself to lose by his clever deception."

XIII. Another case comes up in this way: A certain knight, although he was lacking in every manly virtue so that every woman rejected him as a lover, so impudently demanded a certain lady's love that she granted him the hope of it. By her teaching she developed in this lover so good a character that she gave him a kiss and an embrace and through her he was brought to the highest excellence of conduct and was praised for all the good qualities. After he had been established as a pattern of virtue and a model of good manners, another lady strongly invited him to love her and the knight became wholly obedient to her will, forgetting, so it seems, the gift of the first lady.

On this point we have the response of the Countess of Flanders. She said: "We all think it commendable that the first lady should reclaim from the embraces of any other woman the lover whom she by great

---

[10] Isabelle (sometimes called Elizabeth) of Vermandois was a cousin of Countess Marie; she married Count Philip of Flanders in 1156 and died in 1182. See Introduction, p. 20.

industry raised from the depths of worthlessness to the height of courtesy and the summit of worthiness. We think that a woman has a just and reasonable claim upon a man whom she, by working with him, made worthy, after he had been worthless, and by laborious care made more honorable and set in the way of good manners."

XIV. A certain lady, while her lover was on an expedition overseas and she had no hope of his early return and nearly everybody had given up all hope that he would ever come, sought for herself another lover. But a confidant of the first lover, who was very much grieved by the lady's change of faith, forbade her this new love. The woman did not accept his advice and defended herself by saying, "If a woman who is left a widow by the death of her lover may seek a new love after two years have elapsed, this should be much more permissible for a woman who is left a widow while her lover is still alive and who for this length of time hasn't had the satisfaction of any messenger or letter from him, especially when there has been no lack of messengers." After the question had been disputed pro and con for a long time it was referred to the Countess of Champagne, who settled it with this decision. "It is not right for the lady to give up her love because her lover has been away for a long time (unless she knows that he was the first to fail in his love or that he has clearly been unfaithful) in cases in which it is obvious that his absence is due to necessity or to some especially praiseworthy cause. Nothing should bring more joy to the soul of a woman who is in love than to hear from distant regions the praise of her lover or to know that he is respected by honorable assemblages of great men. That he is said to have refrained from communicating with her by letters or messengers may be considered great prudence on his part, since he may not reveal this secret to any third party. If he had sent letters, even though their contents were kept secret from the bearer, it might easily happen, through the wickedness of the bearer or because he died on the journey, that the secret of their love would be made public."

XV. Still another love case came up. A certain lover, when he has lost an eye or some other ornament of his body while fighting bravely, is rejected by his loved one as unworthy and loathsome, and she denies him the customary embraces. Opposed to this woman is the opinion of the lady of Narbonne, who said on the subject: "We think that a woman is unworthy of any honor if she has decided that her lover ought to be deprived of her love because of some deformity resulting from the common chance of war, which is apt to happen to those who fight bravely. Ordinarily the bravery of men very much incites the love of women and makes them retain this love for a long time. Why, then, should some deformity of the members which naturally and inevitably results from this bravery afflict a lover with the loss of his love?"

XVI. Another problem of this kind was brought before them. A certain knight was suing for a woman's love, and he did not have frequent opportunities of speaking to her, so with the woman's consent he chose a go-between for this purpose, that with his help each of them might the more easily know the other's wishes and in greater secrecy make known his own and that the love between them might forever be managed in even greater secrecy. This go-between accepted the office of legate, but broke faith with his confederate, took upon himself the name of lover, and commenced to look out for himself. The lady in the case had the bad taste to assent to his fraud, and finally she consummated love with him and fulfilled all his wishes. But the knight was wrought up over the fraud and told the whole course of the affair to the Countess of Champagne, asking that the culprit be tried by her decision and that of the other ladies. Even the wrongdoer praised the Countess's verdict. She summoned sixty ladies to her assistance and settled the matter with this decision: "Let that crafty lover who has found a woman suited to his deserts, one who wasn't ashamed to accept so great a villain, enjoy his evilly acquired love if he wants to, and let her enjoy the kind of lover she deserves. But let both be forever deprived of the love of any other person, and let neither be invited henceforward to gatherings of ladies or courts of knights, because he has acted contrary to the honesty of the order of knighthood and she, contrary to the decency of ladies, has disgracefully assented to the love of a go-between."

XVII. Again. A certain knight was in love with a woman who had given her love to another man, but he got from her this much hope of her love—that if it should ever happen that she lost the love of her beloved, then without a doubt her love would go to this man. A little while after this the woman married her lover. The other knight then demanded that she give him the fruit of the hope she had granted him, but this she absolutely refused to do, saying that she had not lost the love of her lover. In this affair the Queen [11] gave her decision as follows: "We dare not oppose the opinion of the Countess of Champagne, who ruled that love can exert no power between husband and wife.[12] Therefore we recommend that the lady should grant the love she has promised."

XVIII. A certain knight shamefully divulged the intimacies and the secrets of his love. All those who were serving in the camp of Love demanded that this offense should be most severely punished, lest if so serious a transgression went unavenged, the example might give occasion to others to do likewise. A court of ladies was therefore assembled in Gascony, and they decided unanimously that forever after he should be deprived of all hope of love and that in every court of ladies or of knights he should be an object of contempt and abuse to all. And if any woman should dare to violate this rule of the ladies, for example by giving him her love, she should be subject to the same punishment, and should henceforth be an enemy of all honest women.

XIX. Another decision very properly belongs with these. A certain knight asked for the love of a certain lady, and she absolutely refused to love him. The knight sent her some rather handsome presents, and these she accepted with eager face and greedy heart; she did not, however, grow any more yielding in the matter of love, but gave him a

[11] Probably Adèle of Champagne, third wife of King Louis of France; she married in 1165 and was left a widow in 1180.

[12] See p. 106.

flat refusal. The knight complained that the woman, by accepting appropriate gifts, had given him a hope of love, which she was trying to take away from him without a cause. To those facts the Queen responded in this fashion. "Let a woman either decline gifts which are offered her with a view to love, or let her pay for them with her love, or let her suffer in patience being classed with the prostitutes."

XX. The Queen was also asked which was preferable: the love of a young man or of one advanced in years. She answered this question with wonderful subtlety by saying, "We distinguish between a good and a better love by the man's knowledge and his character and his praiseworthy manners, not by his age. But as regards that natural instinct of passion, young men are usually more eager to gratify it with older women than with young ones of their own age; those who are older prefer to receive the embraces and kisses of young women rather than of the older ones. But on the other hand a woman whether young or somewhat older likes the embraces and solaces of young men better than those of older ones. The explanation of this fact seems to be a physiological one."

XXI. The Countess of Champagne was also asked what gifts it was proper for ladies to accept from their lovers. To the man who asked this the Countess replied, "A woman who loves may freely accept from her lover the following: a handkerchief, a fillet for the hair, a wreath of gold or silver, a breastpin, a mirror, a girdle, a purse, a tassel, a comb, sleeves, gloves, a ring, a compact, a picture, a wash basin, little dishes, trays, a flag as a souvenir, and, to speak in general terms, a woman may accept from her lover any little gift which may be useful for the care of the person or pleasing to look at or which may call the lover to her mind, if it is clear that in accepting the gift she is free from all avarice. But we wish all of Love's knights to be taught that if a woman receives a ring from her lover as a pledge of love she ought to put it on her left hand and on her little finger, and she should always keep the stone hidden on the inside of her hand; this is because the left hand is usually kept freer from dishonesty and shameful contacts, and a man's life and death are said to reside more in his little finger than in the others,[13] and because all lovers are bound to keep their love secret. Likewise, if they correspond with each other by letter they should refrain from signing their own names. Furthermore, if the lovers should for any reason come before a court of ladies, the identity of the lovers should never be revealed to the judges, but the case should be presented anonymously. And they ought not to seal their letters to each other with their own seals unless they happen to have secret seals known only to themselves and their confidants. In this way their love will always be retained unimpaired."

CHAPTER VIII. THE RULES OF LOVE

Let us come now to the rules of love, and I shall try to present to you very briefly those rules which the King of Love is said to have proclaimed with his own mouth and to have given in writing to all lovers.

One of the knights of Britain was riding alone through the royal forest, going to see Arthur, and when he had got well into the interior of this forest he came unexpectedly upon a young girl of marvellous beauty, sitting on a fine horse and binding up her hair. The knight lost no time in saluting her, and she answered him courteously and said, "Briton, no matter how hard you try you can't succeed in your quest unless you have our help." When he had heard these words he quickly asked the girl to tell him what he had come for, and then after that he would believe what she said to him. The young girl said to him, "When you asked for the love of a certain British lady, she told you that you could never obtain it unless you first brought back that victorious hawk which, men say, is on a golden perch in Arthur's court."[14] The Briton admitted that all this was true, and the girl went on, "You can't

---

[13] John of Salisbury (*Policraticus* VI. xii) records this as a well-known tradition of the ancient Greeks, but he applies it to the finger next to the little finger.

[14] For a list of parallel incidents see the note by William Albert Nitze in *Modern Philology*, XI (1914), 450–51.

get this hawk that you are seeking unless you prove, by a combat in Arthur's palace, that you enjoy the love of a more beautiful lady than any man at Arthur's court has; you can't even enter the palace until you show the guards the hawk's gauntlet, and you can't get this gauntlet except by overcoming two mighty knights in a double combat."

The Briton answered, "I know that I cannot accomplish this task without your aid, and so I will submit myself to your direction, humbly beseeching you to give me your help in the matter and to permit me to claim, in view of the fact that you are directing me, that I enjoy the love of the more beautiful lady."

The young girl said to him, "If your heart is so stout that you are not afraid to carry out those things of which we have spoken, you may have from us what you ask." The Briton answered, "If you will grant my request, I know that I shall succeed in all that I hope for."

The young girl said to him, "Then let what you request be freely granted to you." Then she gave him the kiss of love and said, indicating the horse on which she was sitting, "This horse will take you everywhere you want to go; but you must go forward without any fear and oppose with the highest courage all those who try to stop you. But bear in mind that after you have gained the victory over the first two who defend the gauntlet you must not accept it from them, but must take it for yourself from the golden pillar where it hangs; otherwise you cannot prevail in the combat at the palace or accomplish what you desire."

When she finished speaking, the Briton put on his arms and, after she had given him leave to depart, began to go at a walk through the wood. At length, as he was passing through a wild and lonely place, he came to a certain river of marvellous breadth and depth, with great waves in it, and because of the great height of its banks it was impossible for anyone to reach it. But as he rode along the edge of the bank he came to a bridge which was of gold and had one end fastened to each bank; the middle of it, however, rested in the water, and he could see that it was so shaken that great waves often covered it. At that end of it which the Briton was approaching there was a knight of a ferocious aspect who was sitting on a horse. The Briton greeted him courteously enough, but the knight scorned to return the greeting and said, "Armed Briton, who come from such distant regions, what are you seeking?"

The Briton answered, "I am trying to cross the river by the bridge"; and the bridge keeper said, "Then you must be seeking death, which no stranger here has been able to escape. But if you want to go back home and leave all your arms here, I will take pity on your youth which has led you so rashly and so foolishly into other men's countries and into strange realms."

The Briton replied, "If I were to lay down my arms, you would gain little credit for the victory of a man in arms over an unarmed man; but if you can keep an armed man from going along the public way, then you may consider that your victory has won you glory. If you do not make way peaceably for me to go across the bridge, I shall simply try to force a passage with my sword."

When the bridge keeper heard that the young man was trying to force a passage with his sword, he began to gnash his teeth, and he fell into a great rage and said, "Young man, Britain sent you here in an evil hour, since you shall perish by the sword in this wilderness, and you will never be able to bring back news of the country to your lady. Woe to you, wretched Briton, who have not been afraid to seek the place of your death at the persuasion of a woman!" Then spurring his horse against the Briton he began to attack him with his sharp sword and to hammer him so cruelly that one stroke, glancing off his shield, cut through two folds of his hauberk and into the flesh of his side so that the blood commenced to flow in abundance from the wound. The young man, stung by the pain of his wound, directed the point of his lance at the knight of the bridge, and with a mighty thrust pierced him through, bore him from his horse, and stretched him shamefully upon the ground. But when the Briton was about to smite off his head, the bridge keeper, by the most humble entreaties, sought and obtained mercy.

But on the other side of the river there stood a man of tremendous size, who, seeing the bridge keeper overcome by the Briton and this same Briton starting to cross the golden bridge, began to shake it so violently that much of the time it was hidden by the waves. But the Briton, having great confidence in the excellence of his horse, did not cease to press forward manfully over the bridge, and at length, after great difficulty and many duckings, he arrived at the farther end of it by virtue of his horse's efforts; there he drowned beneath the water the man who had been shaking the bridge and bound up the wound in his own side as well as he could.[15]

After this the Briton began to ride through very beautiful fields, and after he had ridden for about a mile [16] the path came out into a pleasant meadow, fragrant with all sorts of flowers. In this meadow was a palace, marvellously built in a circular form and very beautifully decorated. He could not find a door anywhere in the palace, nor could he see any inhabitants; but in the fields he found silver tables, and on them were all sorts of food and drink set among snow-white napkins. In the same pleasant meadow was a shell of the purest silver in which there was sufficient food and drink for a horse. He therefore drove his horse off to feed, and he himself walked completely around the palace; but finding no sign of any entrance to the dwelling or any evidence that the place was inhabited, he drew near to the table and, driven by his hunger, began ravenously to devour the food he found there. A very little while after he had begun to eat, a door of the palace opened quickly with such violence that the shock of it resounded like near-by thunder, and suddenly out of this door came a man of gigantic size, brandishing in his hands a copper club of immense weight,

[15] Helaine Newstead (*Bran the Blessed*, New York, Columbia University Press, 1939, p. 141) suggests that this is the story to which Chrétien referred in *The Knight of the Cart*, ll. 670–71, but which he did not tell.

[16] Ten stades.

which he shook like a straw without the least effort. To the youth at the table he said, "What sort of man are you, so presumptuous that you were not afraid to come to this royal place and so coolly and disrespectfully to eat the food on the royal table of the knights?" [17]

The Briton answered, "The royal table should be freely open to everybody, and it is not proper that anybody should be refused the royal food and drink. Moreover it is right for me to partake of the rations prepared for the knights, since knighthood is my sole care and a knightly task has brought me to this place. You are therefore doubly discourteous in trying to forbid me the royal table."

To this the doorkeeper replied, "Although this is the royal table, it is not proper for anyone to eat at it except those who are assigned to this palace, and they allow no one to go beyond this point unless he fights with the palace guards and defeats them. And if anyone is beaten by them, there is no hope for him. Therefore get up from the table and hurry back to where you belong, or tell me that you want to fight your way onward and why you have come this far."

The Briton said to him, "I am seeking the hawk's gauntlet; that is why I came. When I get it I shall try to go further and as victor in Arthur's court take the hawk. Where is this palace guard you mention who will keep me from going on?"

The doorkeeper replied, "You fool! What madness possesses you, Briton! It would be easier for you to die and come to life again ten times than to get those things you mention. I am the palace guard who will deprive you of your reputation and spoil Britain of your youth. I am so strong that when I an angry two hundred of the best knights of Britain can hardly withstand me."

The Briton answered, "Although you say you are very powerful, I would like to fight with you to show you what sort of men Britain produces; however, it isn't proper for a knight to fight with a footman."

[17] Miss Newstead (*op. cit.*, p. 142) suggests that this giant is derived (although not directly) from Welsh legends concerning Bran. Thomas Jones (in his review in *Modern Language Review*, XXXV, 402–4) points out that Bran was sometimes called "Brangaled," which means "Bran the Niggardly."

The doorkeeper said to him, "I see that your bad luck has brought you to death in this place where my right hand has felled more than a thousand. And although I am not reckoned among the knights, I would like to fight with you while you are on horseback, because then if you yield to the valor of a footman you will have good reason to know what sort of person would be overcome by the boldness of a man like me if I were on horseback."

To this the Briton answered, "God forbid that I should ever fight on horseback against a man on foot, for against a foot soldier every man should fight on foot," and grasping his arms he rushed bravely at the enemy before him and with a blow of his sword slightly damaged the latter's shield. The guardian of the palace, greatly enraged at this and contemptuous of the Briton's small size, shook his brazen club so furiously that the Briton's shield was almost shattered by the concussion, and he himself was greatly terrified. Thinking that a second blow would finish the Briton, the guard raised his hand to strike again, but before the blow could fall the other quickly feinted and with his sword caught him on the arm, so that the right hand, still holding the club, fell to the ground. But as he was about to put an end to him, the guard cried out, "Are you the one discourteous knight that sweet Britain has produced, you who would slay a wounded man? If you will spare my life I can easily get for you what you want, but without me you can gain nothing."

The Briton said, "Porter, I will spare your life if you will do what you promise."

The guard said, "Wait a bit and I will quickly get you the hawk's gauntlet."

The Briton answered, "You robber and deceiver of men! Now I see plainly that you are trying to cheat me. If you want to save your life just show me the place where that gauntlet of yours is kept."

The guard then led the Briton into the innermost part of the palace where there was a very beautiful golden column that held up the whole weight of the palace, and on this column hung the gauntlet he was seeking. As he grasped it boldly and held it firmly in his left hand he heard a great noise, and although he saw nobody, a wailing began to resound throughout the palace, and a cry, "Woe! woe! in spite of us the victor enemy is carrying away the spoil."

He left the palace and, mounting his horse which was already saddled, continued his journey until he came to a delightful place where there were more of those beautiful fields filled with flowers, and in the fields was a palace finely built of gold. Its length was six hundred cubits, and its width two hundred. The roof and all the outer walls were of silver, and the inside was all of gold set with precious stones. The palace was divided into a great many rooms, and in the hall of state King Arthur was sitting on a golden throne surrounded by beautiful women, more than I could count, and before him stood many splendid knights. In this palace was a beautifully fashioned golden perch on which was the hawk he was seeking, and chained near by lay two hawking dogs. But before he could get to the palace his way was blocked by a heavily fortified barbican, raised to protect the palace, and to the defense of it were assigned twelve very strong knights who permitted no one to pass unless he showed them the gauntlet for the hawk or forced his way sword in hand.

When the Briton saw them, he quickly showed them the gauntlet and they fell back, saying, "Your life isn't safe if you go on this way; it will lead you to great trouble." But the Briton continued on to the interior of the palace and saluted King Arthur. When the knights pressed him to know why he had come there, he replied that he had come to carry off the hawk. One of the knights of the court asked him, "Why are you trying to get the hawk?" and he replied, "Because I enjoy the love of a more beautiful woman than any knight in this court has." The other answered him, "Before you can take away the hawk you will have to fight to prove that statement." "Gladly!" said the Briton. After a suitable shield had been given him both took their places armed within the lists; setting spurs to their horses, they rushed together violently, shattering each other's shields and splintering their lances; then with their swords they smote each other and hewed to pieces the iron armor. After they had fought in this fashion for a long time, the vision of the knight of the palace, whom the Briton had struck on the head with two shrewd blows in rapid succession, began to be so disturbed that he could see almost nothing. When the Briton perceived this, he leapt boldly upon him and quickly struck him, beaten, from his horse. Then he seized the hawk, and, glancing as he did so at the two dogs, he saw a written parchment, which was fastened to the perch with a little gold chain. When he inquired carefully concerning this, he was told, "This is the parchment on which are written the rules of love which the King of Love himself, with his own mouth, pronounced for lovers. You should take it with you and make these rules known to lovers if you want to take away the hawk peaceably." He took the parchment, and after he had been given courteous permission to depart, quickly returned, without any opposition, to the lady of the wood, whom he found in the same place in the grove where she was when he first came upon her as he was riding along. She rejoiced greatly over the victory he had gained and dismissed him with these words, "Dearest friend, go with my permission, since sweet Britain desires you. But, that your departure may not seem too grievous to you, I ask you to come here sometimes alone, and you can always have me with you." He kissed her thirteen times over and went joyfully back to Britain. Afterward he looked over the rules which he had found written in the parchment, and then, in accordance with the answer he had previously received, he made them known to all lovers. These are the rules.

    I. Marriage is no real excuse for not loving.

   II. He who is not jealous cannot love.

  III. No one can be bound by a double love.

  IV. It is well known that love is always increasing or decreasing.

   V. That which a lover takes against the will of his beloved has no relish.

  VI. Boys do not love until they arrive at the age of maturity.

VII. When one lover dies, a widowhood of two years is required of the survivor.

VIII. No one should be deprived of love without the very best of reasons.

IX. No one can love unless he is impelled by the persuasion of love.

X. Love is always a stranger in the home of avarice.

XI. It is not proper to love any woman whom one would be ashamed to seek to marry.

XII. A true lover does not desire to embrace in love anyone except his beloved.

XIII. When made public love rarely endures.

XIV. The easy attainment of love makes it of little value; difficulty of attainment makes it prized.

XV. Every lover regularly turns pale in the presence of his beloved.

XVI. When a lover suddenly catches sight of his beloved his heart palpitates.

XVII. A new love puts to flight an old one.[18]

XVIII. Good character alone makes any man worthy of love.

XIX. If love diminishes, it quickly fails and rarely revives.

XX. A man in love is always apprehensive.

XXI. Real jealousy always increases the feeling of love.

XXII. Jealousy, and therefore love, are increased when one suspects his beloved.

XXIII. He whom the thought of love vexes eats and sleeps very little.

XXIV. Every act of a lover ends in the thought of his beloved.

XXV. A true lover considers nothing good except what he thinks will please his beloved.

XXVI. Love can deny nothing to love.

XXVII. A lover can never have enough of the solaces of his beloved.

[18] Compare Cicero *Tusculan Disputations* IV. xxxv.

XXVIII. A slight presumption causes a lover to suspect his beloved.

XXIX. A man who is vexed by too much passion usually does not love.

XXX. A true lover is constantly and without intermission possessed by the thought of his beloved.

XXXI. Nothing forbids one woman being loved by two men or one man by two women.

These rules, as I have said, the Briton brought back with him on behalf of the King of Love to the lady for whose sake he endured so many perils when he brought her back the hawk. When she was convinced of the complete faithfulness of this knight and understood better how boldly he had striven, she rewarded him with her love. Then she called together a court of a great many ladies and knights and laid before them these rules of Love, and bade every lover keep them faithfully under threat of punishment by the King of Love. These laws the whole court received in their entirety and promised forever to obey in order to avoid punishment by Love. Every person who had been summoned and had come to the court took home a written copy of the rules and gave them out to all lovers in all parts of the world.

BOOK THREE

The Rejection of Love

Now, FRIEND WALTER, if you will lend attentive ears to those things which after careful consideration we wrote down for you because you urged us so strongly, you can lack nothing in the art of love, since in this little book we gave you the theory of the subject, fully and completely, being willing to accede to your requests because of the great love we have for you. You should know that we did not do this because we consider it advisable for you or any other man to fall in love, but for fear lest you might think us stupid; we believe, though, that any man who devotes his efforts to love loses all his usefulness. Read this little book, then, not as one seeking to take up the life of a lover, but that, invigorated by the theory and trained to excite the minds of women to love, you may, by refraining from so doing, win an eternal recompense and thereby deserve a greater reward from God. For God is more pleased with a man who is able to sin and does not, than with a man who has no opportunity to sin.

Now for many reasons any wise man is bound to avoid all the deeds of love and to oppose all its mandates. The first of these reasons is one which it is not right for anyone to oppose, for no man, so long as he devotes himself to the service of love, can please God by any other works, even if they are good ones. For God hates, and in both testaments commands the punishment of,[1] those whom he sees engaged in the works of Venus outside the bonds of wedlock or caught in the toils of any sort of passion. What good therefore can be found in a thing in which nothing is done except what is contrary to the will of God? Alas what

[1] Lev. 20:10; Prov. 6:32; Apocalypse 21:8.

an affliction it is and what bitterness to our hearts when we grieve constantly to see men reject the things of heaven for the sake of the foul and shameful acts of Venus! O wretched and insane, to be looked upon as lower than a beast, is that man who for the sake of a momentary delight of the flesh will reject eternal joys and strive to hand himself over to the flames of ever-burning Gehenna! So, Walter, you can see, and you are clever enough to understand, how much honor a man deserves who because of his fondness for some light woman scorns heaven's King and pays no attention to His commandments, and does not fear to enmesh himself in the toils of his ancient enemy. For if God had wished the act of fornication to be without blame, he would have had no reason to order the solemnization of marriage, since God's people could multiply faster without it than by marrying. We must therefore wonder at the folly of the man who because he embraces the lowest and most earthly love loses that eternal heritage which the heavenly King, with His own blood, restored to all men after it had been lost. Indeed, for a mortal man we consider it a very great disgrace and an offense against Almighty God if by following the enticements of the flesh and the pleasures of the body he slips back again into the snares of Hell, from which the Heavenly Father Himself once redeemed him by shedding the blood of His Only-Begotten Son.

We all know, moreover, that there is a second argument against love, for by it we injure our neighbor whom, according to the divine mandate, every man is bidden to love as himself.[2] But even without the divine mandate and considering only worldly convenience, we are bound to love our neighbors, for no one can get along without neighbors even for a short time.

There is still a third thing which persuades everybody to avoid love: by it one friend is estranged from another and serious unfriendlinesses grow up between men, and these even lead to homicide or many other evils. No one is so bound to another by the bonds of affection or friendship that if he finds out that the other man is suing urgently for the

[2] Luke 10: 27.

love of his wife or his daughter or some near relative he will not at once be filled with a spiteful hatred toward him or conceive a venomous anger. He who neglects the honor of his friend for the sake of serving the flesh is thought to live for himself alone, and so, it seems, every man should turn from him as an enemy of human kind and should flee from him as from a venomous beast. For what do we find so necessary or so useful to men as to have reliable friends? According to Cicero [3] not even the use of fire or water seems so necessary to men as to have the comfort of friends. If out of all mankind one finds a single friend, he has found something more precious than any treasure, since there is nothing in the world so valuable that it can be compared to a real friend. Many, however, are called by the name "friend" who lack the quality that the name denotes, for their friendship is dissolved by the accidents of time. But a true friend becomes even more faithful in his friend's adversities and more constant in every misfortune. It is to this sort of thing that the old saying refers:

While you are fortunate you will number many friends,
  When the skies grow dark you will be alone. [4]

The eloquent Tully shows you in his book on friendship what is the value of a true friend and how useful he is. From this you can clearly see the utility and the convenience of friendship, and how little reputation, and of what sort, a man deserves to have among his fellow men if he makes friendship secondary to wallowing in the pleasures of the flesh.

Still another argument forbids us to indulge in the crime of love. Although all sins, by their very nature, stain the soul, this is the only one that defiles both body and soul, [5] and therefore it is more to be avoided than any of the others; clearly, then, it is not without reason that the divine authority declares there is no sin more serious than fornication.

---

[3] *On Friendship*, sec. 22.   [4] Ovid *Tristia* I. ix. 5–6.
[5] "Other sins stain the soul alone . . . fornication stains not only the soul but the body." Peter Lombard *Commentary on First Corinthians* vi. 18.

But it seems that there is still another reason why we should avoid love. The man who is in love is bound in a hard kind of slavery and fears that almost anything will injure this love of his, and his soul is very much upset by a slight suspicion, and his heart is greatly troubled within him. Because of love's jealousy he is afraid every time his beloved talks with any other man, or goes walking with one, or stays out of sight longer than usual, because "Love is a thing full of anxious fear." [6] He does not dare to do or to think anything that is in the least contrary to what his beloved wants, because a lover is always afraid that his beloved may change her desire for him, or her faithfulness, and whether waking or sleeping a lover can never get rid of this thought. He whom the sword of Love has really wounded is shaken all the time by the constant thought of his beloved, and he cannot be happy over wealth, or any honor in the world, or any dignity, so much as he is if he really enjoys his love just as his soul desires it. For even if a lover should gain the whole world, but suffer some detriment or hindrance in his love, he would look upon all the rest as the deepest poverty, but he would think that no penury could harm him so long as his love was as he wished it to be. A lover is afraid to do or to say anything which might for any reason make his beloved angry or give her a grievance against him. Who, then, is so foolish and mad as to try to get that which forces a man into such cruel servitude to another person and submits him to her will in everything? Besides, even if your friend happens not to be offended by your love because it is directed toward some person in whom he is not interested, still he can never feel real friendship for you until true love dominates him too. For he whom Love's darts hit thinks about nothing else, and he does not think that anything is of any use to him except to please his beloved and be always devoted to her service, and he renders a poor return to his friend whom, in his love, he neglects or loses. That wretch is considered to live only for himself and his beloved who neglects being useful or friendly to everyone else and puts all his reliance on

[6] Ovid *Heroides* I. 12.

the love of one woman; so with good reason he should be dropped by all his friends, and all men should avoid him.

There is yet another argument that seems hostile to the lover. From love comes hateful poverty, and one comes to the prison of penury. For love inevitably forces a man to give without regard to what he should give and what he should not; and this is not generosity, but what ancient common sense calls prodigality,[7] a vice which sacred Scripture teaches us is a mortal one [8]—one for which no abundance of goods can suffice—and thus it brings every man, regardless of who he is, to the depths of poverty. Thus it forces a man to pile up wealth, honestly or dishonestly, so that his poverty may have something on which to feed his love [9] and something to keep his honor unharmed in the world. For if a man who is used to having plenty of money or to enjoying the pleasures of the flesh and the world afterwards comes to the shades of want, the whole world seems dark to him, and he is not afraid to commit any crime in order to regain the fortune he has lost, so that he may indulge in pleasures like those he formerly enjoyed, and no one can think of a sin in the world that a lover would hesitate to commit if by so doing he could turn his poverty into wealth with which to feed his love. Be careful, therefore, not to seek such an antecedent cause, the consequences of which you cannot easily avoid.

You can see now what people will think of a man after he has committed robberies and thefts and other furtive and wicked acts and with what a face a man can mingle with men after he has been found guilty of any of these crimes. Besides, what renders a man more contemptible to other men than for him to be compelled to suffer the obscurities of poverty for the love of a woman?

There is another argument, weighty enough, which stands in the way of every lover, and this is that love brings intolerable torments to all men during their lifetimes, and after they are dead it makes them suffer infinitely greater ones. O what a marvellously good thing should

---

[7] Aristotle *Nicomachean Ethics* IV. sec. 1.   [8] Luke 15: 18, 21.

[9] Compare Ovid *The Cure for Love*, l. 749.

everybody consider that which promises to the living unremitting pain and threatens the dying with everlasting torment, and provides for all lovers that heritage which the Holy Scripture shows us is situated in outer darkness where there shall be weeping and gnashing of teeth! [10] If you will take my advice, Walter, you will leave good things like that for someone else. But although I have said a great deal about the pains that lovers suffer while still alive, I do not think that anybody can fully appreciate them unless he has been taught by experience.

Men maintain that there is still another reason why we should wholly avoid love; chastity and the restraining of carnal desires are reckoned among the virtues, and so their opposites, lust and the delight of the flesh, must necessarily be reckoned among the vices. Therefore every man must flee from them, because there is nothing that men more desire while they live on earth than to have a praiseworthy name among their fellows and to have their reputation spread widely throughout the world. But nobody can keep his reputation bright and unharmed or have a good name among men unless he is adorned with the virtues. And no one can have the adornment of the virtues if he is spotted with the tiniest black speck of vice, for virtue and vice "do not go well together or dwell in the same abode." [11] I will go even further and say that in old or young, clerk or layman, footman or knight, man or woman, men praise chastity and virtue and bodily purity and condemn the corruption of the flesh. For no man can gain the love of a woman of such an exalted position that his good name will not on this account suffer greatly, and with good reason, among good and prudent men in every court. Why then do you seek for love, when because of it you will be considered by God and men false and a blasphemer? Surely for no other reason than that you may lose God as well as your worldly reputation.

It is not considered to a woman's credit either if she begins to devote herself to the employments of love, even if she is loved by one of royal

---

[10] Matt. 8: 12; 22: 13; and 25: 30; Apocalypse 21: 8.
[11] Ovid *Metamorphoses* II. xiii. 846.

race. Indeed, although in men an excess of love or of lechery is tolerated on account of the boldness of the sex, in women it is considered a damnable offense; a woman's good name is ruined by it, and every wise person looks upon her as an unclean harlot and holds her in utter contempt.

And for still another reason we blame love; if you consider the thing rightly and trace it out diligently, you will find that there is not a criminal excess that does not follow from this same love. Now, it is admitted that homicide and adultery very often come from it; perjury, too, comes from it, because often when one betrays a woman with respect to love, he swears oaths which according to the rules of the holy fathers are to be considered, not as oaths, but rather as perjuries. That theft, too, comes from love is shown by the seventh of the reasons for rejecting love that we have already given. From it comes also false witness; there is no kind of lie that lovers will not tell when compelled by the necessity of love. That wrath, too, and likewise hate come from it is clear enough to everybody. It is admitted, too, that incest very often comes from it, for we cannot find a man so well versed in the divine mandates that if the evil spirit incites him to love he can keep under control his passion for women related to him by blood or marriage or for women dedicated to God, as we see from constant experience. Idolatry, too, very clearly comes from love, as is shown by the case of Solomon, the wisest of men, who from love of women did not fear to go after strange gods and like a beast make sacrifice to dumb idols.[12] If this could happen to a man whom God wished to have excel all others in the ripeness of his wisdom and in his temperateness, what protection can we have, who in comparison with him are considered ignorant and who live, as it were, under the guidance of someone else? For where you see green wood become dry, dry wood is consumed by the fire.

But still another argument seems very much opposed to love. Many evils come from love, but I do not see that anything that is good for

[12] III Kings (I Kings) 11: 1–10.

men comes from it; that delight of the flesh which we embrace with such great eagerness is not in the nature of a good, but rather, as men agree, it is a damnable sin which even in married persons is scarcely to be classed among the venial faults which are not sins, according to the word of the prophet, who said, "For behold I was conceived in iniquities and in sins did my mother conceive me." [13]

Again we confound love with an argument of this kind: Not only does love cause men to lose their celestial heritage, but it even deprives them of all honor in this world. For there is no cleric so noble or of such a distinguished family that he can easily attain honors in the church if it is known that he indulges in the rites of love and is devoted to the pleasures of the flesh; indeed he deserves to be deprived of all the honors he already has and to be looked upon by men as infamous. There is not even any layman with such a reputation for good sense and good character that he will not lose the good fame that he has and be considered unfit for any office of honor if he is found to be tainted with any vice of the flesh. So, too, a woman, no matter how noble, prudent, and beautiful she may be, is looked upon with contempt if she is known to have given her love to anyone, and every man of good character refuses to have anything to do with her.

Besides this we find that any lover is slow and lazy about everything except what may seem to be of service to his love. A man in love pays no attention to his own affairs or to those of any of his friends, and if anybody talks to him about something he has done he will not lend an attentive ear to what the man is saying, nor will he really hear the words of a suppliant unless the latter says something that has to do with his love. In such a case, however, you could talk to him for a whole month and he wouldn't miss one iota of what you said, for he is so eager to hear words about his beloved that he would never grow tired of listening, no matter how long you talk.

Besides this we know beyond a doubt that God Himself is the fountainhead and origin of chastity and of modesty, and from Scripture we

[13] Psalm 50: 7 (51: 5 in the Protestant version).

know that the Devil is really the author of love and lechery.[14] And so, because of their sources, we are bound forever to observe modesty and chastity and to shun lechery completely, because we agree that that which the Devil has given rise to cannot be at all wholesome for men or give them anything that we can praise. But that which God gives rise to can by no means result in anything that is bad for men or prove evil for them. You ought to know, then, what mental blindness a man suffers who leaves God's service and busies himself with that of the Devil. For the Devil promises to his soldiers many things, and pleasant ones, too, but afterwards he pays them with very bitter ones; he always does the opposite of what he has promised, since he has been a liar from the beginning and he stood not in the truth.[15] He is indeed in the habit of giving his servants a wretched retribution, for the more they serve him the greater are the torments that they deserve to earn from him and the greater the tortures they deserve to suffer. On the other hand, the more a man insults the Devil the more he sees him his subject. The Devil is also to be compared to a robber who offers to guide a traveler safely, and after he has taken pay for so doing leads him to a place where there are enemies and leaves him there, sharing the spoil and the booty with these enemies. In this way the Devil offers sweet and pleasant things to his soldiers and to those who want to follow after him, and somehow he makes them confident that they will have immunity from punishment and will enjoy a long life; then, after he has taken pay for his guidance—that is, when they are firmly bound to him by the sinners' coin—he leads them to a place of ambush —that is, to death—where the hostile snares of the demons are laid for mankind. There he leaves them in the toils of the enemy, and with this enemy he divides the spoils and the booty; because after he has led them by his frauds and tricks into hell and the power of the demons, then with the other powers of hell he afflicts them by the torments he

---

[14] St. Jerome, in his letter to Eustochium (xxii, 11) and in his various Biblical commentaries, points out that this is the meaning of Job 40:11 (40:16 in the Protestant version).

[15] John 8:44.

hands out to them. But God is not like this; in place of the good and pleasant things He has promised us, He gives us very much better and very much sweeter ones; because He is the Way, the Truth, and the Life,[16] and so with good reason He pays us more richly than He has promised to. Whoever will with full confidence entrust himself in His company will never fall into the toils of any enemy, but will be led safely to his desired goal and to eternal glory. With good reason, therefore, every man is bound to reject love and deeds of wantonness and to strive for complete bodily chastity.

Love, moreover, regularly leads men to deadly, inescapable warfare and does away with treaties of perpetual peace. Often, too, it overthrows great cities and mighty fortresses and the safest of castles and changes the good fortune of wealth into the evil fortune of poverty, even though a man may not give away anything that he has; and it drives many to commit crimes, which they must atone for, but of which neither they nor their relatives are by any means guilty.

Even more evils than this may be noticed in love, for love wickedly breaks up marriage and without reason turns a husband from his wife, whom God, in the law He gave us, firmly bade not to separate from her husband. For the Scripture says, "Whom God hath joined together, let not man put asunder." [17] Indeed, we have known many lovers who have been driven by love to think of killing their wives, and they have even put them to a very cruel death—a thing which all will agree is an infamous crime. A man ought not to love anything in this world as much as the wife to whom he is lawfully bound, for God has told us that the wife is one flesh with her husband, and he bade her, forsaking all others, to cleave only to him; for he said, "For this cause shall a man leave father and mother and shall cleave to his wife, and they two shall be in one flesh." [18] Besides, with a wife we overcome our passion without sinning, and we do away with the incentives to wanton-

[16] John 14 : 6.   [17] Matt. 19 : 6; Mark 10 : 9.
[18] Matt. 19 : 5–6; Mark 10 : 7–9.

ness without staining our souls; and we have by our wives legitimate
offspring who will worthily comfort us both living and dying, and
in them God can see that we bear Him worthy fruit. But even if at
times a man does get offspring through fornication, such a son can
be of no comfort to his father, since he cannot even inherit from him.
Indeed, the Scriptures tell us that sons born of fornication are the
shame of their parent, and we do not think that they are acceptable to
God; Holy Scripture seems to make this clear to us when it says, "The
sons of adulterers are abominable to God." [19]

Since, then, all sorts of wickednesses come from love and nothing
good can be found to spring from it, but only untold torments for mankind—why, O foolish young man, do you seek to love and to deprive
yourself of the grace of God and of your everlasting heritage? You
must learn, then, dearest of friends, to retain your purity of body and
to overcome the pleasures of the flesh by strength of character and to
keep your vessel unspotted for the Lord.[20] Even though you may be of
so ardent a nature that it seems to you too hard a thing to keep your
body pure, still, if you will give heed to my advice it will straightway
be easy for you to embrace bodily continence and chastity, and you can,
without great difficulty, turn your back upon carnal pleasures. Never
let your thoughts, therefore, lead you to the delight of the flesh, and
always take care wholly to avoid places, times, and persons which may
excite your passions or give occasion for lust. If a convenient place and
some unexpected happening urge you on to the work of the flesh by
putting the thought of some woman into your head, be careful to restrain your passion like a man and to get away from the tempting place.
Even if carnal incitements have commenced to vex you, take care that
they do not lead you to action, or that the combination of circumstances
does not cause you to sin. If you prove faithful and victorious a few
times in the conflict with lust, you will rarely, if ever, be troubled by
it after that. For lust is the sort of thing that overcomes us if we follow

[19] Possibly Ecclus. 41: 8.   [20] I Thess. 4: 3–4.

it, but is driven away if we flee from it.[21] It will therefore be easy for you to avoid its assaults if you will give sincere attention to what we have said. We hope that your noble birth and excellence of character may never be spotted by the infection of Venus or stained by illicit commerce with a woman or soiled with her filthiness, for there is nothing in the world more loathsome or more wearisome than to meditate too intently on the nature or the characteristics of a woman.

But let us pass by these things for the present, lest we be thought in some way to accuse nature and also because they are clear enough to any sensible man. Our present intention is merely to dissuade you wholly from love and to advise you to keep your body chaste. If with divine help we can accomplish our design, you must realize that nothing could happen to us in this life that would please us better, because bodily purity and fleshly abstinence are things that every man should have in the presence of God and of men, and he should preserve them by all means, because if they are neglected no good in a man can be completely perfect. But if it is known that any man has these virtues, a great many excesses are overlooked in him and even manifold crimes are tolerated. If a man proves to be chaste and generous, he is not easily harmed by the detractions of anyone else or deprived of the praise that is due him. You will be wise, therefore, if you make great efforts to attain that which adorns all the good qualities that are to be found in a man, and has the power to cover up many excesses in anyone. Do not be surprised that I said "chaste" and added "and generous," for without generosity all virtue in a man seems to lie dead and to bear no fruit of praise according to the word of the Apostle James, who said, "All faith without works is dead." [22] So, too, all virtue without generosity is considered nothing.

Another argument, too, seems clearly to oppose lovers. By love and

---

[21] "We must fight lust in Parthian fashion; as the Parthians put their enemies to flight by fleeing and conquer by turning their backs, so lust must be fought by fleeing and vanquished by retreating." Alanus de Insulis *Epitome of the Art of Preaching*, chap. v.

[22] Jas. 2: 20.

the work of Venus men's bodies are weakened, and so they are made less powerful in warfare. By love men are weakened in three very logical ways: by the mere act of Venus, as the physiologists tell us, the powers of the body are very much lessened; love causes one to eat less and drink less, and so not unreasonably the body, being less nourished, has less strength; finally, love takes away a man's sleep and deprives him of all rest. But lack of sleep is followed in a man by bad digestion and great weakening of the body, as we can see from the rational physiological definition of the word sleep, for, as Johannicius [23] says, "Sleep is a rest of the animal powers with an intensification of the natural powers," and therefore lack of sleep is merely a wearying of the animal powers with weakening of the natural ones. In a fourth way, too, it may not unfittingly be said that the human body is weakened, for we believe that through sin all of God's gifts in a man are lessened and the span of man's life is shortened. Since, therefore, bodily strength is a great and especial gift to man, you will do wrong if you strive after things which can for any reason cause this particular gift to fail in you or to be in any way decreased. But from love come not only the things we have mentioned, but bodily sickness also; for a bad digestion upsets the humors within us, and so fevers and numberless illnesses arise. The loss of sleep also causes frequent alterations in the brain and in the mind, so that a man becomes raging mad. But too much brooding by day and by night, which all lovers indulge in, also brings on a certain weakness of the brain, and from this come many illnesses of the body. But I remember that I once found in certain medical books that because of the works of Venus men quickly grow old, and so I try by my entreaties to warn you not to love.

For yet another reason I urge you not to love: that is because in a wise man wisdom loses its function if he loves. No matter how full of wisdom any man may be, if he is seduced to the work of Venus he

[23] Honeïn-ben-Ishaq (809–873) wrote a sort of introduction to medicine, which developed into the much-read *Isagoge Iohannicii ad Artem Parvam Galeni*. According to Bossuat this passage is not found in Johannicius, but comes from Avicenna; Drouart la Vache's translation substitutes the name Avicenna for Johannicius in this passage.

cannot be moderate or restrain by his wisdom the impulse of wantonness or keep from doing things that lead to death. Indeed, it is said that wise men become more wild with love and indulge more ardently in the pleasures of the flesh than those who have less knowledge to control them. But wise men, after they have sinned in love are accustomed to despise the excesses of lust more than those who have little knowledge to support them. Who was filled with greater wisdom than Solomon, yet he sinned by wantoning beyond measure, and because of his love for women he did not fear to worship strange gods. And who was found greater or more famous for wisdom than David the Prophet, who, although he had innumerable concubines, lusted after the wife of Urias and dishonored her in adultery and like a perfidious homicide killed her husband? [24] What lover of women, then, can moderate his own desire if men so strong in the precepts of wisdom could make no use of it when the love of women was in question, and could not restrain their wantonness?

Again we confound lovers with another argument. The mutual love which you seek in women you cannot find, for no woman ever loved a man or could bind herself to a lover in the mutual bonds of love. For a woman's desire is to get rich through love, but not to give her lover the solaces that please him. Nobody ought to wonder at this, because it is natural. According to the nature of their sex all women are spotted with the vice of a grasping and avaricious disposition, and they are always alert and devoted to the search for money or profit. I have traveled through a great many parts of the world, and although I made careful inquiries I could never find a man who would say that he had discovered a woman who if a thing was not offered to her would not demand it insistently and would not hold off from falling in love unless she got rich gifts in one way or another. But even though you have given a woman innumerable presents, if she discovers that you are less attentive about giving her things than you used to be, or if she learns that you have lost your money, she will treat you like a

[24] II Kings (II Samuel), chap. 11.

perfect stranger who has come from some other country, and everything you do will bore her or annoy her. You cannot find a woman who will love you so much or be so constant to you that if somebody else comes to her and offers her presents she will be faithful to her love. Women have so much avarice that generous gifts break down all the barriers of their virtue. If you come with open hands, no women will let you go away without that which you seek; while if you don't promise to give them a great deal, you needn't come to them and ask for anything. Even if you are distinguished by royal honors, but bring no gifts with you, you will get absolutely nothing from them; you will be turned away from their doors in shame.[25] Because of their avarice all women are thieves, and we say they carry purses. You cannot find a woman of such lofty station or blessed with such honor or wealth that an offer of money will not break down her virtue, and there is no man, no matter how disgraceful and low-born he is, who cannot seduce her if he has great wealth. This is so because no woman ever has enough money—just as no drunkard ever thinks he has had enough to drink. Even if the whole earth and sea were turned to gold, they could hardly satisfy the avarice of a woman.

Furthermore, not only is every woman by nature a miser, but she is also envious and a slanderer of other women, greedy, a slave to her belly, inconstant, fickle in her speech, disobedient and impatient of restraint, spotted with the sin of pride and desirous of vainglory, a liar, a drunkard, a babbler, no keeper of secrets, too much given to wantonness, prone to every evil, and never loving any man in her heart.

Now woman is a miser, because there isn't a wickedness in the world that men can think of that she will not boldly indulge in for the sake of money, and, even if she has an abundance she will not help anyone who is in need. You can more easily scratch a diamond with your fingernail than you can by any human ingenuity get a woman to consent to giving you any of her savings. Just as Epicurus believed that the highest good lay in serving the belly, so a woman thinks that the only things

[25] Ovid *Art of Love* II. 279–280.

worth while in this world are riches and holding on to what she has. You can't find any woman so simple and foolish that she is unable to look out for her own property with a greedy tenacity, and with great mental subtlety get hold of the possessions of someone else. Indeed, even a simple woman is more careful about selling a single hen than the wisest lawyer is in deeding away a great castle. Furthermore, no woman is ever so violently in love with a man that she will not devote all her efforts to using up his property. You will find that this rule never fails and admits of no exceptions.

That every woman is envious is also found to be a general rule, because a woman is always consumed with jealousy over another woman's beauty, and she loses all pleasure in what she has. Even if she knows that it is the beauty of her own daughter that is being praised, she can hardly avoid being tortured by hidden envy. Even the neediness and the great poverty of the neighbor women seem to her abundant wealth and riches, so that we think the old proverb which says

> The crop in the neighbor's field is always more fertile,
> And your neighbor's cow has a larger udder.[26]

seems to refer to the female sex without any exceptions. It can hardly come to pass that one woman will praise the good character or the beauty of another, and if she should happen to do so, the next minute she adds some qualification that undoes all she has said in her praise.

And so it naturally follows that a woman is a slanderer, because only slander can spring from envy and hate. That is a rule that no woman ever wanted to break; she prefers to keep it unbroken. It is not easy to find a woman whose tongue can ever spare anybody or who can keep from words of detraction. Every woman thinks that by running down others she adds to her own praise and increases her own reputation—a fact which shows very clearly to everybody that women have very little sense. For all men agree and hold it as a general rule that words of

[26] Ovid *Art of Love* I. 349–350.

dispraise hurt only the person who utters them, and they detract from the esteem in which he is held; but no woman on this account keeps from speaking evil and attacking the reputation of good people, and so I think we must insist that no woman is really wise. Every quality that a wise man has is wholly foreign to a woman, because she believes, without thinking, everything she hears, and she is very free about insisting on being praised, and she does a great many other unwise things which it would be tedious for me to enumerate.

Every woman, likewise, is sullied by the vice of greediness, because every woman tries with all her might to get everything good for herself, not only from other men but even from a husband who is very suitable for her, and when she gets them she tries to keep them so that they are of no use to anybody. So great is the avarice by which women are dominated that they think nothing of running counter to the laws, divine and human, and they try to enrich themselves at the expense of others. Indeed, women think that to give to no one and to cling with all their might to everything, whether rightly or wrongly acquired, is the height of virtue and that all men ought to commend it. To this rule there are no exceptions, not even in the case of the Queen.

Woman is also such a slave to her belly that there is nothing she would be ashamed to assent to if she were assured of a fine meal, and no matter how much she has she never has any hope that she can satisfy her appetite when she is hungry; she never invites anybody to eat with her, but when she eats she always seeks out hidden and retired places and she usually likes to eat more than normal. But although in all other respects those of the feminine sex are miserly and hold with might and main to what they have, they will greedily waste their substance to gobble up food, and no one ever saw a woman who would not, if tempted, succumb to the vice of gluttony. We can detect all these qualities in Eve, the first woman, who, although she was created by the hand of God without man's agency, was not afraid to eat the forbidden fruit and for her gluttony was deservedly driven from her home in Paradise.[27] So if that woman who was created by the hand of God without sin could not refrain from the vice of gluttony, what about the others whom their mothers conceived in sin and who never live free from fault? Therefore let it be laid down for you as a general rule that you will rarely fail to get from a woman anything you desire if you will take the trouble to feed her lavishly and often.

Woman is commonly found to be fickle, too, because no woman ever makes up her mind so firmly on any subject that she will not quickly change it on a little persuading from anyone. A woman is just like melting wax, which is always ready to take a new form and to receive the impress of anybody's seal. No woman can make you such a firm promise that she will not change her mind about the matter in a few minutes. No woman is ever of the same mind for an hour at a time, so that Martianus had good reason to say, "Come now, cease your delay, for a woman is always fickle and changeable." [28] Therefore you must not hope to get any satisfaction from any woman's promise unless you are sure you already have the thing she promises you; it is not expedient to rely upon the civil law for what a woman promises, but you should always bring your bag with you, ready to take it. When dealing with women there seems to be no exception to that old saying, "Don't delay; putting off things you are ready for always does harm." [29]

We know that everything a woman says is said with the intention of deceiving, because she always has one thing in her heart and another on her lips. No man can pride himself on knowing a woman so well or on being on such good terms with her that he can know her secret thoughts or when she means what she says. No woman ever trusts any of her men friends, and she thinks every one of them is a

[27] "Adam, set in Paradise, lost the glory of immortality through gluttony. . . . Adam was made of mud by the hands of God." Augustine *Sermon cxlvii* (referring to Genesis iii. 17).

[28] The passage comes ultimately from Vergil's *Aeneid* IV. 569; Trojel says that he has been unable to find the passage in the works of Martianus Capella.

[29] The passage is from Lucan's *Pharsalia* I. 281, but it is quoted by Hildebert of Le Mans in his *Moral Philosophy* (I. 28), from which Andreas seems to get other ideas.

downright deceiver; so she always keeps herself in the mood for deception, and everything she says is deceitful and uttered with a mental reservation. Therefore never rely upon a woman's promise or upon her oath, because there is no honesty in her; always be careful to keep your intentions hidden from her, and never tell her your secrets; in that way you may cheat one trick with another and forestall her frauds. Samson's good character is well enough known to everybody, but because he couldn't keep his secrets from a woman he was, we read, betrayed by her in the duplicity of her heart, was overcome by a troop of his enemies, and was captured and deprived of both his bodily strength and his eyesight.[30] We learn, too, of innumerable other women who, according to the stories, have shamefully betrayed husbands or lovers who were not able to keep secrets from them.

Every woman is likewise stained by the sin of disobedience, because there isn't in the world a woman so wise and discreet that, if anyone forbids her to misuse anything she will not strive against this prohibition with all her might and do what she is told not to. Therefore the remark of the wise man, "We strive for what is forbidden, and always want what is denied us,"[31] should be applied to all women without exception.

We read, too, of a very wise man who had a wife whom he hated. Because he wanted to avoid the sin of killing her with his own hand, and he knew that women always strive eagerly after what is forbidden them, he prepared a very valuable flask into which he put wine of the best and most fragrant kind, mixed with poison, and he said to his wife, "My sweetest wife, be careful not to touch this vessel, and don't venture to taste any of this liquor, because it is poisonous and deadly to human beings." But the woman scorned her husband's prohibition, for no sooner had he gone away than she drank some of the forbidden liquor and so died of the poison. But why should we mention this, since we know of worse cases? Wasn't it Eve, the first woman, who, although she was formed by the hand of God, destroyed herself by

[30] Judg. 16:15–21.   [31] Ovid *Amours* III. iv. 17.

the sin of disobedience and lost the glory of immortality and by her offense brought all her descendants to the destruction of death? Therefore if you want a woman to do anything, you can get her to do it by ordering her to do the opposite.

The feminine sex is also commonly tainted by arrogance, for a woman, when incited by that, cannot keep her tongue or her hands from crimes or abuse, but in her anger she boldly commits all sorts of outrages. Moreover, if anybody tries to restrain an angry woman, he will tire himself out with a vain labor; for though you may bind her, hand and foot, and fasten her into any kind of instrument of torture, you cannot keep her from her evil design or soften her arrogance of soul. Any woman is incited to wrath by a mild enough remark of little significance and indeed at times by nothing at all, and her arrogance grows to tremendous proportions; so far as I can recall no one ever saw a woman who could restrain it. And no woman has been found who is an exception to these rules.

Furthermore, every woman seems to despise all other women—a thing which we know comes only from pride. No man could despise another unless he looked down upon him because of pride. Besides, every woman, not only a young one but even the old and decrepit, strives with all her might to exalt her own beauty; this can come only from pride, as the wise man showed very clearly when he said, "There is arrogance in everybody and pride follows beauty." [32] Therefore it is perfectly clear that women can never have perfectly good characters, because, as they say, "A remarkable character is soiled by an admixture of pride." [33]

Vainglory also mightily possesses woman, since you cannot find a woman in the world who does not delight in the praise of men above everything else and who does not think that every word spoken about her has to do with her praise. This fault can be seen even in Eve, the first woman, who ate the forbidden food in order to have knowledge of good and evil. Furthermore, you cannot find a woman so lowly-born

---

[32] Ovid *Fasti* I. 419.   [33] Claudian *The Fourth Consulship of Honorius*, l. 305.

that she will not tell you she has famous relatives and is descended from a family of great men and who will not make all sorts of boasts about herself. These are the things that vainglory seeks for its own.

You will find, too, that every woman is a liar, because there isn't a woman living who doesn't make up things that are untrue and who doesn't boldly declare what is false. Even for a trifle a woman will swear falsely a thousand times, and for a tiny gain she will make up innumerable lies. Women indeed try by every means to support their lies, and they usually cover up the sin of one with that of others that are elaborately concocted. No man can have such a strong case against a woman that she will confess her fault unless she is caught in the very act.

Again, every woman is a drunkard, that is, she likes to drink wine. There is no woman who would blush to drink excellent Falernian with a hundred gossips in one day, nor will she be so refreshed by that many drinks of undiluted wine that she will refuse another if it is brought her. Wine that is turned she considers a great enemy, and a drink of water usually makes her sick. But if she finds a good wine with no water in it, she would rather lose a good deal of her property than forgo drinking her fill of that; therefore there is no woman who is not often subject to the sin of drunkenness.

Every woman is also loud-mouthed, since no one of them can keep her tongue from abuses, and if she loses a single egg she will keep up a clamor all day like a barking dog, and she will disturb the whole neighborhood over a trifle. When she is with other women, no one of them will give the others a chance to speak, but each always tries to be the one to say whatever is to be said and to keep on talking longer than the rest; and neither her tongue nor her spirit ever gets tired out by talking. We even see many women who are so anxious to talk that when they are alone they talk to themselves and speak out loud. A woman will boldly contradict everything you say, and she can never agree with anything, but she always tries to give her opinion on every subject.

Moreover, no woman knows how to keep a secret; the more she is told to keep it to herself, the harder she tries to tell it to everybody. No one to this day has been able to find a woman who could keep hidden anything confided to her, no matter how important it was or how much it seemed that to tell it would be the death of somebody. Whatever you intrust as a secret to the good faith of a woman seems to burn her very vitals until she gets the harmful secrets out of her. You cannot avoid this in a woman by ordering her to do the opposite, as in the case mentioned above, because every woman takes great pleasure in gossip; therefore be careful to keep your secret from every woman.

Every woman in the world is likewise wanton, because no woman, no matter how famous and honored she is, will refuse her embraces to any man, even the most vile and abject, if she knows that he is good at the work of Venus; yet there is no man so good at the work that he can satisfy the desires of any woman you please in any way at all.

Furthermore, no woman is attached to her lover or bound to her husband with such pure devotion that she will not accept another lover, especially if a rich one comes along, which shows the wantonness as well as the great avarice of a woman. There isn't a woman in this world so constant and so bound by pledges that, if a lover of pleasure comes along and with skill and persistence invites her to the joys of love, she will reject his entreaties—at any rate if he does a good deal of urging—or will defend herself against his importunity. No woman is an exception to this rule either. So you can see what we ought to think of a woman who is in fortunate circumstances and is blessed with an honorable lover or the finest of husbands, and yet lusts after some other man. But that is what a woman does who is too much troubled with wantonness.

Woman is also prone to every sort of evil. Whatever evil in this world is greatest, that any woman will commit without fear and for a trivial reason; by a little persuading anyone can easily incline her mind toward any evil. Besides there is not a woman living in this world, not even the Empress or the Queen, who does not waste her whole life on auguries and the various practitioners of divination, as the heathen do, and so long as she lives she persists in this credulousness and sins without measure again and again with the art of astrology. Indeed, no woman does anything without considering the proper day and hour for beginning it and without inaugurating it with incantations. They will not marry, or hold funeral rites for the dead, or start their sowing, or move into a new house, or begin anything else without consulting this feminine augury and having their actions approved by these witches. Therefore Solomon, that wisest of men, who knew all the evils and the misdeeds of womankind, made a general statement concerning their crimes and wickednesses when he said, "There is no good woman." [34] Why therefore, Walter, are you striving so eagerly to love that which is bad?

Indeed, a woman does not love a man with her whole heart, because there is no one of them who keeps faith with her husband or her lover; when another man comes along, you will find that her faithfulness wavers. For a woman cannot refuse gold or silver or any other gifts that are offered her, nor can she deny the solaces of her body when they are asked for. But since a woman knows that nothing so distresses her lover as to have her grant these to some other man, you can see how much affection she has for a man when, out of greed for gold or silver, she will give herself to a stranger or a foreigner and has no shame about upsetting her lover so completely and shattering the jewel of her own good faith. Moreover, no woman has such a strong bond of affection for a lover that if he ceases to woo her with presents she will not become luke-warm about her customary solaces and quickly become like a stranger to him. It doesn't seem proper, therefore, for any prudent man to fall in love with any woman, because she never keeps faith with any man; everybody knows that she ought to be spurned for the innumerable weighty reasons that have already been given.

Besides this there is another reason why Love seems very hateful,

[34] Perhaps Andreas has in mind Eccles. 7: 29.

and this is that he very often carries unequal weights [35] and always makes a man fall in love with some woman whom he cannot by any amount of solicitation obtain, since she does not return his love, not having been wounded by Cupid's arrow. Therefore you should not choose to commit yourself to him who compels you to seek with all your might something which he himself arranges shall be utterly denied you. If Love wanted to be considered a just ruler, he would make only those people fall in love who could, either at once or after a proper amount of suffering, have their love returned; since he does not do this, it would seem proper to refuse to enter into his service. It does not seem as though you ought to love the company of a man who would lead you forth to battle and then when the fighting begins go over to the enemy and help him to defend himself against you. Therefore it is not advisable, my respected friend, for you to waste your days on love, which for all the reasons already given we agree ought to be condemned. For if it deprives you of the grace of the Heavenly King, and costs you every real friend, and takes away all the honors of this world as well as every breath of praiseworthy reputation, and greedily swallows up all your wealth, and is followed by every sort of evil,[36] as has already been said, why should you, like a fool, seek for love, or what good can you get from it that will repay you for all these disadvantages? That which above all you seek in love—the joy of having your love returned—you can never obtain, as we have already shown, no matter how hard you try, because no woman ever returns a man's love. Therefore if you will examine carefully all the things that go to make up love, you will see clearly that there are conclusive reasons why a man is bound to avoid it with all his might and to trample under foot all its rules.

Now this doctrine of ours, which we have put into this little book

---

[35] See p. 47.

[36] "This [love] is a plague more pernicious than any monster, for it empties the purse, enervates the body, intoxicates the soul, weakens the dominion of the mind, stains the soul, destroys one's good name, offends one's neighbor, separates one from God." Alanus de Insulis *Epitome of the Art of Preaching*, chap. v.

for you, will if carefully and faithfully examined seem to present two different points of view. In the first part we tried to assent to your simple and youthful request and did not wish, on this subject, to give in to our indolence; so we set down completely, one point after another, the art of love, as you so eagerly asked us to do, and now that it is all arranged in the proper order, we hand it over to you. If you wish to practice the system, you will obtain, as a careful reading of this little book will show you, all the delights of the flesh in fullest measure; but the grace of God, the companionship of the good, and the friendship of praiseworthy men you will with good reason be deprived of, and you will do great harm to your good name, and it will be difficult for you to obtain the honors of this world.

In the latter part of the book we were more concerned with what might be useful to you, and of our own accord we added something about the rejection of love, although you had no reason to ask for it, and we treated the matter fully; perhaps we can do you good against your will. If you will study carefully this little treatise of ours and understand it completely and practice what it teaches, you will see clearly that no man ought to mis-spend his days in the pleasures of love. If you abstain from it, the Heavenly King will be more favorably disposed toward you in every respect, and you will be worthy to have all prosperous success in this world and to fulfill all praiseworthy deeds and the honorable desires of your heart, and in the world to come to have glory and life everlasting.

Therefore, Walter, accept this health-giving teaching we offer you, and pass by all the vanities of the world, so that when the Bridegroom cometh to celebrate the greater nuptials, and the cry ariseth in the night,[37] you may be prepared to go forth to meet Him with your lamps filled and to go in with Him to the divine marriage, and you will have no need to seek out in haste what you need for your lamps, and find it too late, and come to the home of the Bridegroom after the door is shut, and hear His venerable voice.

[37] Matt. 25: 6.

Be mindful, therefore, Walter, to have your lamps always supplied, that is, have the supplies of charity and good works. Be mindful ever to watch, lest the unexpected coming of the Bridegroom find you asleep in sins. Avoid then, Walter, practicing the mandates of love, and labor in constant watchfulness so that when the Bridegroom cometh He may find you wakeful; do not let worldly delight make you lie down in your sins, trusting to the youth of your body and confident that the Bridegroom will be late, since, as He tells us Himself, we know neither the day nor the hour.

BIBLIOGRAPHY

PRINTED EDITIONS

LATIN

1. Incipiunt tituli capitulorum tractatus amoris & de amoris remedio Andree capellani pape jnnocencij quarti. Et habet iiij. partes. [Page 3]. Tractatus amoris & de amoris remedio Andree capellani pape Jnnocencij quarti ad Gualterum. Incipit feliciter Et habet quatuor partes. (No date or place of publication is given, but the *Gesamtkatalog der Wiegendrucke*, item 1759, assigns it to C. W., in Strasburg, in 1473 or 1474.)

2. Erotica seu Amatoria Andreae Capellani regii vetustissimi scriptoris ad venerandum suum amicum Gvvalterum scripta, nunquam ante hac edita sed saepius a multis desiderata, nunc tandem fide diversorum MSS codicum in publicum emissa a Dethmaro Mulhero [Dietmar Müller] Dorpmundae [Dortmund], typis Westhovianis, anno Vna Caste et Vere aManDa [1610].

3. Erotica sive amatoria diu multumque desiderata iucundissimis historiis referta, cum frugifera amoris reprobatione. Denua à Detmaro Mulhero in publicum emissa. Tremoniae [Dortmund] 1614.

4. Andreae Capellani regii Francorum De amore libri tres. Recensuit E. Trojel. Havniae [Copenhagen] in Libraria Gadiana. 1892.

5. Andreae Capellani regii Francorum De amore libri tres. Text llatí publicat per Amadeu Pagès. Castelló de la Plana: [Sociedad Castellonense de Cultura], 1929.

5a. Item 5 was reprinted in the following year with the Catalan version. See item 17.

FRENCH

6. Fiebig, Werner, Das "Livre d'Enanchet" nach der einzigen Handschrift 2585 der Wiener Nationalbibliothek herausgegeben. Jena

& Leipzig: Gronau, 1938. "Berliner Beiträge zur romanische Philologie," Band 8.

7. Li Livres d'Amours de Drouart la Vache; texte établi d'après le manuscrit unique de la Bibliothèque de l'Arsenal par Robert Bossuat. Paris: Champion, 1926.

ITALIAN

8. Regole bellissime d'amore in modo di dialogo . . . Tradotte di Latino in volgare da . . . Angelo Ambrosini. Venetia, 1561.
9. Dialogo d'amore di M. Giovanni Boccaccio. Interlocutori: il signor Alcibiade e Filaterio giovane. Tradotto di latino in volgare da M. Angelo Ambrosini. Apud I. Barilettum. Venetiis, 1574.
10–14. This was reprinted in Venice by G. B. Bonfadino in 1586, 1592 and 1597, and in Paris by S. Thiboust in 1624. Trojel lists an edition in Venice in "MDCXI," which may be an error for 1592, as I have found no further trace of it.
15. Un Capitolo d'amor del Libro d'Amor di Mes. Andrea . . . ora per la prima volta interamente pubblicato, con una prefazione di V. Savorini. Bologna, 1876.

CATALAN

16. Regles de amor i parlament de un hom i una fembra, obra atribuïda al canceller Mossèn Domingo Mascó (segle XIV), ab un estudi crític de Eduard Julià. Castelló de la Plana: [Sociedad Castellonense de Cultura], 1926.
17. Andreae Capellani regii Francorum De amore libri tres. Text llatí amb la traducció catalana del segle XIV. Introducció i notes per Amadeu Pagès. Castelló de la Plana: [Sociedad Castellonense de Cultura], 1930.

GERMAN

18. Hie hebt sich an das bůch Ouidy von der liebe zů erwerben. auch die liebe zeuerschmehen Als doctor hartlieb vou [sic] latein zeteütsch

gepracht hat. durch bete vnd geschäffte eines fürsten von österreych als hernach geschriben steet.

[The colophon]: Gedruckt vnn volenndet in der keyserlichen statt augspurg von Anthoni Sorgen an der mittwochen vor sant Pauls bekerung tag Anno domini 7c̄ jm lxxxij jar.

This edition is in folio and has nineteen woodcut illustrations. See *Gesamtkatalog der Wiegendrucke,* item 1760.

19. Hie hebt sich an das bůch Ouidij die liebe zů erwerben. vnd ouch die liebe zů uerschmehen et cetera.

[Page ii]: Hie hebt sich an das bůch Ouidy von der lieb zů erwerben Ouch die lieb zeuerschmehen Als doctor hartlieb von latin zetütsch bracht hat. durch bet vnd gescheffte eines fürsten von österich als hernach geschriben steet.

[The colophon]: Getrückt vnd volendet zů Strassburg von Martino Schotten noch Cristus gburt M. cccc lxxxiiij. jor. Uff zinstag noch Sant Gertruten tag Aber nit darumb das volbracht werd schand vnd übel sunder ver-vermitten werd. Wann nit böss ist böss künden aber böss zůuolbringen Dann vnwissent übel mag nit vermitten werden.

Folio; contains nineteen woodcuts; *Gesamtkatalog,* item 1761.

20. Hie hebt sich an das bůch Ouidy von der liebe zů erwerben. auch die lieb zeuerschmehen. Als doctor hartlieb von latein zů teütsch gepracht hat durch bete vnnd geschäffte eines fürsten von österreich als hernach geschriben steet.

[The colophon]: Getruckt vnd volendet in der keiserlichen stat Augspurg von Anthoni Sorg am mit wochen vor Simonis vnd Jude. Anno domini .M.CCCC. LXXXJJJJ.

Folio; contains nineteen woodcuts; *Gesamtkatalog,* item 1762.

21. Hans Georg Wieczorek, Johann Hartliebs Verdeutschung von des Andreas Capellanus Liber de reprobatione amoris. Breslau dissertation, 1929.

22. Der Minne Regel von Eberhardus Cersne aus Minden, 1404. Mit einem Anhang von Liedern. Herausgegeben von Franz Xaver Wöber. Wien: Wilhelm Braumüller, 1881.

23. Das königlich fränkischen Kaplans Andreas 3 Bücher über die Liebe aus dem Lateinischen übertragen und herausgegeben von Hanns Martin Elster. Dresden: Aretz, 1924.

SECONDARY SOURCES

Anglade, Joseph, Les Troubadours; leurs vies—leurs œuvres—leur influence. 2ᵉ éd. Paris: Colin, 1919.

Appel, Carl, [Review of Nykl's "Abu Muhammad"], *Zeitschrift für romanische Philologie*, LII (1932), 770–91.

—— [Review of Nykl's "Aben Guzman"], *Zeitschrift für romanische Philologie*, LV (1935), 725–37.

Bossuat, Robert, Drouart la Vache; traducteur d'André le Chapelain. Paris: Droz, 1926.

Cohen, Gustave, Chrétien de Troyes et son œuvre. Paris: Boivin, 1931.

Cross, Tom Peete, and William Albert Nitze, Lancelot and Guenevere: a Study on the Origins of Courtly Love. Chicago: University of Chicago Press, 1930.

Drescher, Karl, "Johann Hartlieb: über sein Leben und seine schriftstellerische Tätigkeit," *Euphorion*, XXV (1924), 225–41; 254 (i. e., 354)–370; 569–90.

Fauriel, C., "André le Chapelain, auteur d'un traité de l'amour," *Histoire littéraire de la France*, XXI (1895), 320–32.

Grabmann, Martin, "Das Werk *De amore* des Andreas Capellanus und das Verurteilungsdekret des Bischofs Stephan Tempier von Paris vom 7. März, 1277," *Speculum*, VII (1932), 75–79.

Graf, Arturo, Roma nella memoria e nelle immaginazioni del medio evo. Torino: Loescher, 1882.

Grimes, E. Margaret, "Le Lay du Trot," *Romanic Review*, XXVI (1935), 313–21.

Guyer, Foster E., "The Influence of Ovid on Crestien de Troyes," *Romanic Review*, XII (1921), 97–134; 216–47.

Holmes, Urban Tigner, Jr., A History of Old French Literature from the Origins to 1300. Chapel Hill: Linker, 1937.

Jeanroy, Alfred, La Poésie lyrique des troubadours. Toulouse: Privat, 1934.

Kelly, Amy, "Eleanor of Aquitaine and Her Courts of Love," *Speculum*, XII (1937), 3–19.

Kirby, Thomas A., Chaucer's Troilus; a Study in Courtly Love. University, La.: Louisiana State University Press, 1940.

Lewis, C. S., The Allegory of Love: a Study in Medieval Tradition. Oxford: Clarendon Press, 1936.

Lot-Borodine, Myrrha, "Sur les origines et les fins du *service d'amour*," Mélanges de linguistique et de littérature offerts à M. Alfred Jeanroy par ses élèves et ses amis (Paris: Droz, 1928), pp. 223–42.

Manitius, M., "Beiträge zur Geschichte des Ovidius und anderer römischer Schriftsteller im Mittelalter," *Philologus*, Supplementband VII (1899), 721–67.

—— Geschichte der lateinischen Literatur des Mittelalters. Vol. III. München: Beck, 1931.

Marçais, Georges, "La Poésie andalouse du XIe siècle," *Journal des savants*, 1939, pp. 14–30.

Menéndez-Pidal, Ramón, "Poesía árabe y poesía europea," *Revista cubana*, VI (1937), 5–33. Reprinted Habana, Secretaria de Educación, 1938.

—— "Poesía árabe y poesía europea" [not the same article], Bulletin hispanique, XL (1938), 337–423.

Morley, S. Griswold, "A Note on Arabic Poetry and European Poetry," *Hispanic Review*, VII (1939), 344–46.

Mott, Lewis Freeman, The System of Courtly Love. Boston: Athenaeum Press, 1896.

Neilson, William Allen, The Origins and Sources of the Court of Love. Boston: Ginn and Company, 1899. [Harvard] *Studies and Notes in Philology and Literature*, VI.

—— "The Purgatory of Cruel Beauties," *Romania*, XXIX (1900), 85–93.

Nykl, A. R., Abū Muḥammad, 'Alī ibn Ḥazm al-Andalusī: a Book Containing the Risāla Known as the Dove's Neck-Ring about Love and Lovers. Paris: Geuthner, 1931.

—— "The Latest in Troubadour Studies," *Archivum Romanicum*, XIX (1935), 227–36.

Painter, Sidney, French Chivalry: Chivalric Ideas and Practices in Mediæval France. Baltimore: Johns Hopkins Press, 1940.

Paris, Gaston, La Littérature française au moyen âge (XIe–XIVe siècle). 2e éd. Paris: Hachette, 1890.

—— "Etudes sur les romans de la Table Ronde: Lancelot du Lac," *Romania*, XII (1883), 459–534.

—— [Review of Trojel's "Middelalderens Elskovshoffer"], *Journal des savants*, 1888, pp. 664–75, 727–36.

P[aris], G[aston], "La comtesse Élisabeth de Flandres et les troubadours," *Romania*, XVIII (1888), 591–95.

Pérès, Henri, La Poésie andalouse en arabe classique au XIᵉ siècle: ses aspects généraux et sa valeur documentaire. Paris: Maisonneuve, 1937.

Rajna, Pio, "Tre studi per la storia del libro di Andrea Cappellano," *Studj di filologia romanza*, V (1891), 193–272.

Rand, Edward Kennard, Ovid and His Influence. New York: Longmans, 1928.

—— "The Classics in the Thirteenth Century," *Speculum*, IV (1929), 249–69.

Rougemont, Denis de, L'Amour et l'Occident. Paris: Plon, 1939. A translation by Montgomery Belgion was published in London by Faber and Faber under the title *Passion and Society* (1940) and in New York by Harcourt Brace as *Love in the Western World* (1940).

Sandys, J. E., A History of Classical Scholarship. 3d ed. Cambridge: Cambridge University Press, 1921.

Schevill, Rudolph, "Ovid and the Renascence in Spain," *University of California Publications in Modern Philology*, IV (1913), 1–268.

Steiner, Arpad, "The Date of the Composition of Andreas Capellanus' De amore," *Speculum*, IV(1929), 92–95.

—— "The Identity of the Italian 'Count' in Andreas Capellanus' *De amore*," *Speculum*, XIII (1938), 304–308.

Tatlock, J. S. P., "Interpreting Literature by History," *Speculum*, XII (1937), 390–95.

Trojel, E., Middelalderens Elskovshoffer; Literaturhistorisk-kritisk undersøgelse. Kjøbenhavn: Reitzel, 1888.

—— "Sur le Chevalier Raembaud, de Francesco da Barberino," *Revue des langues romanes*, XXXII (1888), 286–88.

Vigneras, Louis-André, "Chrétien de Troyes Rediscovered," *Modern Philology*, XXXII (1935), 341–42.

Voretzsch, Karl, Introduction to the Study of Old French Literature; translated by Francis M. DuMont. Halle: Niemeyer, 1931.

Wilcox, John, "Defining Courtly Love," *Papers of the Michigan Academy of Science Arts and Letters*, XII (1930), 313–325.

Wulff, August, Die frauenfeindlichen Dichtungen in den romanischen Literaturen des Mittelalters bis zum Ende des XIII. Jahrhunderts. Halle: Niemeyer, 1914.

Zonta, Giuseppe, "Rileggendo Andrea Cappellano," *Studi medievali* (old series), III (1908), 49–68.